Bruce Philip Smith

Francis Frank Sinkwich

Angelo Bortolo Bertelli

Leslie Horvath

Richard William Kazmaier

Billy Dale Vessels

John Joseph Lattner

Alan Dante Ameche

THE
HEISMAN

Earnest Randolph Davis

Terry Wayne Baker

Roger Thomas Staubach

John Gregory Huarte

Patrick Joseph Sullivan

John Stephen Rodgers

John Raymond Cappelletti

Archie Mason Griffin

Herschel Junior Walker

Michael Thomas Rozier

Douglas Richard Flute

Vincent Edward Jackson

Gino Louis Torretta

Charlie Ward Jr.

Rashaan Salaam

THE HEISMAN

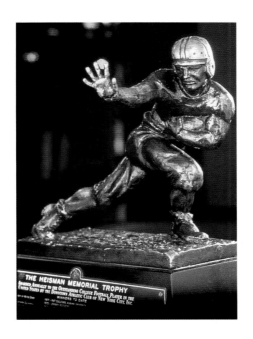

Sixty Years of Tradition and Excellence

ADVENTURE
QUEST
INC.

THIS FIRST EDITION IS PUBLISHED IN 1995 BY
ADVENTURE QUEST, INC.
BRONXVILLE, N.Y. 10708
Library of Congress Cataloging - in- Publication Data
PRINTED IN THE USA
BY JOSTENS PRINTING AND PUBLISHING

FIRST EDITION
10-9-8-7-6-5-4-3-2-1
ISBN 1- 888170-00-X
All worldwide rights reserved by Adventure Quest, Inc.

ACKNOWLEDGMENTS

The research and compilation of a book of this magnitude requires the assistance of a large number of people who have taken the extra time to go through their files and help locate those long-ago written newspaper and magazine stories that many have forgotten about or misplaced, or the nostalgic photos that have been rarely seen or were tucked in an envelope and buried in a desk drawer many years earlier.

Now as we celebrate the glorious history of those fabulous ballplayers whose heroic feats earned them The Heisman Memorial Trophy®, we should also celebrate those historians, researchers and others who have allowed us to enjoy and perhaps cherish once again those rekindled memories of a special time long ago.

First, I'd like to thank Frank Powers, President of The Downtown Athletic Club, Carmine Ragucci, the chairman of The Heisman Memorial Trophy Committee and Rudy Riska, the Executive Director of the Heisman Memorial Trophy Trust, who opened up the D.A.C.'s archives for me to go through and discover much of its unexplored past. I also greatly appreciate the assistance of Sean Ingram, Mark Palladino and Rob Whalen of the D.A.C. who handled all of my day-to-day requests for research materials.

Also, I'd like to thank the sports information directors of the various schools of the Heisman winners and at which John Heisman coached along with the others who poured through their archives on numerous occasions on my behalf and whom I'm greatly indebted to: Marc Dellins of U.C.L.A.; Jim Schneider and Bruce Madej at the University of Michigan; Ted Nance at the University of Houston; Ester Livingstone and Linda Venzon at the University of Miami; Steve Buzzard at Oklahoma State University; John Heisler at the University of Notre Dame; Jeff Nelson and Budd Thalman at Penn State University; Kerry Tharp at The University of South Carolina; Sam Scuillo and Larry Eldridge Jr. at the University of Pittsburgh; Wayne Hogan at Florida State University; Mare Ryan at the University of Minnesota; Tim Tessalone at the University of Southern California; Bill Little at the University of Texas; John Humenik at The University of Florida; Bill Franques and Herb Vincent at Louisiana State University; Kent Partridge at Auburn University; Claude Felton at the University of Georgia; Colin Killian and Alan Cannon at Texas A & M University; Bob Vazquez at Stanford University; Dave Hilbert at the University of Chicago; Tom Bates at the U.S. Naval Academy; Bob McKinney at the U.S. Military Academy; Steve Malchow at the University of Wisconsin; Glen Stone at Texas Christian University; Ed Wisneski at Southern Methodist University; Steve Snapp at Ohio State University; Allison George at Georgia Tech University; Hal Cowan at Oregon State University; Steve Urich and Sara Hoffman at Yale University; Gail Stasulli at the University of Pennsylvania; Kurt Kehl at Princeton University; George Wine at the University of Iowa; Mike Treps at the University of Oklahoma; Bill Cousins at Rice University; Bob Bradley at Clemson University; Bo Carter, the Media Relations Director of the Southwest Conference; Charlie Fiss, the Media Relations Director of the Mobil Cotton Bowl; Michael Sims, a research assistant at Vanderbilt University Archives; Chris McKosky at the National Football League Public Relations Office; Brad Koplowitz at the University of Oklahoma Archives; Joe Horrigan at the Pro Football Hall of Fame and Jorge Jaramillo at Wide World Photos. Special thanks should go to President Gerald Ford for his contribution and cooperation in this effort.

I'd like to thank the writers, editors and research assistants who pulled this project together in the final stages. Most importantly, I'm very appreciative of the many long hours that Darcy Olson and Mary Dunn put in while typing and re-typing on their computers the many drafts of this manuscript and Maribeth Waddell and Elizabeth A. Girard for Assistant Editorial work.

Finally to Robert W. Bass, Lawrence A. Jordan, Jan Russo and Jim Toomey for their tremendous support.

The Publishers

THE WRITERS

Bob August
Dave Anderson
Tony Barnhart
Sam Blair
Furman Bisher
Charles Bullard
Dwight Chapin
Arthur Daley
Pat Harmon
Ivan Maisel

David McNabb
Jim Murray
Bob Oates
Cooper Rollow
Ed Sherman
Red Smith
Robert McG. Thomas Jr.
George Vecsey
William N. Wallace
Rick Warner
Gordon S. White Jr.
Gene Wojciechowski

EDITORIAL & RESEARCH

Jack Bell
Assistant Editor

David Fischer
Research Assistant

Elizabeth A. Girard
Assistant Editor

Jasmine M. Hallberg
Research and Editorial
Assistant

Kathleen McElroy
Assistant Editor

Maribeth Waddell
Assistant Editor

John W. Heisman was first athletic
director of the Downtown Athletic Club

*"In any fight for glory, it's
the heart that tells the story."*

—John W. Heisman

For Nile Kinnick and Ernie Davis,
who had only begun to achieve a small
measure of their greatness when Fate
interceded.

CONTENTS

INTRODUCTION

by Gerald R. Ford

Through the years, during my association with both athletics and politics, I have been fortunate to meet and get to know many of the Heisman Trophy winners. Each possessed tremendous talent and rare courage. A few of them, however, made a memorable impact that I will never forget.

I had just graduated from Michigan and begun my tenure as a freshman football and boxing coach at Yale, when Chicago's Jay Berwanger won the first of the Downtown A.C.'s Heisman Trophy in 1935. Berwanger was big, powerful and fast and could pass and kick—a real triple-threat back. He scored two touchdowns while leading Chicago to a 27-0 victory over Michigan in my senior year, in 1934, and I still have the scar to prove how good a ballplayer he was.

Once, during the game, while trying to make a tackle on Berwanger, I was unable to get a good grasp on him and as I fell to the ground his heel hit my cheekbone, opening a nice 3-inch gash. Luckily, there wasn't a lot of bleeding, but I still had to go to the sideline and get it bandaged. Within a few weeks the cut healed. Now, however, when I stand in front of a mirror to shave, I am confronted with this little souvenir reminding me of the time I tried to bring down the great Berwanger—and lost.

As with many of the Heisman winners, I owe a lot to football. It is a marvelous game and means a great deal to me. Beginning with my years at South High School in my home town of Grand Rapids, Mich., it was football that took me to the University of Michigan at Ann Arbor, and later to law school at Yale.

At Michigan, during the early 1930's, we used the short-punt formation, which looked like a modified single-wing formation. I played the center position and almost every center snap was a lead pass to the tailback who would already be in motion. During this era we labored under limited-substitution rules, which usually meant total exhaustion after every game. In a close contest, no more that 15 or 16 men would play. I only averaged playing about 15 minutes per game during my first two years on the Michigan varsity because we had an undefeated team and won the national championship.

My senior year, when I was a regular starter, we didn't run up any scores. Instead, we were too busy trying to keep our opponents from running up the score on us. The starters on our team were usually the finishers. We weren't too good either—with a record of 1 win and 7 losses—and we weren't too exciting.

After the 1934 season, I was invited to play in the East-West Shrine Game in San Francisco and later in the College All-Star Game in Chicago. Following these two games, Curly Lambeau of the Green Bay Packers made me an offer of $200 a game for 14 games to play the next season. This offer was later matched by the Detroit Lions. But Ducky Pond, the Yale coach, had asked me to be on his staff at New Haven and this was an opportunity for me to realize two dreams—to stay in football and to pursue a law degree.

Gerald R. Ford named to the 1959 Sports Illustrated Anniversary All-American roster while he played for University of Michigan

So I went to Yale and coached there for six seasons, from 1935 through 1940. This was at the end of the Eli's last rule over Eastern football.

Yale was led by Larry Kelley and Clint Frank during my first three seasons and they were a spectacular sight to behold. Kelley was an end who was noted for his brash manner and daring acrobatic catches. He was also a big favorite of the sportswriters who loved to quote him and write about his on-the-field exploits. Frank was a triple-threat tailback and a smart field general. Together, they formed a splendid passing threat, and against the best teams in the East—Princeton, Penn, Dartmouth and Harvard—Yale usually came out the winner.

Kelley, almost single-handedly, led Yale to a 7-0 win over Fritz Crisler's Princeton team in 1935, which was the Tiger's first loss in three seasons. He had the same kind of game against Penn the following season. In memorable contests against Princeton and Dartmouth in 1937, it was Frank's standout performance that proved to be the much-needed difference for victory.

At the end of the 1936 season Kelley was voted the second recipient of the Heisman Trophy. Frank would be awarded the same honor a year later.

Bo Schembechler discusses sideline strategies with Gerald Ford, then assistant coach at University of Michigan.

Prior to the 1938 season, Coach Pond promoted me to the position of head jayvee coach. Along with this promotion came the responsibility of scouting all of the varsity's opposition.

One of the teams that I scouted that fall was my alma mater, Michigan, that had a promising sophomore tailback named Tom Harmon. Michigan barely defeated us in this contest, 15-13, but you couldn't help but notice Harmon and his dazzling football skills. Blessed with a swift stride and the ability to change his direction on a dime, very few people could catch Harmon. In 1939, he would be runner-up to Heisman winner Nile Kinnick of Iowa. In 1940, the trophy would be his outright.

When World War II began, Harmon traded in his Michigan uniform for that of an Army Air Corps bomber pilot. Although his plane was shot down twice, he courageously survived both times and became just as big a war hero as he had been a football hero.

There would be many other Heisman winners who greatly impressed me, including Doc Blanchard, Glenn Davis and Pete Dawkins at Army, Hopalong Cassidy at Ohio State and Ernie Davis of Syracuse. But none probably made a bigger impact on my life than John Cappelletti, the brilliant tailback from Penn State who won the Heisman Trophy in 1973.

I was attending the Heisman Dinner in New York City that year and had been looking forward to meeting Cappelletti, the big, rugged running back whose hard-hitting, bulldozer style had propelled the Nittany Lions to an 11-0 record, and whom I h watched on television all season. That evening after Cappelle was presented his Heisman Trophy, he made perhaps the fine and most passionate speech that I have ever heard, dedicating l trophy to his younger brother, Joey, age 11, who was battli leukemia and didn't have long to live. He told us, "If I c dedicate this trophy to Joey tonight and give him a couple of da of happiness, this is worth everything."

As one might expect there wasn't a dry eye in the house th night. We were all moved by Cappelletti's sincerity and love f his younger brother. Finally, when Cappelletti was finished w his acceptance speech, Archbishop Fulton J. Sheen was asked give the dinner's closing prayer. It was then that somethi unique happened to an already unique evening. After arriving the podium, Archbishop Sheen told us, "There is no need fo benediction tonight for God has already blessed you with Jo Cappelletti."

Yes, we were indeed blessed. And my heart, like most of t audience of more than 1,500 in the banquet hall, was bei tugged at quite heavily.

It has now been more that 20 years since I witnessed Jo Cappelletti's Heisman speech, but it was an evening that I w always remember.

John Cappelletti and Vice President Gerald Ford at 1973 Heisman dinner.

These days, when I am watching college football on televisic and hear the sportscasters refer to certain college players as possible Heisman candidate, I sometimes find myself compa ing these current superstars to the Heisman winners whom I ha known such as Berwanger, Kelley, Frank, Harmon or Cappelle and I wonder if they, too, have that rare character and ability achieve a standard of excellence that only a special group h been able to obtain.

This Heisman story is about that pursuit of excellence and t fortunate few who have obtained it.

EDITOR'S NOTE

uring the mid - and late 1920's the illuminating neon lights that ring life and the evening to Broadway would never burn righter.

ew York City had now become the Mecca of the Sportsworld— id perhaps the rest of the world. Everybody who was anybody ade their way there to showcase their talents and to visit the ncy restaurants, the theatres and the speakeasies that lined the avernous White Way, where the celebrities of art, finance, olitics, the literary circles and the underworld were sure to be ound.

he Golden Age of Sport, which began when Jack Dempsey had nocked out Jess Willard with lead fists at Tex Rickard's keshore extravaganza in Toledo, Ohio, in July 1919, had now ourished into a national mania and with it a new era of great hletic achievement was ushered in. The newspapers and oviehouse newsreels all bragged of the growing successes of abe Ruth, Red Grange, Bobby Jones, Big Bill Tilden, Johnny 'eismuller, Jim Thorpe, Knute Rockne and Jack Dempsey until ley eventually became athletic gods for an entire admiring ation.

he sportswriters who did all the bragging, mixing both fact and ction until it became illusion, were among the finest to ever sit ehind a typewriter; a group of guys named Runyon, Rice, allico, Trevor, Kiernan, Wallace and Danzig.

was during this crazed milieu that a group of New York City's 1ost prominent investment bankers and maritime operators roposed building the world's largest athletic club. This mega ructure, which was to be called The Downtown Athletic Club, as to be 44 stories tall and located at the tip of Manhattan Island, ear Battery Park, City Hall, Wall Street and the real center of ew York City influence and power.

he legal incorporation paperwork for The Downtown Athletic 'lub had first been drawn up in 1926 and after their membership nrollment had reached 1,000 members in March 1928, plans for 1e elaborate athletic facility were soon announced. Construc- on on the clubhouse would begin nearly a year later, with the uilding's cornerstone being laid in November 1929.

1n Sept. 26, 1930, the $4.5 million D.A.C. building, which pped out in final form at 35 floors, was finally opened. Its 1embership stood at 3,286 and a former football coach—and uite successful one—by the name of John W. Heisman was hosen to be the club's athletic director.

he new club wasted little time in trying to establish itself as an qual to the older and more prominent New York Athletic Club

in squash, racquetball, swimming and track & field competition. Over the next few years the rivalry between the two clubs would prove to be very stiff.

Finally, in the late summer of 1935, the brazen D.A.C. member- ship decided to up the ante a bit against the New York A.C. and voted to inaugurate an award which would be given to the most outstanding college football player at a school located east of the Mississippi River.

The award, which would carry the club's name, was known as The Downtown Athletic Club Trophy and would hopefully bring a lot more recognition to the fledgling club. Although the award would be renamed in 1936 in honor of Heisman, following his unexpected death, few at the time could have anticipated its eventual success.

From the beginning it would be the sportswriters who would determine The D.A.C. Trophy's—and later The Heisman Me- morial Trophy's—outcome. Gathering at such popular Gotham haunts as Billy LaHiff's, Toot Shor's, Perry's, Mama Leone's and The 21 Club, Grantland Rice and his memorable gang of writers would often remain until early in the morning recounting and toasting the gridiron exploits of popular college stars such as Jay Berwanger, Larry Kelley, Tom Harmon, Glenn Davis, Doc Blanchard and others until, in time, they were elevated to mythical folklore.

These tales were then fed to an awaiting nation who followed the daily and weekly accounts of their football heroes on radio and in the sports pages.

Later, similar awards such as the Maxwell and Walter Camp trophies would also be inaugurated. But through the years, The Heisman Memorial Trophy and its recipients would set the standard of excellence for all others to emulate.

Now, in the sixtieth anniversary celebration of The Heisman Memorial Trophy, twenty of America's finest sportswriters, the successors of Runyon, Rice, Gallico et al, have gathered once again to swap tales about college football's greatest ballplayers and those privileged few who have won this prestigious award.

In many ways this book on The Heisman Memorial Trophy and the memorable ballplayers who won it, will be a reunion of sorts for most of us. It will recall those salad days of our youth, when everything seemed so wondrous and magical and anything was possible and when a group of football immortals ran, hurdled and passed their way into a special place in our hearts.

Hopefully, it will be a journey that we will all fondly enjoy.

The patriotic bunting was appropriate for Nile Kinnick, one of the Heisman's most all-American recipients.

The Trophy

OWNTOWN A.C.
Welcomes KINNICK

John Heisman

The Man Behind the Trophy

On October 7, 1916, the Georgia Tech team defeated Cumberland College 220–0, a score that has never been equaled or even approached and probably never will.

The coach of the winning team was John William Heisman. Did he run up the score that day? Yes, he did. Was arrogance, or ego, involved? Yes, it was. And money? Yes, indeed.

The Heisman Memorial Trophy, college football's most renowned prize, is named correctly, for the man whose life was so representative of this contentious game. Better Heisman than Camp or Warner, Rockne or Wilkinson, Bryant or Hayes, whose teams won far more contests than Heisman's did.

Heisman had warts and poultices all over his career. His teams, representing eight different colleges, won 185 times, lost 70 and tied 17. Not bad … not gaudy.

He was never quite fired, always moving on when the time became ripe. He moved for money a few times and once on account of an impending divorce. He had been a player, no All-America but a stumpy little lineman, 5' 10", 155 pounds. He was irascible, something of a yeller, had a good opinion of himself and made his own enemies. But above all else there was his zeal for football. Did he love the game? He was consumed by it.

That match against Cumberland had been a revealing one. The little college in Lebanon, Tennessee, earlier something of a power in Southern football, had can-celed its 1916 schedule for lack of players. But the spring before, the Cumberland baseball team had defeated Georgia Tech 22–0—one zero from the grid-iron score—and Heisman had been coach of the humiliated Tech team. Later it came out that the players representing Cumberland were in truth professionals from Nashville who had been recruited by some students to give the college a little athletic esteem. Heisman was furious.

There may have been another motive. Dan McGugin was the well-regarded coach at Vanderbilt and a rival of Heisman's. McGugin's Commodores had played a weak schedule in 1915 and ran up some attention-grabbing high scores. Heisman disapproved—perhaps out of envy. After the Cumberland rout, for which he was criticized, the coach wrote an essay for the college annual in which he said that adding up points and comparing scores between teams was "a useless thing." The Cumberland outcome was there, Heisman said, "to show folks it was an easy thing to run up a score in one easy game."

It certainly was easy. There were no first downs in the match. Georgia Tech scored within three downs every time it got the ball, and it attempted no passes. Cumberland had only 19 players, a motley collection that had been rounded up one week before the game by George Allen, the team manager. Only a few of them had ever played football. Allen, who was to become a

The Trophy Winners

1936
The award rendered even Larry Kelley speechless.

1938
Small in size only, Davey O'Brien was a man of big talents and big rewards.

1939
No one knows what the future may have held in store for Nile Kinnick after his Heisman days.

No icon of ice, Heisman was an intense competitor throughout his lengthy career as a college football coach.

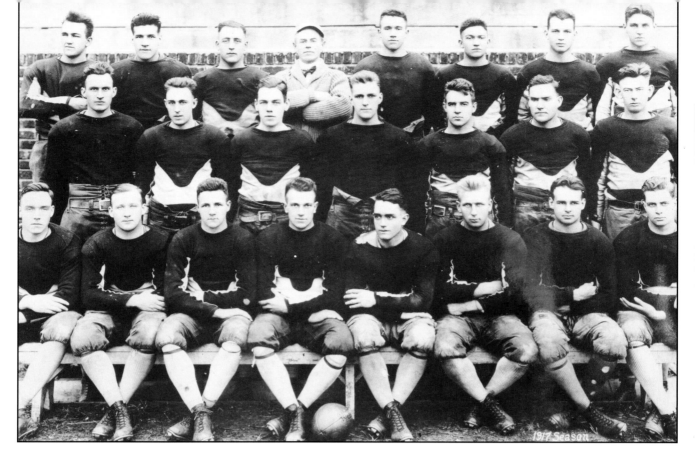

crony of Dwight Eisenhower's and a member of the general's White House "kitchen" cabinet, spun tales about the game in later years, telling his listeners that he had been lured into the contest with the promise of an expense-paid trip to Atlanta to play the game, plus a $500 guarantee proffered by Heisman. The coach had baited the trap.

The score at halftime was 126–0, prompting these immortal words from Heisman in the locker room: "Men, don't let up. You never know what those Cumberland players have up their sleeves."

Heisman knew a thing or two about deception. In the game against Vanderbilt that autumn, the 25-year-old Heisman, newly installed at Auburn in his first coaching position, had his quarterback, Reynolds Tichenor, tuck the football under his jersey as he bent over as though to tie his shoelaces. A back faked taking a handoff, other teammates circled and then scattered, the Commodores could not locate the football and Tichenor tiptoed up the field for a touchdown.

Heisman used the same play later against Georgia and its celebrated coach, Glenn (Pop) Warner, who promptly appropriated it. This hidden-ball play showed up on Warner's teams at Cornell and later at Carlisle in the professional ranks.

Southern football was full of high jinks in those years.

The Winners, continued

1940
Offense, defense, running, passing, kicking—Tom Harmon was a genuine multiple threat for the Michigan Wolverines.

1942
Frank Sinkwich was flat-footed only to the Marines, who released him soon after he accepted his Heisman in full regalia.

Heisman, originally from Pennsylvania, moved in 1900 from Auburn to Clemson, where Georgia Tech was the big rival. In 1902 a Clemson team arrived in Atlanta by train, accepted their host's many invitations and went out on the town. John Heisman's famous training rules were ignored, and the Clemson players wined and dined far into the night. The next day the Tech supporters wagered heavily on their team against Clemson's surely under-the-weather bunch. Later in the morning another train arrived carrying the real Clemson varsity, which had spent a safe and restful night in nearby Lula, Georgia, far from the temptations of the big city. Georgia Tech lost the game 44–5.

That Clemson team was small but blessed with great speed and quickness. Those were Heisman's preferred qualities in his teams, in part because there were so few big players available to him at Auburn, Clemson and Georgia Tech. He knew what to do with quickness. As a college player at Brown and Penn between 1887 and '91, Heisman had been part of the flying-wedge era, when players massed as in a rugby scrum, a rough, disorganized kind of football that he deplored.

Like Walter Camp, Amos Alonzo Stagg and Dr. Harry Williams, Heisman was an imaginative pioneer of this evolving game. He was perhaps the first to institute a shift, setting his backs in a line at a right angle to the scrimmage line and then shifting them horizontally with a quick snap of the ball, thus producing a forerunner of Knute Rockne's famous Notre Dame shift.

Heisman was scouting the Georgia–North Carolina game played at Atlanta's Brisbane Park in 1895 when a Tar Heel punter was overrun and could not get his kick away. So he flung the football down the field. A teammate caught the pass and ran 70 yards for a touchdown.

However, the rules of this era stated that throwing the ball was illegal. "I didn't see the ball thrown," said the referee, and the play was legal that day. Heisman took note, and after the forward pass became a legalized maneuver in 1906, he was one of its first and few exploiters.

It was with the Golden Tornado, later also called the Yellow Jackets, that Heisman had his greatest success. He came to Atlanta from Clemson for the 1904 season with the generous annual salary of $2,250 plus 30% of the athletic gate receipts. This coach could count.

A huge banner was lofted in Piedmont Park jubilantly proclaiming "Tech Gets Heisman for 1904," a coup for the Tech faithful, who no doubt recalled the pastings that Heisman's teams had handed the Yellow Jackets over the years. Heisman went to work on the program immediately, persuading city officials to provide convict labor to create a stadium of sorts in a wooded tract. Out went the stumps and up went the fences. Now there would be a gate with gate receipts.

Heisman stayed for 16 seasons, through 1919. The Yellow Jackets enjoyed a 33-game winning streak that ended in 1918, and his 1917 team was acknowledged to be the national champion. It ran up scores, too: 41–0 over Penn in an intersectional match that drew an astonishing crowd of 10,000 to Atlanta; 63–0 against Washington & Lee; 83–0 in a crushing defeat of Vanderbilt; a 98–0 wallop of Carlisle; and a 68–7 blowout of Auburn.

Gene Griessman, in a penetrating biography of Heisman, wrote, "Heisman's teams did not huddle during the Georgia Tech years. The quarterback would call the plays and, sometimes, the teams would run a series of plays without any call. Then there were times when Heisman called the plays himself from the sidelines—

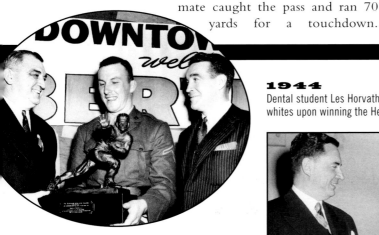

1943
Angelo Bertelli was the first of four Heisman winners for Notre Dame coach Frank Leahy (right).

1944
Dental student Les Horvath flashed his pearly whites upon winning the Heisman.

1945
Doc Blanchard's unstoppable force on the field made him a household name off it.

even though it was illegal—by taking out his handkerchief, by letting it fall, by adjusting his cap or by putting his hand in his pocket."

Atlanta loved the excitement, the show, the precision of the Yellow Jackets. One newspaper account stated, "The Tech band could discard its leader and play by the jump-shift timing of the team." Yes, the famous Heisman shift was in vogue.

After the United States entered World War I in April 1917, most college sports programs were curtailed. Heisman hardly noticed. His critics gossiped that the coach had been slow to encourage his players to enlist, although several of them did. That he came from German-American ancestry—his given name was Johann Wilhelm Heisman—did not help.

In 1903, while at Clemson, Heisman met and married Evelyn McCollum Cox, a widow with a son. Cox was an actress with a summer stock company in which Heisman took an interest. He had long sustained a passion for the theater and had even tried a few Shakespearean roles, an effort that provoked one writer to describe him as "a terrible Thespian." There is no record of how the marriage went, although Heisman may have had some difficulty maintaining his modesty as he became more and more successful. At the end of the 1919 season Heisman asked a few members of the Tech athletic board to drop by his house. The coach, now 50, sat at a breakfast table on which lay a sheaf of stocks and bonds. Heisman then asked Lawrence (Chip) Robert, an old friend, to help with an equitable division of the assets. "A most unfortunate thing has happened," he told his guests. "Mrs. Heisman and I have decided to divorce. There are no hard feelings, and I have agreed that wherever Mrs. Heisman wishes to live, I will live in another place."

Mrs. Heisman chose to stay in Atlanta, and Heisman left town. Never again would he match the success or fame he enjoyed in Atlanta. He would coach for eight more years, at Penn, Washington & Jefferson and at Rice, years that would be marred by squabbles with his superiors, his associates and his players. Then he moved to New York City, where he became a contributor to *Colliers* magazine, a special football writer for *The New York Evening Journal* and, eventually, the athletic director of the new Downtown Athletic Club.

Heisman's football voyage had begun in Titusville, Pennsylvania, an oil town where his father worked as a cooper—a maker and repairer of the barrels in which the precious crude was transported. Heisman's father, who had been disowned by his German father, Baron von Bogart, for marrying a peasant girl, had come to America and had settled first in Cleveland. He took his wife's family name, Heisman. Heisman Sr.'s business prospered, and John D. Rockefeller's Standard Oil was one of his customers.

Young Johann Wilhelm went out for football at Titusville High School but not with the approval of his father, who called the game "bestial," and with reason. Johann played that rough brand of football whose centerpiece was the flying wedge and later said himself, "The human frame is unequal to the wedge."

Heisman went to Brown University for two years and then to the University of Pennsylvania to earn a law degree. His hopes for a law career were ended during the Penn-Princeton game in 1891, when the crude lighting system of New York's Madison Square Garden injured his eyes. The team physician told the young man he should rest his eyes for two years, so Heisman went to Ohio to become the first football coach at Oberlin

The Winners, continued

1946
Coach Earl Blaik (center) created a juggernaut both "Inside" and "Outside" at Army with Doc Blanchard and '46 Heisman winner Glenn Davis.

1947
Notre Dame lost prized quarterback Johnny Lujack for two years while he served in the Navy during WWII.

1948
The largest man to win the Heisman, Leon Hart towered over his competitors.

College. He took a postgraduate course in art, and because of loose eligibility rules that allowed graduate students to play ball, Heisman played end on his own team, which went undefeated, beat Ohio State twice and outscored the opposition 262–30.

Perhaps it was at Oberlin that Heisman honed his introductory speech to his players, one always delivered on the first day of practice. Holding up a football, Heisman would ask, "What is it?" and then answer, "A prolate spheroid—that is, an elongated sphere—in which the outer leather casing is drawn over a somewhat smaller rubber tubing."

He paused, and then added with theatrical effect, "Better to have died as a small boy than to fumble this football."

The next season Buchtel College, which eventually became the University of Akron, offered Heisman a salary of $750, while at Oberlin the hat had been passed yielding only $400. So Heisman went to Buchtel for a year. But the faculty was upset when he spirited away the squad for a rigorous two-week training program prior to the final game. While Heisman credited the team's better conditioning for its overtime win against Ohio State, the faculty disapproval meant he was out of a job.

By then he had developed training and dietary programs plus lists of one-sentence dos and don'ts relating to the game and life away from the game. "Always be where the ball is." "Don't forget to stiff-arm."

In 1895, after another season back at Oberlin, Heisman went on to Alabama Polytechnic (which would become Auburn). He stayed five happy seasons in the pleasant college town, later saying, "I never had a team at Auburn I did not love, nor did I have one quarrel with any player during the whole five years. There is not one man with me during those five years that is not still my very warm friend."

He could not say the same about the Georgia Tech players. He called one "a flaming jackass," another, "you little idiot." His speech was clear, nasal and high-pitched, easy to hear, and in later years he used a small megaphone for practices to be sure his words weren't missed. He sometimes talked to his players in exaggerated, theatrical language as in this piece of advice on tackling. "Thrust your projections into their cavities, grasping them about the knees and depriving them of their means of propulsion."

Heisman was not fooling. A Tech player once said of him, "He was a czar on the field. No one dared question him. There was no horsing around or laughing. It was strictly business." Another said, "He may have had some humor about him but not that I ever saw." A Georgia Tech scrub was elevated to the varsity and on his first day found the coach demonstrating how to hold the football. Heisman cradled the ball and asked one of the players, named Six Carpenter, to try to dislodge it.

A teammate recalled, "Old Six, who had a fist like a calf's head, took one punch, and the ball shot five feet up in the air." When the recently elevated varsity member let out a giggle, the coach scowled and said to him, "Stop that laughter and run around the field 10 times."

After three so-so seasons at Penn (16-10-2 overall) Heisman quit on December 18, 1922, but not before he turned to his squad and said, "I have taught you all I know and still you know nothing."

He next became head coach at Washington & Jefferson, a small-college power in Washington, Pennsylvania, that had played in the 1922 Rose Bowl and that had a great halfback in Charles (Pruner) West, who happened to be black. There was a commendable

1952
Billy Vessels blazed into America's living rooms in college football's first televised year.

1954
An immigrant's son, Alan (the Horse) Ameche achieved the American dream with his Heisman success.

moment when Washington & Lee came north from Virginia to play and demanded that West not be used. Heisman and the college authorities refused to cave in, and the game was canceled.

Heisman kept moving, next to Rice Institute in Houston, a small college in the tough Southwest Conference with only 400 students. He also remarried in 1924. His new wife was Edith Maora Cole, whom he had known years before when she was a student at Buchtel.

Rice was generous, giving Heisman a five-year contract at $9,000 per year. Heisman had only to be on campus for the spring practices and fall seasons. A new enterprise, a sporting goods business in New York City, had his attention, too.

Heisman displayed his usual innovative streak at Rice, creating an athletic dormitory, perhaps the first one for college sports, where the athletes resided, took meals and studied. However, there were not enough players—only 30 or 40—to compete with the powers such as Texas, Texas Christian and Southern Methodist. Heisman had faced a similar problem before. Once at Georgia Tech during chapel Heisman had said to the students, "Gentlemen, we are destitute of people. If you weigh 150 pounds or more, please come out for football." Such entreaties failed at Rice, and the coach resigned after a 2-6-1 season in 1927. His overall record there was 14–21, and he had lost the respect of his players. He was accused of favoritism, of ordering quarterbacks not to give the ball to players he disliked. Thirty-six years of coaching had come to an end.

The New York years, however, would prove to be quite pleasant. The Heismans lived in an apartment on Park Avenue and had money, although they lost some in the Florida land bust of 1929. At the behest of his old Atlanta friend Bobby Jones, Heisman took up golf and played often, especially on vacations to his wife's hometown of Rhinelander, Wisconsin, where he would eventually be buried.

His association with the Downtown Athletic Club began in 1930 when the new club opened its 35-story, $3 million clubhouse. Heisman was to be its athletic director, which meant some fact-finding missions to athletic clubs in Detroit and Chicago to determine exactly what it was that an athletic director was supposed to do.

The idea of a football award was conceived by D.A.C. executive William Prince, not Heisman, in 1935. The award was to be given in the club's name and go to the best player east of the Mississippi River. Initially Heisman balked at the idea of giving such an award. However, he would later give the award his support and predict correctly that the selectors, of whom he was to be one, would name Jay Berwanger of Chicago as the first recipient of the Downtown Athletic Club Trophy.

Heisman was planning to write a history of football when he died suddenly of bronchopneumonia on October 3, 1936, in his apartment. A few weeks later the Downtown Athletic Club voted to rename the D.A.C. Trophy in Heisman's honor.

In time, the award—like the man it was named for—would become something very special.

—*WILLIAM N. WALLACE*

The Winners, continued

1960

The fleet legs of Joe Bellino carried him to one glorious year and four records for Navy.

1962

Attorney general Robert Kennedy took part in the award ceremony for Terry Baker, Oregon State's hardworking Heisman winner.

Fordham coach Jim Crowley (right, with running back Warren Mulrey in the pose) was one of three men to approve the trophy design.

Ed Smith

A Model for the Ages

It was in 1982, almost half a century after the fact, that Ed Smith learned that he had posed for the Heisman Trophy. It wasn't that it had slipped his mind. He remembered the sessions with Frank Eliscu well enough. He just never knew the sculpture Eliscu was working on would become a trophy.

"I just thought it was something he was doing for himself," Smith said.

1965
The first great Trojan tailback to win the Heisman, Mike Garrett later returned to his alma mater as athletic director.

1967
UCLA's Gary Beban made big plays at big moments to narrowly defeat O.J. Simpson for the Heisman.

21

The Trophy

The mistake was understandable. Smith, a New York University fullback when he posed for Eliscu after the 1934 season, only knew at the time that he was doing a favor for a fellow he had known since high school. One who was always fooling around with clay for his own amusement.

Smith had no idea that the statue he posed for would become perhaps the most famous trophy in the land and that a bit of its fame would one day rub off on him.

Until he, was brushed with the Heisman mystique, Smith had been an emblem of the thousands of football players who never won a Heisman.

Edward Robert Smith was born in Harlem on June 17, 1913, and moved to Washington Heights when he was about 12. It was at George Washington High School that he got to know Eliscu. "He was a little fellow," Smith recalled in an interview in the spring of 1994, "a track man." Indeed, Eliscu was a 120-pound sprinter on a team that came in second in the Penn Relays.

As a distinctly big fellow, one who grew to 6'1", 209 pounds in college, Smith gravitated to football and was good enough in high school to make the Public School Athletic League all-star team his junior and senior years. A year younger than Eliscu, Smith went on to play for NYU, which was beginning to deemphasize football in the wake of a mini-scandal involving payments to players.

Even so, NYU continued to play its home games in Yankee Stadium against formidable opponents, and from the time he was a sophomore in 1933, Smith was a star, known for his long, booming punts that frequently made the difference between victory and defeat, or at least between defeat and debacle as NYU went through two mediocre seasons, including a 3-4-1 record his junior year.

Smith, who had already missed several games with torn ligaments in his left leg ("It still bothers me"), recalls the "1" in that 3-4-1 record especially well.

"I banged the other leg up," he said. "It was the Georgetown game at the Stadium, and I got hit on the thigh. It blew up to twice its size. They had to cut the pants off me." Smith, who was in the hospital for several days, did not mention that his punts that day were critical in holding the favored Hoyas to a scoreless tie.

The next year, 1935, with Smith in better health, NYU went through the season undefeated, until the final game against Fordham.

Although it would seem appropriate that a fullback should pose for a statue depicting a ballcarrier, Smith didn't see it that way. "I did more passing and kicking than running," he said. "In those days, with the single wing and the double wing, you had to be a triple threat.

"I'd run off and on to keep the other team on edge," he added.

Whatever he did, he did so well that after graduation in 1936 he joined the Boston Redskins of the National Football League, earning $125 a game, a salary that seems more generous than it actually was. "We had to supply our own equipment, shoes and pads," he said. "They only gave us our helmets and jerseys."

Smith was a starter but got hurt after seven games. He recovered well enough to return by the end of the season and probably would have followed the team to Washington, D.C., in 1937 if it hadn't been for one thing. "They signed Sammy Baugh," he said, "so they traded me to Green Bay."

What Smith remembers best about Green Bay was getting there: "I flew to Chicago. It was my first trip on an airplane. Then I took a train and got to Green Bay in

The Winners, continued

1970
Despite 11 operations and a career mired in pain, Jim Plunkett continued to throw long, beautiful touchdown spirals until his retirement at the age of 40.

1972
Johnny Rodgers lifted himself out of Omaha's northside ghetto and into the elite of his sport.

the middle of the night. I didn't know where I was."

Smith, happy to be getting $200 a game from the Packers, lasted only a few weeks, until coach Curly Lambeau called him in and told him that the cost of his transportation from New York to Green Bay would be deducted from his pay.

"I hollered murder," Smith said. "I wrote the NFL, but they were nothing in those days, so I just took a train and got out of there."

Smith finished the 1937 season playing for the semi-pro Newark Bears, but when his injuries began to get the best of him he quit football (returning for a brief comeback in 1941 when he played for a semipro team in Springfield, Massachusetts, where he was a teammate of Vince Lombardi).

Steady jobs weren't easy to come by during the Depression, but Smith had a hook. His father was Edward A. Smith, a business agent for Local One of the Elevator Constructors Union, who eventually became president of the International. His son had been working summers in elevator construction since his high school days.

"I remember working on the Empire State Building in 1930," said Smith, who began working on elevators full-time after his pro career ended, eventually becoming a Local One business agent and in time assistant to the International's president in Philadelphia.

Smith stayed with the union until his retirement in 1976. Six years later he got a call from Joe Goldstein, a well-known New York public relations man, who had been delegated to track down Smith for the filmmaker Bud Greenspan. Greenspan was making a documentary

on the Heisman and thought it would round out the project to include the man who had posed for the trophy.

Until Goldstein mentioned Eliscu, Smith had no idea what he was talking about. Since then he has frequently told the story about how he got the NYU equipment man to lend him a full uniform, which he took, with his own football shoes, "to the little shop Eliscu had down in Greenwich Village."

As a result of Goldstein's phone call, Smith has stepped out of the football mists and is now invited every year to attend the Heisman ceremonies. He was even presented with a Heisman Trophy of his own, which he keeps on the desk in his office at his home in Lynbrook, Long Island. "I'm looking at it right now," he said during a telephone call in May 1994.

It should be noted that posing for the Heisman Trophy is not the same thing as being the model for the Heisman Trophy. Eliscu has made it clear that the form and face of the statue were molded from his own imagination. He needed Smith for the details of the uniform, to get the high-top shoes, the socks, the pants, the shirt and the leather helmet just right.

Still, it cannot be denied that Smith is entitled to a full footnote in football history. The face and the body of the Heisman may not be his, but the shoes are pure Smith.

—*Robert McG. Thomas Jr.*

1975
Just one more, please: With two Heismans, Archie Griffin got accustomed to striking the pose.

1976
Tony Dorsett transformed the Pittsburgh fortunes during his four exhilarating, All-American years.

Frank Eliscu

From Feet of Clay to Greatness in Bronze

Time is running out. His team is behind, and he has gotten the call. He has taken the handoff, broken through the line and bulled his way past the linebackers until he is now in the open field with only a single determined defender between him and the goal line. The game is in the balance. As the defender closes in from the right, sure that he can bring the ballcarrier down, the runner shifts the ball from his right hand and tucks it firmly into the crook of his left arm, pressing it close to his body. Then, in one fluid motion just as the tackler arrives, he takes a sudden graceful sidestep and throws his right arm out, shoving the tackler away with his open hand.

As quickly as he appeared the tackler is gone, now merely an implicit fallen figure as the runner surges forward. The touchdown is made. The game is won.

A beautiful run, but this is the moment we remember: the runner alone in full stride, his arm outstretched, moving away toward football immortality.

If ever there was a run and a moment worthy of the Heisman Trophy, this is it, but then, of course, this *is* the Heisman Trophy.

That the Heisman Trophy is at once one of the world's most recognized and respected awards for individual athletic achievement and an actual trophy—cast in bronze and standing on a black onyx base on a marble pedestal—may be more than happenstance.

It is tempting to wonder whether the club's annual

presentation could have attained its present preeminence if the committee of founders had decided to honor the year's outstanding college football player by establishing, say, a Heisman Award, symbolized by a suitably imposing plaque, or even a Heisman Cup, complete with graceful handles.

But the actual unassailable fact is that when the members of the Downtown Athletic Club created the annual award in 1935 they also decreed that a trophy depicting a football player would be created along with it.

And Frank Eliscu is the man they chose to create it.

It is also tempting to wonder what the Heisman may have become if the founders had entrusted the trophy to another sculptor.

They could hardly have known at the time that the Heisman would be the first of hundreds of celebrated works by Eliscu ranging in scale from the inaugural medals of President Gerald Ford and Vice President Nelson Rockefeller to the monumental "Cascade of Books" above the entrance to the James Madison Building of the Library of Congress.

At the time he was assigned to create what became known as the Heisman Trophy, Eliscu was an impoverished 23-year-old graduate of Pratt Institute whose sole professional output had been depart-

The Winners, continued

1977
Few Heisman winners were more desrving than NCAA rushing and scoring champion Earl Campbell.

1979
The storied legacy of Tailback U did not hamper USC's Charles White in his quest for a Heisman.

24

ment store mannequins and dolls' heads.

To be sure, he was not the first choice. To a man, those who were considered the leading sculptors of the day either turned up their noses at the very idea of creating a sports trophy or hid their disdain behind a demand for payment far beyond the club's means.

Eliscu was different. He needed the money.

He no longer remembers exactly how he came to the committee's attention, but as the 82-year-old Eliscu recalled in an interview from his home in Sarasota, Florida, in the spring of 1994, "It was my first commission."

If there seems to be a prayerful veneration in Eliscu's work, it may be no accident. Eliscu, who was born in Brooklyn on July 13, 1912, and grew up in the Washington Heights section of Manhattan, recalled that

1980
George Rogers overcame tremendous personal hardship and a paucity of media coverage to win the Heisman.

1981
Marcus Allen's performance at USC was bested only by the ongoing excellence of his play in the NFL.

1982
A Heisman candidate almost from his first game as a freshman, Herschel Walker elicited the awe of a nation.

the first tentative explorations of what was to become his art were made with the residue of his great-grandmother's prayer candles. "I would take the paraffin with me into the tub when I took a bath and work it underwater," he said.

His first figures were of horses' heads. "I loved to make animals," he said. Eliscu's horses seemed so real, so alive that his talent was instantly apparent. "I became something of a local celebrity," he said.

In time, word of his talent spread beyond Washington Heights to Harrison Tweed, one of New York's most prominent lawyers and a major patron of the arts. Tweed, who operated what amounted to a summer arts colony for talented youngsters at his estate in Montauk, Long Island, invited Eliscu to spend 10 weeks at the camp, and a lasting friendship was born.

"He became the closest thing next to my own father," Eliscu said.

Tweed introduced the young Eliscu to leading American artists and gave Eliscu's own art an important boost by paying the production costs of his first work in bronze, "Diana and the Fawn," which was exhibited at the National Academy of Design while Eliscu was still in high school.

Unable to afford college after graduation from George Washington High School, Eliscu worked for a mannequin maker and a toy company before he won a scholarship covering the first year of a three-year art program at Pratt. When the scholarship ran out, Tweed came to the rescue, paying for the last two years in exchange for art lessons every Monday night in his apartment at 10 Gracie Square.

Tweed, whose name has been preserved in the law firm, Milbank, Tweed, Hadley & McCloy, also performed a critical service when Eliscu was offered the

Heisman assignment. "He insisted on looking over the contract before I signed it," Eliscu said. After it passed muster, Eliscu signed it and went to work.

Much as he needed the $200 fee, Eliscu has always insisted that he approached the work not as a commercial venture but as a labor of love, which is to say, a labor of art.

"I wanted to make the best thing I could," he said. "I worked and I changed, and I gave it everything I could."

Working entirely from his imagination, his only guidance from the club was to produce a football player in action, Eliscu made three wax "sketches," about four inches high, of different poses. It is interesting to speculate how well defensive players might have fared in the annual balloting if the club had selected Eliscu's favorite. It was of a lineman tackling a ballcarrier, their conjoined bodies rising into a graceful S.

When the sketches were completed, a three-coach delegation from the club, Lou Little of Columbia, Jim Crowley of Fordham and John Heisman himself, paid an inspection visit to Eliscu's studio at the old Clay Club at 4 West 8th Street.

All agreed on the straight-arming ballcarrier, but after studying the figure, it was suggested that the outstretched arm, which Eliscu had pointed straight ahead, would be more natural if it extended out to the side, to better mimic how a runner would push a tackler away.

To drive their point home, as Eliscu watched open-mouthed, three of the most famous figures in the world of football held an impromptu mock scrimmage right there in his studio, taking turns stiff-arming each other.

Eliscu got the point and simply pushed the pliable wax arm back until it pointed in the correct direction. "It

The Winners, continued

1983
Nebraska's Mike Rozier rushed for his Heisman yardage with seemingly effortless ease.

1985
His opponents— on the track, the gridiron and the baseball field—can attest to Bo Jackson's prodigious talents.

1987
Fans serenaded Tim Brown with chants of "Heisman" throughout his heralded senior season.

To translate the form into the ultimate trophy, Eliscu worked in clay attached to an armature made of lead wire. He used his own imagination, "artistic license," he calls it, in forming the body and shaping and detailing the powerful biceps and calf muscles that are so prominent on the muscular figure. Even the face, he said, was of his own imagining.

The one area he was not willing to trust to his artistic vision was the figure's costume. Knowing that Ed Smith, a high school classmate, was a football player at New York University, Eliscu asked Smith to bring his uniform to the studio and pose in it.

The Heisman may have been Eliscu's first professional work, but it was hardly his last. Since then there has rarely been a day that Eliscu has not spent creating.

He even rendered crucial artistic service to the nation in World War II. Assigned to an Army engineering unit at Fort Belvoir in Virginia, he spent the early part of the war making invasion maps and models for landings from Salerno to Normandy.

Then, after a flood of war casualties began arriving back in the United States, he was transferred to a medical unit at Valley Forge, Pennsylvania, where he assisted in the grisly work of assisting in plastic surgery and cutting cartilage to form into noses and chins.

Eliscu, by then a sergeant, gained an unusual footnote in the history of plastic surgery when he developed a technique of tattooing to remove birthmarks and provide color to reconstructed lips.

Since the war Eliscu has not only been one of the nation's most acclaimed and honored artists, he has also been one of the most prolific. He has turned out hundreds of pieces from the studio he maintained first at his home in Ossining, New York, and more recently in Sarasota, Florida, where he lives with his wife, Mildred.

Whatever his subject and whatever his medium, Eliscu, who has worked in everything from wax to stone, strives to satisfy his lifelong passion for breathing movement into otherwise inanimate objects.

"To me, movement is almost giving life to bronze," he said. "I try to put [in] action even if a thing is stilled or seated, through expression or a tilt of the head."

He also shuns abstract art in favor of realistic forms, which allow him to achieve, as he puts it, "a sense of recall, where you look at something and you're moved to recall what it makes you feel."

Ask him to name his favorite works, and Eliscu, who can choose them from museums all over the country, mentions his original, "Diana and the Fawn," "Holocaust," in Orlando; "Cascade of Books," in Washington, D.C.; the "Shark Diver," at Brookgreen Gardens in South Carolina; and, yes, the Heisman.

"It's an honest work," he said. "I think that the Heisman has a feeling. I think that you can feel not only the movement but the intensity of the piece. That's what I call honesty."

It is true that the statue depicts a run that never literally happened. Yet it symbolizes a run that happens every fall, year after year, just as Frank Eliscu imagined it.

For him the Heisman is more than a trophy. It is a work of art.

"I liked it then," he said, "and I like it now."

—ROBERT MCG. THOMAS JR.

1988
With the NCAA's all time greatest single rushing season, Barry Sanders lifted the game to new heights.

1989
Andre Ware made history when he became the first black quarterback to win the Heisman.

Selecting the Winner

The Winners, continued

1990

Ty Detmer's bionic arm led him to an out-of-this-world 29 NCAA records.

1991

The acrobatic Desmond Howard defied gravity in his spectacular catches for Michigan.

It is late afternoon on a Saturday early in December. In the Heisman Room on the 13th floor of the Downtown Athletic Club overlooking the Hudson River in lower Manhattan you can almost feel the suspense. As the television lights go up and the president of the club steps to the lectern, the hubbub dies and there is a hush in the room.

The five leading candidates for the Heisman Memorial Trophy sit nervously in the front row. Behind them are scores of club officials and invited guests, some standing at the back, blocking the door and spilling out into the elevator lobby.

Four floors above, a horde of reporters keep their eyes on the television monitor as they await the announcement now moments away. If the excitement seems palpable, there is a reason. It has been building for 60 years.

Bill Prince, what have thou wrought!

It was not John W. Heisman, the club's athletic director, but Willard B. Prince, the editor of *The D.A.C. Journal*, who dreamed up the idea of an annual award honoring the year's outstanding college football player. Indeed, Heisman was actually cool to the idea, believing that it would be inappropriate to honor individual achievement in a team sport. But when Heisman mentioned Prince's idea at a lunch with a group of sportswriters, their response was so enthusiastic he changed his mind.

Still, Heisman rejected Prince's idea that the award be named for him, so the first award, given in 1935 and limited to players east of the Mississippi, was known as The Downtown Athletic Club Trophy.

The next year, after Heisman's death, it became The Heisman Memorial Trophy and was broadened to include the entire country.

From the beginning, sportswriters and broadcasters have determined the winner, and to balance sectional favoritism they have been divided evenly among geographic regions. The number of regions and selectors have varied, but since 1988 there have been a total of 870 media voters, 145 from each of six regions. Since 1988 former Heisman winners have also voted.

Prince died in 1949, but many of the principles he laid down have not varied. Each elector is still required to vote for three players, with points awarded on a 3-2-1 basis and the winner being the player who receives the most points, whether or not he has received the most first-place votes.

Part of Prince's methodology though has changed a lot. For the first award his son John helped him address hundreds of envelopes mailed to the initial electors. When the ballots came back, Prince's daughter helped him count them at the dining room table.

Now the ballots are received and tallied by auditors at the accounting firm of Deloitte & Touche, who are sworn to secrecy. Although they give the club a list of top vote getters so the leading candidates may be invited to the announcement ceremony, only the auditors know the winner until an afternoon in December when the club president steps to the lectern, opens a sealed envelope and reads the name to an expectant nation.

Like each award for 60 years, Bill Prince, this one's for you.

The envelope, please.

—*Robert McG. Thomas Jr.*

1992
Gino Torretta held off nearly all of Miami's opponents, losing only one regular-season game during his career.

1993
Charlie Ward, now with basketball's New York Knicks, led the Seminoles to a national title and established himself as one of the Heisman's most versatile winners.

1935

Jay Berwanger

The Reluctant Pioneer

If Grantland Rice had needed a fifth horseman to go along with the four members of the Notre Dame team that Rice once canonized, the honor might well have gone to Jay Berwanger.

Jay who?

Jay Berwanger, the University of Chicago's incredible "one-man gang," who gained more than a mile from scrimmage before becoming the very first winner of the Heisman Memorial Trophy, in 1935. How good was Berwanger? Rice, the legendary sportswriter, recalled hearing Berwanger's high school coach in Dubuque, Iowa, say, "If Berwanger isn't another Jim Thorpe, there'll never be one."

Rice may be allowed a touch of hyperbole, but it would not be an exaggeration to say that Berwanger's status as the first Heisman winner has made him one of the more important—if not one of the more well-known—names in sports. What few remember is just how obscure the trophy was in those days. In fact, Berwanger was far more intent on winning the Silver Football, presented to him by *The Chicago Tribune* as the Big Ten's most valuable player of 1935, than he was on winning the Heisman, an award he had frankly never heard of. The trophy would not even be named the Heisman until the following season, making the two-time All-America halfback for Chicago the first and last player to win the Downtown Athletic Club Trophy. None of this should detract from the talent of Berwanger, who was widely recognized as the best football player not only in the Midwest but also in the entire nation.

How much did the first Heisman winner really care about the award? So little that when Berwanger, who was senior class president at Chicago's prestigious university, returned to the Psi Upsilon fraternity house on a blustery November day in 1935 and found a telegram telling him of his latest honor, he was less than thrilled.

"It said I had won some trophy," Berwanger said, "and that there would be two tickets waiting to take a guest and me to New York.... It didn't seem like a real big deal. No one at school said anything much to me about it. I was more excited about the trip than the trophy, because it was my first flight."

Berwanger selected his coach, Clark Shaughnessy, as his guest on the trip to New York. Berwanger learned nearly as much about the eastern metropolis as he had learned about football from Shaughnessy, one of the game's great innovators and strategists. The two took in all the standard tours, watched a performance of the Rockettes and had lunch at the 21 Club.

It wasn't until later Heisman winners began cashing in on the award in negotiating rich professional contracts that Berwanger realized the trophy's value. Said Berwanger recently: "When television came on the scene and college football began getting exposure, it became a big deal that I had won the first one.

"The difference between winning the first Heisman in 1935 and winning it now is like the difference between nothing and a million dollars. For 20 years I had no requests for autographed pictures. Then, after World War II, I started getting 10 or 12 letters a week. I have a good supply of pictures. I autograph them and send them out myself."

Berwanger's trophy disappeared, for all intents and purposes, for nearly a decade after he received it. After all, where do you store a huge bronze statue that weighs 25 pounds but feels like 50? So he asked his Aunt Gussie to keep it for him until after graduation.

It seems that Aunt Gussie's coffee table wasn't big enough, nor her mantelpiece wide enough to accommodate the monster trophy. But she finally found a use for it, and for nearly 10 years the trophy served as Aunt Gussie's doorstop, providing her with cool breezes off Lake Michigan. It also became a convenient floor-level hat rack for Berwanger and other guests.

Obscure as the trophy might have been, Berwanger was nonetheless a most worthy first recipient. At 6'1" and 195 pounds, he led the Maroons' relatively weak squad to an 11-11-2 record during three varsity campaigns, gaining 1,839 yards on the ground, passing for another 926 and scoring a total of 22 TDs. During his Heisman season of 1935, he rushed for 577 yards on 119 carries and completed 25 of 67 passes for 405 yards. A true all-round performer, Berwanger did the Maroons' punting and kicking, scored six touchdowns, caught two passes, intercepted four, and returned punts and kickoffs.

Berwanger was perhaps the first example of a franchise player. Without him on the field the Maroons had virtually no chance to win. Their strategy was simple: If Berwanger could hold the game close, maybe he could win it as well. Four years after Berwanger played his last game, during which time the Maroons won only one Big Ten contest, the school dropped football.

The first Heisman winner was a deserving one: Berwanger was a virtual one-man gang for Chicago.

His finest moments came in his senior year. He nearly beat Ohio State by himself, scoring both touchdowns to give the Maroons a 13–0 lead early in the second half. On one TD, an 85-yard dazzler, Berwanger reversed his field three times, eluded 10 Buckeyes, just missed going out of bounds on either sideline, stopped dead twice so that his interference could form and finally picked up a blocking convoy to the end zone. Alas, despite Berwanger's artistry, Ohio State went on to win. But the freewheeling halfback beat Illinois in his college finale, returning a punt 50 yards to the one-yard line, diving over for a touchdown and kicking the extra point in a 7–6 Chicago victory.

Berwanger launched not only the Heisman, but also the National Football League draft, in which he was the first player ever selected. Although the Philadelphia Eagles drafted Berwanger in 1936, the Chicago Bears' venerable, tightfisted owner-coach, George Halas, obtained the signing rights. When Papa Bear asked the Chicago star how much money he wanted, Berwanger, who had no interest in pro ball and had already mapped out a business future that was to make him a millionaire, replied, "Twenty-five thousand dollars over two years."

"We'll see you around, Jay," said Halas, whose highest-paid Bear, Bronko Nagurski, was making $7,000 a year and being paid in IOUs.

"I gave him a figure I knew he wouldn't agree to," Berwanger said. "I've never regretted the decision. The Depression was on, and I didn't think I could get a good job while playing pro football.

"Halas held no grudge against me. We became friends in later years. He left $25,000 in his will to the University of Chicago for athletic facilities."

Berwanger's "good job" with a sponge-rubber company paid $25 a week. After serving in the Navy Air Force during World War II, he started his own manufacturing business, selling molded rubber and plastics. He and his wife, Jane, now divide their time between homes in Oak Brook, Illinois, and Mexico.

"My strengths were speed and elusiveness," Berwanger said. "A fullback is a brave man. He likes to run over people. A halfback, by nature, has to be a coward. He runs away from others. I had 9.9 speed in the 100-yard dash, so I ran away."

No opponent who ever faced Berwanger considered him a coward. That would have been still another first.

—*Cooper Rollow*

Larry Kelley

Remarks of a Winner

On October 17, 1936, a good Yale team took on a talented Navy team in Baltimore's Municipal Stadium. By the third quarter the Midshipmen were leading 7–6. Yale punted and Navy's Snead Schmidt fumbled the return at his 20-yard line. Larry Kelley of Yale was charging at Schmidt, and the bouncing football struck Kelley's foot. Was it accidental or did Kelley intentionally kick the ball?

Whatever his intention, the deflection proved propitious as the ball bounced down to the Navy two-yard line, where Kelley himself recovered it. The officials, apparently without any suspicion of subterfuge, awarded possession to Yale. Clint Frank scored from there, and Yale went on to a 12–7 victory. It took a few days for the idea to sprout that perhaps Navy had been jobbed by the Kelley fellow, who so often was in the middle of one brouhaha or another.

At first Kelley denied that he had deliberately kicked the ball—"I'm not that smart," he said—but the denials grew weaker as time went by, and in truth he didn't mind the play being assessed as a clever ruse by an opportunistic Yale man. By the next season the rules committee had added a rule prohibiting the kicking of a free ball, intentionally or not, and so Kelley, in addition to being in the Heisman pantheon and the College Football Hall of Fame is, in spirit anyway, also in the rule book.

Historians such as rules authority David Nelson later stated that Kelley's kick was intentional. No one knows for sure, but that sort of skepticism came to surround much of the lore associated with Kelley. In fact, over the years, Kelley, bright though he was, was given credit for a number of wisecracks, gags and one-liners that he didn't say or commit. Call him the Yogi Berra of his day.

But Lawrence Morgan Kelley *was* a deserving Heisman winner and a superb offensive football player. A big receiver for his era at 6'2" and 185 pounds, Kelley was a master at disguising his considerable speed, strolling into the secondary from right

The Kelley legend became as laden with unreliable anecdote as that of a man named Yogi many years later.

1936 Larry Kelley

end and then with a sudden burst accelerating past an unwary defender. He had a strong vertical leap and great hands for bringing in high, almost unreachable passes. Blocking, tackling and practice were of less interest to him. This was a big-play performer.

The first big play of his illustrious college career came against the 1934 Princeton Tigers and produced the only loss in 26 games from 1933 through 1935 for Tiger coach Fritz Crisler's deep and talented squads. During the week leading up to the game there had been speculation among the Princeton students that the team might consider a bid to play in the Rose Bowl on January 1.

Under a stunning blue sky on November 17, 1934, 11 Yale men played 60 minutes against an unbeaten Princeton team, which was seeking to extend a 17-game unbeaten streak. The Elis, with a 3–3 record, had only 23 players in uniform that day, while the Tigers squad was four deep. This was single-position football with limited substitution, no platoons.

Princeton's Ken Sandbach fumbled the opening kick-off and barely made it out of his own end zone. It was a play that set the tone for Princeton's performance throughout the day as the Tigers mishandled the ball on seven of their first 10 plays, prompting a Yale player to say, "I hope the Rose Bowl has handles on it." The crack was attributed later to Kelley, but the source was actually guard Ben Grosscup.

Yale soon found itself on the Princeton 43, and it was time to strike. Kelley went deep. The pass by Jerry Roscoe, the tailback, looked overthrown.

"I leaped, snared the ball with one hand and circled," Kelley said. "Kats Kadlic and Gary LeVan tried to head me off. I decided to stop dead and then cut back. My sudden stop sent the two Princeton tacklers tripping over each other's legs, one of them brushing my knees as he slid by."

Kelley's touchdown set off a wave of celebration among the Eli faithful. "I was as much surprised as anyone else," he said. "I was so nervous, I dropped the ball as I handed it to the referee."

Yale won 7–0, and Kelley went on to score a touchdown in every other game during his career against the Bulldogs' Big Three rivals, Princeton and Harvard. A notable feat in an era when completing just half a dozen passes in a game was considered remarkable.

The upset at Princeton was monumental, and the Kelley fame mounted and mounted. The next year, at Franklin Field, Yale faced a Pennsylvania team composed of players from a more ethnic, public high school background than Yale's WASPy, prep-school stocked team (Kelley had a year at the Peddie School in New Jersey).

A different battlefield: After college, Kelley (right) met Jay Berwanger in a rugby match in Chicago.

With the Bulldogs trailing early, 20–6, a Penn player is alleged to have said, "I thought you were a gabby guy, Kelley. A little bashful today?"

The world was told the Yale end replied, "Oh, do you fellows speak English?" This feisty putdown was repeated by many writers, but Kelley never said it. In all probability the quip was the invention of Gould Martin, an alumnus who hung around the Yale Club bar in New York with sportswriters such as Joe Williams of the *World-Telegram*. Williams, after Kelley's last game, confessed, "I started giving publicity to those cracks he was supposed to be uttering down on the playing field. Most came to

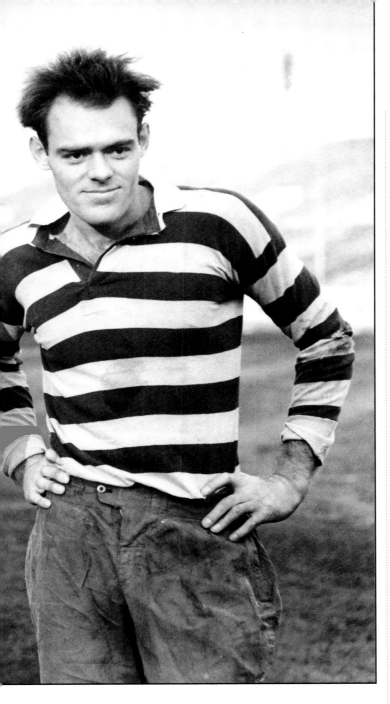

me from the barroom humorists of the Yale Club, harmless enough and for all I knew authentic."

More brazen was George Trevor, Yale '15, who wrote beautiful and imaginative prose for *The New York Sun*. With Trevor as Kelley's self-appointed Boswell, the Yale athlete seemingly could do no wrong. When the Heisman ballots were counted, 219 were for Kelley and 47 for runner-up Sam Francis of Nebraska. Many of the Eli's votes surely had been inspired by Trevor's iconography.

Against Harvard, when a sweep around Kelley's end failed, he was said to have shouted at the Harvard quarterback, "What judgment, trying Kelley's end on fourth down." He later offered his hand to an official after scoring a touchdown. "I thought you'd want to shake hands with me. Everyone else does."

Fiction. "He was no-nonsense when we were playing ball," said fullback Bud Miles. "I don't think he ever said anything cutting or nasty," said Clint Frank. "If someone from the other team made a wisecrack, Larry always had the right word to put him in his place."

Said Kelley in an interview years later, "I may have said some things on the field, but not like you've read. I really cared about winning. I'm like Vince Lombardi. 'Winning is everything.' " Kelley cried when he walked off the field after his last game.

The Yale teams were no juggernauts, but they did win 18 of 25 in Kelley's three seasons and were 7–1 when he was captain, in 1936. A 26–23 comeback victory over Princeton, which had led 16–0, was the gem that senior year, highlighted by a key 60-yard touchdown grab by Kelley. After catching the pass from Frank at the 25, Kelley realized he could never outrun the closing Princeton sprinter, Jack White. So he ran directly at White and knocked him on his back with a stiff arm. He had attacked the defender. "Amazing," said Crisler, who called it the greatest game he had ever seen.

Everything came easy for this Williamsport, Pennsylvania, native. He was captain and first baseman for the Yale baseball team and an honors student who won scholarships that paid his way.

After college Kelley flirted with pro football, spurning an offer from the Boston Shamrocks of the short-lived American League, and had a brief fling in the glove business. But most of his adult life was spent as a prep school master, happy and contented years at Peddie and Cheshire Academy.

Kelley has been a devoted Heisman alumnus, having attended many of the Heisman dinners and served as a member of the Heisman Foundation. His humor has delighted many, beginning at the modest Downtown Athletic Club luncheon on December 16, 1936, when he received his award. His acceptance speech was classic Kelley. The audience roared when he began. "Fellow Rotarians," he said.

—*WILLIAM N. WALLACE*

1937
Clint Frank

When Yale Last Ruled the East

That the second and third Heisman Trophy winners came from Yale was not a matter of that institution's tony elitism, great gridiron history or proximity to the hero-making machinery of New York's press. Larry Kelley and Clint Frank were good football players; in the opinion of NFL Hall of Famer Earle Neale, Frank was a great one.

"Greasy" Neale, who spent a long lifetime in football, was by title merely an assistant coach at Yale during the Kelley-Frank era. In reality, however, he was co–head coach with Ducky Pond and the mastermind behind a clever offense that blended the double wing's deception with the single wing's power. It was this innovative attack that Frank used over three seasons, from 1935 to 1937, to lead the Elis to 19 wins in 25 games.

Neale never forgot Frank. Years later Neale would call Frank and Steve Van Buren, who helped Neale's Philadelphia Eagles win NFL championships in 1948 and '49, the two best backs he had ever known. "If I had to pick between them, I might choose Frank because he was so strong on defense," said Neale.

Greasy, famous for bungling names, called Frank Cliff rather than Clint throughout their association, and so did Kelley, for affection and affect, whenever the teammates met over the next 55 years. "Cliff," said Neale, "was a miracle on defense. I saw him play back to break up passes and still make tackles on the line of scrimmage. He was all over the field—knocking down passes, smashing line plays, often tackling back of the line for heavy losses."

But defense never won a Heisman Trophy. Col. Russell (Red) Reeder Jr., the former Army scout, in 1994 at the age of 92 remembered Clint Frank as "a forceful, vertical runner. He generated tremendous power and always gained." That was the mark he left.

Neither Neale, Pond nor anyone else expected Clinton Edward Frank to become a great gridiron hero when he came out for the varsity in 1935. Because of a shoulder injury, Frank had not played as a freshman or at Lawrenceville, where he prepped for a year after leaving Evanston Township High School in Chicago's suburbs.

Frank, in addition to his great athletic ability, was a master at play selection.

With Jerry Roscoe as the Elis' No. 1 tailback, Frank played little as a sophomore, but the next two seasons he ran the team. Four games in particular stand out—one against Dartmouth, two against Princeton and one against Harvard.

The first of these was at Princeton in 1936 in which the Tigers went ahead early 16–0. The late Tim Cohane, author of *The Yale Football Story*, picks up the story at that point.

"Charlie Ewart got Yale going by running a quick kick back to the Tiger 35. Frank now began to mix his plays in a way that completely befuddled the Orange and Black. He passed to Flick Hoxton for 17. He made four himself. Al Wilson circled end on a trick play to the 1. Princeton stiffened but on third down Frank charged across with

Tigers clinging to him. They left the field with Princeton ahead, 16–7, and everybody in the crowd of 57,000 knew the second half would be a dilly. It was."

Al Hessberg, the wingback and the fastest Bulldog, ran 22 yards for a touchdown on a delayed buck and hand-off from Frank. On Yale's next possession Frank called for a Neale special, a spread pass formation, with Ewart the target because Kelley was being blanketed so well by the Tigers. But the team captain and end spoke up in the huddle.

"Wait a second, Clint," he said. "Try me this time. I think I can give them the slip from this spread."

Frank dropped way back and simply flung the ball with all his might, never seeing Kelley but anticipating where his end would be. Kelley caught the pass, stiff-armed Jack White and completed a 60-yard touchdown play.

But Princeton came back and went ahead, 23–20, in the fourth quarter. Again Frank's mix of plays fooled Nassau as the Elis drove to the Yale 13. Cohane, who was there, wrote, "Frank had by now played himself nearly into exhaustion. But he called his own signal off-tackle.

"The Princeton left side backer rose up and jammed his way. It looked as if Frank must surely be piled up. Instead, with a mighty wrench, he broke away from the nearest tackler, stiff-armed another and with a last wild burst of speed veered out around the left flank and went pounding into the end zone."

Yale won 26–23, and Fritz Crisler, the Princeton coach, said, "If the teams could have gone on playing, it might have ended 79–76. But Yale would have won."

After Yale beat Harvard the next Saturday, thanks to Frank's 44-yard run and 41-yard touchdown pass, the Crimson's new coach, Dick Harlow, sought out Frank in

In 1981, when Yale honored its back to back Heisman winners, Larry Kelley and Clint Frank, legendary sportswriter Red Smith was on hand to offer his thoughts on a bygone era in college football.

John W. Heisman was born in Cleveland, played football at Brown and Pennsylvania and coached at Oberlin, Akron, Auburn, Clemson, Georgia Tech, Pennsylvania, Washington and Jefferson, and Rice. At Georgia Tech he set a record for coachly compassion when his team defeated Cumberland 222–0. This display of selfless clemency won him such warm affection among his fellows that when an award was established for individual excellence in undergraduate ranks, the trophy was named for Heisman.

After Jay Berwanger of Chicago won the first Heisman Trophy, in 1935, Yale produced winners back to back. Its glib end, Lawrence Morgan Kelley, won in 1936, and Clinton Edward Frank, the unsinkable halfback, in 1937. [In photo on opposite page, Frank is on the left, Kelley on the right.] Last Friday, on the eve of the Harvard game, Kelley and Frank found a permanent home for their trophies. They presented the bronze statuettes to Yale, where they will be displayed in the Kiphuth Trophy Room in the Yale gym until fission do them part.

"My little friend here has meant much to me in 45 years," Larry Kelley said. "His headgear has been worn smooth by my friends and me rubbing it for luck. I'll miss him, but now there's a time to make better use of him. I hope some potential Rhodes scholars visiting Yale gain some inspiration. And I hope they can run, pass and kick."

Frank, too, hoped the trophies might be some inspirational force "to encourage and help stimulate excellence." Yet when he spoke of his own football days he spoke not of victory but of his bitterest defeat—the 13–6 Harvard victory in the last game of a season that had seen Yale go undefeated.

"I've thought about that game through a lot of sleepless nights," Frank said. "I've been told to forget it, that perhaps it was the best thing that ever happened to me, but I can't believe that."

Frank, known as the "most taped player of our time," played the Harvard game on one leg, made tackles all over the field and kept Yale fighting to the end. Said Tom Thorp, the umpire, "He stuck it out when two iron men would have called it a day."

The presentation took place in the President's Room in Woolsey Hall, a round room of quiet elegance. Carmen Cozza, the Yale coach, who attended the cradle of American coaches, Miami of Ohio, gazed at the bronze running backs.

"Gee," he said, "this is the first time I ever saw a Heisman Trophy, let alone two of them."

Kelley addresses his old schoolmate as Cliff Frank. That's what their coach, Greasy Neale, called him, because Greasy couldn't pronounce Clint or didn't want to.

Kelley has been a teacher at prep schools like Peddie and Cheshire. He never was interested in coaching, and pro football didn't offer much as a career in his day. Anyway, Larry was better known for his opportunistic plays and impromptu remarks than for sustained excellence, though he was a gifted pass catcher, had rare speed afoot and could block and tackle superbly when he felt like it.

More often, though, when somebody of his era mentions Larry, he'll tell about the Penn game on Franklin Field in Philadelphia in 1935, Kelley's junior year. With Penn leading, 20–8, Kelley was quiet.

"I thought you were a gabby guy, Kelley," said the Penn tackle opposite him. "What's the matter, a little bashful today?"

Larry looked up in courtly surprise. "Oh," he said, "do you fellows speak English?"

Frank is a prosperous adman in Chicago who used to head a Chicago mob running Midwestern scholar-athletes to Yale. That traffic seems to have ended. Maybe scholarship has declined in the corn belt. Maybe Yalies consider Midwestern scholars subversive.

the locker room and told him, "You're the greatest competitor I've ever seen."

In Frank's senior year, the only one for which we have his statistics, he was captain and gained 667 yards rushing in eight games, averaging 4.24 yards per carry. He completed 30 of 105 pass attempts, good by the standards of that run-dominated era. The team came within one game of an unbeaten season. Perhaps the season's most notable contest was a hard-fought 9–9 tie with Ivy powerhouse Dartmouth.

The Green seemed to have Yale beaten 9–2 near the end, with the Elis stuck on fourth-and-eight at their 47 before Frank hit Hessberg for a 28-yard gain. With 36 seconds left three Yale passes fell incomplete. Frank, ever

of 79 and 51 yards. His team won 26–0.

Harvard was ready for Yale the next week at Cambridge and won 13–6 in the snow. Frank was injured but would not leave. At the end he limped off the field, and Tom Thorp, the umpire, said, "His knee was badly swollen, and he was barely able to move. I couldn't see how the fellow could make another play. He could stand only on one leg. But he stuck it out when two iron men would have called it a day."

Stanley Woodward, a noted football writer for *The New York Herald Tribune*, wrote, "Clint Frank is the best football player we have seen since the war. He was the greatest defensive player on the field. He made 50 tackles. He kept the Yale team fighting to the finish. He drove and he fought and, ultimately, for the first time this season, he lost."

And he never played again. Pro football was a suspect sport for Yale men and many others in those days, and Frank never gave it a thought. In an elegant acceptance speech at the Downtown Athletic Club, he told his Heisman audience, "To me football has always been a sport and a game. I began it as such. I played it as such. And I leave it as such."

Frank had almost twice as many Heisman votes, 524 to 264, as runner-up Byron (Whizzer) White of Colorado, who went on to become a Supreme Court justice. Pittsburgh's Marshall Goldberg came in third with 211 votes.

After Yale, Frank returned to his native Chicago and took a job in advertising. He served with distinction in World War II as an aide to Brigadier General Jimmy Doolittle, becoming a lieutenant colonel. When he resumed his advertising career, he went on to a success even greater than he had found in football. Before he sold it in 1977 to Interpublic, the Clinton E. Frank Agency had become the 23rd largest in the United States.

Frank stayed close to football until his death in 1992. The varsity practice field at Yale is named after him, and the National Football Foundation, which he supported generously, awarded him its highest honor in 1988.
—*WILLIAM N. WALLACE*

Clint said he had given up skiing, too. He had two knee operations last year, and although a doctor told him, "Listen, you can't get any worse," sliding down a hill hurts too much.

A welcome and unexpected attendant at the presentation was Jordan Olivar, the Villanova tackle and son of a Staten Island club fighter, who succeeded the late Herman Hickman as Yale coach. He had a successful insurance business going in California before, during and after his coaching days. He is a lovely man, as bald as Carmen Cozza.

"Jordan came by this morning to look at our office," Cozza said. "I told him, 'Nothing's changed. I'm still using your comb.'"

Speaking of the possibility that the trophies on display might inspire some undergraduate of the future, Larry Kelley said, "After last week's game against Princeton (in which Princeton's Bob Holly completed passes for more than 500 yards), I hope they inspire some defensive backs to enroll here."

cool, threw once more, in the right flat to Hessberg, who got the jump on the secondary. Hessberg raced to a touchdown, Gil Humphrey kicked the conversion, and Yale remained unbeaten.

Against a lesser Princeton team, in the rain at New Haven, Frank put on his greatest statistical show—191 yards gained rushing on 19 carries, which included runs

The late Bart Giamatti is flanked by the two Yale Heisman winners years later.

"He wins great honors and wears them well."

Just eight words, but they were all that was needed to describe Robert David O'Brien in the 1935 Woodrow Wilson High School yearbook. He was only 17 then, but that brief verse spoke volumes about the little guy who became one of football's greatest legends.

So did the picture above it. His dark, shining eyes suggested rare spirit, intensity and leadership. Nearly all of his senior classmates smiled happily in their pictures, but O'Brien's expression was more serious. One senses the integrity and ambition that were already present in this young man.

As Flem Hall, the retired sports editor of *The Fort Worth Star-Telegram,* who chronicled the dynamic quarterback's Heisman Trophy–winning career at TCU, said, "Davey was a prince in every sense."

Wade Thompson, an assistant coach from O'Brien's Woodrow Wilson days, confirmed that even as a teenager, O'Brien exuded quality. "On the field, every move he made was the right one," said Thompson. "Off the field, he was everyone's friend. Davey never was one to get the big head."

Great deeds, small ego. O'Brien was a most unusual package.

He was one of the finest football players in Dallas high school history. Though he stood slightly under 5'7" and weighed only 118 pounds, he brought the first great acclaim to the then new East Dallas school, which was destined to become the only high school in America to produce two Heisman Trophy winners (the other was Tim Brown of Notre Dame in 1987). Anyone who watched O'Brien play then wasn't surprised to see him lead TCU to a perfect season and a national championship in 1938 or set NFL passing records with the Philadelphia Eagles.

In those Depression-era days, a good football team was something a community could hold close to its heart when many families were just scraping by. The Wildcats played their big games with older Dallas rivals in Fair Park Stadium, site of the future Cotton Bowl. Across the street was the racetrack, where pari-mutuel betting flourished during its first fling in Texas.

Herschel Forester, Woodrow Wilson's coach, had his own stable of winners. The most spectacular was built like a Shetland pony. "David was strong and tough. He had big arms and legs. If he had been taller, he would have

1938
Davey O'Brien

Great Deeds, Small Ego

weighed 190," said Rusty Cowart, who met O'Brien when they attended Lipscomb Elementary and Davey started spending most of his time playing football in a field behind the Juliette Fowler Home, an orphanage where Cowart, I. B. Hale and other future athletic stars grew up.

O'Brien lived with his mother, Ella Mae Keith O'Brien, in a handsome two-story house in the prestigious new Lakewood section. His parents divorced when he was a toddler, and his mother reared him with the help of her brother, who was a florist and the financial director at the Fowler Home. O'Brien thrived in the public schools of East Dallas and found his special family among the Fowler Home kids.

"He was like a brother to me," Cowart said. "We'd eat lunch together at school, and he knew that all a Home boy had was a peanut-butter sandwich. He would split his Hershey bar and milk with me."

At Woodrow Wilson the diminutive O'Brien and Hale, the towering 200-pound tackle from the Home whom O'Brien nicknamed Big Boy, were good enough to star as sophomores in 1932, when the Wildcats lost in the state quarterfinals to Fort Worth Masonic Home 40–7. In the next two years O'Brien developed into an all-city, all-state and all-Southern player. But he never forgot the embarrassment of that loss to Masonic Home, a legendary Texas schoolboy power of that era.

O'Brien committed one of the few lapses of his football career that day. Masonic Home had exploded for two quick touchdowns to break open a close game, 27–7. On the ensuing kickoff O'Brien allowed the ball to land in the end zone without downing it. An alert Masonic Home player covered the ball for another touchdown, making it 33–7 at the half.

O'Brien learned from that experience, gaining a maturity that served his teams well through the years. At TCU, he understudied Sammy Baugh as a sophomore in 1936, when the Horned Frogs were invited to play in the first Cotton Bowl Classic on January 1, 1937. TCU beat Marquette 16–6, and Baugh moved on to a Hall of Fame career with the Washington Redskins. The torch was passed to O'Brien, and by 1938 he was setting college football ablaze with his passing, running, kicking and defense. He weighed only 155 then, but he

From the fields of Fowler Home to the stadiums of the NFL, O'Brien was a man who knew how to win.

seemed indestructible in body and spirit.

"He was a tough little nut," said teammate Connie Sparks, who played fullback in coach Dutch Meyer's wide assortment of wingback and spread formations. "Dutch was pretty young and gruff then, and he never bragged much on Davey until his later years. But he must have had great confidence in Davey as a quarterback. Dutch gave us a game plan, and we always had some special plays. Then on game day he turned it over to David."

Which was exactly how O'Brien wanted it.

"Davey was so modest about his public success that he hid his plaque for making the Kate Smith All-America team behind a dresser in the dorm," Cowart said. "But he took great pride in running the team on the field. We were in the locker room before our game at A&M when Dutch walked over to him and said, 'O'Brien, the first play will be 40 Sucker!' Davey just nodded. When Dutch walked away, Davey told me, 'That will be the last play that little square-headed s.o.b. will call today.' "

TCU would win 34–6.

By New Year's Day the Frogs were 10–0, O'Brien had 19 touchdowns and 1,733 yards for the season and had not only won the Heisman but also the Maxwell and Walter Camp awards, the first such grand slam in college football. So great was his national fame that he finished fourth in the Associated Press's annual ranking of outstanding U.S. athletes, amateur and pro, ahead of such immortals as Joe Louis, Hank Greenberg and Jimmie Foxx. But TCU still had to play Carnegie Tech in the Sugar Bowl.

At halftime the faltering Frogs trailed 7–6, and Meyer asked if any of the players had something to say. Finally, O'Brien stood up.

"It was the only time Davey ever did anything like that," Meyer would recall years later. "He calmly told the kids to keep their poise and play like they knew how to play, and they'd win the game. That was all, but it was enough. Davey threw a touchdown pass and kicked a field goal. We won 15–7."

There was a splendid feeling of brotherhood among those TCU players. They cleaned offices in the administration building in the evening and on weekends to earn room and board, and they were always ready to help each other.

"Nobody had any money," said Don Looney, a junior end on the 1938 national champions who worked with Davey in the South Texas oil fields during the summer and joined the Eagles in 1940, becoming O'Brien's favorite receiver. "If one guy had a dollar, you knew you could borrow a quarter from him."

Despite his upper-middle-class background, O'Brien always fit in. He shared the work, and whenever he had some money, he shared that, too.

Looney later became wealthy in the oil business in Houston, but he never forgot how much O'Brien cared. Before O'Brien died in 1977 after a long battle with cancer, his savings and insurance had been wiped out, and his family was faced with a large debt. Old friends dug in. Teammates say Looney was one of the greatest contributors.

O'Brien, who graduated from TCU in the spring of 1939 with a degree in geology, at first balked at turning pro. Bert Bell, the Eagles' owner-coach, lured him into the NFL with the biggest contract given a rookie since Red Grange's day: a $12,000 signing bonus, $10,000 per season and a percentage of the gate receipts. But O'Brien said he would sign for only two years, after which he planned to join Hale in attending F.B.I. training school at Quantico, Virginia.

So on December 1, 1940, O'Brien played his final game. It was at Washington against Baugh and the Eastern Conference champion Redskins.

"Before the game Davey told me, 'I'll be looking for you,'" Looney said. "Our team was crippled. The NFL rules required you to suit up 18 players for a game, and we had to put three guys who were too hurt to play in uniform to meet the minimum."

The Redskins won 13–7, but O'Brien set an NFL record by completing 33 passes. Looney caught 14, another record, for 180 yards.

"Davey hung around the locker room a little while after the game, telling all the guys goodbye, then he went on to Quantico to report to the F.B.I.," Looney said. "He and I.B. did a good job there, too. They became the best marksmen in the F.B.I.", Which surprised no one who ever knew them. O'Brien had taken a large salary cut—down to $3,200—but he was happy. He and Big Boy, his lifelong friend, were doing something special together again.

By his standards, that was the best reward of all.
—*SAM BLAIR*

O'Brien, the pride of Texas, gratefully received his award from Walter Holcombe of the D.A.C.

A Hero Lost

John Greenleaf Whittier, the noted American writer of the 19th century once wrote: "For all sad words of tongue or pen, the saddest are these: 'It might have been!'"

Nile Clarke Kinnick Jr. was a modern-day Renaissance man, an exceptional student-athlete who loved poetry and politics as much as football. In 1939 Iowa's "Cornbelt Comet" won the Heisman Memorial Trophy and was named Male Athlete of the Year by the Associated Press, beating out Joe DiMaggio and Joe Louis. But Kinnick, the grandson of a former Iowa governor, had ambitions that went far beyond sports.

World War II, however, ended those plans. When the Navy fighter pilot was lost at sea in 1943, at the age of 24, the nation may have lost a future senator, Supreme Court justice or president. "There is no calculating what he might have done," said Wiley Rutledge, an Iowan who was a U.S. Supreme Court justice in the 1940s.

Kinnick was president of his senior class at Iowa and graduated with honors as a Phi Beta Kappa. He turned down a lucrative offer to play pro football in order to attend law school at Iowa, but with war looming in 1941, he joined the Navy and was called to active duty three days before the Japanese attacked Pearl Harbor.

"Every man whom I've admired in history has willingly and courageously served in his country's armed forces in time of danger," Kinnick wrote in his diary. "It is not only a duty but an honor to follow their example as best I know how."

"May God give me the courage and ability to so conduct myself in every situation that my country, my family and my friends will be proud of me."

Family, friends and teammates always took pride in Kinnick's accomplishments, which included playing almost every minute of the 1939 season until he was hurt in the final game. Though they were usually undermanned, undersized and underdogs, Kinnick and his fellow "Iron Men" went 6-1-1 that year, including an upset of mighty Notre Dame.

"He was the most disciplined young man I have ever met in my life. Nile knew exactly what he wanted and how he wanted to get there.... His dedication was to be the best he could possibly be. Nile was the only person I ever saw in my life who was trying to do that every day and every minute," said Al Couppee, the quarterback of the 1939 squad.

Kinnick and his two younger brothers grew up on a farm in Adel, Iowa. Kinnick developed into an all-around sports star and once played on the same Junior Legion baseball team with future Hall of Fame pitcher Bob Feller, who was from nearby Van Meter. During the Depression the family was forced to leave the farm and move to Omaha, where Kinnick was an A student and made all-state in football and basketball at Benson High.

Kinnick's father had played football at Iowa State, but Nile Jr. decided to attend Iowa, which at the time was the virtual doormat of the Big Ten. The Hawkeyes continued to struggle in Kinnick's first two seasons, winning a total of two games, but it wasn't his fault. A triple threat as a runner, passer and kicker, Kinnick was All–Big Ten as a sophomore and played most of his junior year on a severely injured ankle. Still, Kinnick blamed himself for the Hawkeyes' problems, telling his parents in a letter: "Your son should have stuck to ping-pong and parlor games."

The Hawkeyes' fortunes began to change when coach Irl Tubbs was replaced by Dr. Eddie Anderson after the 1938 season. Anderson, an Iowa native, played under Knute Rockne at Notre Dame and then went to medical school while playing pro football for the Chicago Cardinals. He came to Iowa from Holy Cross, where his teams had gone 47-7-4 during the previous six seasons.

Kinnick was Anderson's kind of player. Despite his small stature (5' 8", 170 pounds), Kinnick was one of the strongest men on the team. "Tough as an iron post," Anderson said. "Slap him in the stomach and he'll break your wrist."

Kinnick displayed his toughness—and versatility—as Iowa opened the season with a 41–0 rout of South Dakota. He ran for three touchdowns, including a 65-yard dash, passed for two more and drop-kicked five conversion points. The next week, he was spectacular again in a seesaw 32–29 victory over Indiana—Iowa's first win over the Hoosiers in 18 years. Kinnick threw three TD passes, ran for another, set a school record by returning nine punts for 201 yards and had 171 yards in kickoff returns.

Iowa lost its next game 27–7 to Michigan and Tom Harmon, who would win the Heisman the following year. Iowa's only score came on a 71-yard touchdown pass from Kinnick to

The widely admired Kinnick was the prototypical golden boy with the golden future.

Fifty years after the death of Iowa legend Nile Kinnick, local columnist Charles Bullard looked back at the unfulfilled promise of a genuine American hero whose talents and character transcended the sport that made him famous.

Fifty years ago this month, Nile Kinnick, the most famous football player in Iowa history, died when the Navy fighter plane he was piloting crashed in the Caribbean Sea off the coast of South America.

Although 8,398 Iowans died during World War II, the death of the University of Iowa's only Heisman Trophy winner shook the state like no other wartime tragedy. The state mourned the loss of its favorite son with the same sorrow the nation felt when President John F. Kennedy was assassinated in 1963.

"From my recollection, it was one of the biggest stories, one of the biggest tragedies to come out of World War II," said WHO sports director Jim Zabel who was editor of *The Daily Iowan* student newspaper at the University of Iowa when Kinnick's Grumman Wildcat developed an oil leak and plunged into the Gulf of Paria between Venezuela and Trinidad.

Zabel remembers remaking page one and devoting the entire front page to coverage of Kinnick's untimely death.

"He was still a gigantic hero on the Iowa campus," he said. "It was an epic thing."

Don Klotz, who was the Hawkeye tennis coach from 1947 to 1970, said Kinnick was so popular that his death was like losing a family member.

"The publicity was so general that you felt that you had seen him and knew him," said Klotz.

Iowans of a certain age can still remember where they were when they heard the news that Kinnick had vanished without a trace within four miles of the carrier *Lexington* on June 2, 1943.

Kinnick's plane sank out of sight before rescue craft could reach him. His body was never recovered. Only paint chips and an oil slick marked his watery grave.

"It just destroyed me," said Al Couppee, who was the quarterback during Kinnick's 1939 Heisman Trophy season. "I've never had such a total shock in my life, nothing. Not Kennedy's assassination, nothing," said Couppee, who now lives in Canyon Lake, California.

Kinnick's death affected the state so deeply because he was more than a football star. Even at age 24, he was already a legend.

In addition to being a great athlete, Kinnick was a Phi Beta Kappa student with personal integrity and leadership qualities so pronounced that his contemporaries say he would have been governor, a U.S. senator, a Supreme Court justice or president had he lived.

"I think he would have become an extremely important man in this state," said Paul Baender, a professor emeritus of English at the University of Iowa who wrote a 1991 book about Kinnick. "If he had lived, I think he could have written his own ticket for the rest of his life"

George (Red) Frye, of Albia, who was a center and a linebacker on the 1939 Hawkeye football team dubbed The Iron Men by sportswriters, said he believes Kinnick would have been president of the United States. "As a matter of fact, I would have been more surprised if he was not president of the United States."

Noting that Kinnick was studying to be a lawyer before he enlisted in the Navy, Des Moines restaurateur Babe Bisignano said he thinks Kinnick would have returned to law school after the war and eventually become a justice on the U.S. Supreme Court.

Floyd (Buzz) Dean. "Kinnick was as tough a competitor as any man I played against," Harmon said. "I don't care how bad you had Kinnick down, he came back at you."

After beating Wisconsin and Purdue, the Hawkeyes shocked undefeated, third-ranked Notre Dame 7–6 in Iowa City. Once again Kinnick was the hero, running over two tacklers to score Iowa's only touchdown. Notre Dame scored late in the game but missed the extra point,

"He could have been anything he wanted to be," said Bisignano. "That's the kind of person he was."

Kinnick, who grew up in Adel, was the grandson of an Iowa governor and was groomed from a very early age to follow in his grandfather's footsteps. The name recognition he earned on the gridiron coupled with his wartime exploits and winning personality would have made him a formidable political force in the state and, perhaps, in the nation. Baender and his faculty friends sometimes amuse themselves with a game of "what if" involving Kinnick. Kinnick was a Republican, but he would not have been old enough to be Dwight Eisenhower's vice-presidential running mate in 1952. However, Kinnick would have been the right age in 1956. If Eisenhower had dumped Richard Nixon in favor of Kinnick, Baender said the 1960 election could have been between Kinnick and John F. Kennedy, the Democratic standard-bearer.

"That would have been really something," said Baender. "Both Navy veterans, both about the same age, both very articulate, both very attractive. Kennedy was a wannabe football player, Kinnick was a Heisman winner."

Couppee, who as a television personality in California knew Nixon and Ronald Reagan, said Kinnick had the right stuff to be president. And he was squeaky clean. "This was a guy you would never be able to trace anything to," said Couppee. "He wasn't a draft dodger. He wasn't a skirt chaser. He wasn't a womanizer. He wasn't anything but a hell of a man.

"He was far beyond the average Phi Beta Kappa, the average Heisman Trophy winner, the average all-around athlete. I've never seen a more disciplined human being." But Couppee said Kinnick's athletic abilities should not be minimized. Although Kinnick was only 5'7" or 5'8" and 170 pounds, the tailback was multitalented. He passed, he punted, he carried the ball, he kicked extra points, he played tenacious defense.

"If Kinnick had come along today, he would be just as great as he was then," said Couppee. "Somehow or other, he'd find a way to be that great. He was just that kind of person."

and Iowa held on for the huge upset.

Next up was mighty Minnesota. The Golden Gophers led 9–0 in the fourth quarter before Kinnick rallied the Hawkeyes with two touchdown passes—a 45-yarder to Erwin Prasse and a 28-yarder to Bill Green with three minutes left. Kinnick clinched the 13–9 victory with an interception in the closing seconds and was carried off the field by joyful fans in his final home game.

Kinnick had played every minute of his last six games. A shoulder injury ended Kinnick's streak in the season finale, a 7–7 tie with Northwestern that dashed Iowa's hopes for a Big Ten title but didn't dim the local enthusiasm for the school's best team in 15 years.

"We couldn't go anywhere without people cheering us," Couppee said. "They even stopped movies to turn on the lights and cheer us. We were forever the Iron Men."

So it was no surprise when Kinnick swept all the major postseason awards, including the Heisman Trophy. In his memorable acceptance speech Kinnick alluded to the war that would eventually take his life. "I thank God that I was born to the gridirons of the Middle West and not to the battlefields of Europe," he said. "I can say confidently and positively that the football players of this country would much rather fight for the Heisman award than for the Croix de Guerre."

Kinnick played one more football game, throwing two touchdown passes for the College All-Stars in a 45–28 loss to the NFL champion Green Bay Packers on August 29, 1940. He turned down a $10,000 offer from the NFL Brooklyn Dodgers so he could study law and pursue his other interests, including politics. That fall he introduced Republican presidential candidate Wendell Willkie at a rally in Iowa Falls. During the speech many people in the crowd chanted, "We want Kinnick!"

But a possible political career was interrupted by World War II.

On June 2, 1943, Kinnick took off on a training flight from the U.S.S. *Lexington* in the Caribbean Sea. The plane started to leak oil, and Kinnick was forced to make a water landing four miles from the ship. When rescuers reached the spot a short time later, there was no trace of Kinnick or the plane. Although no one is sure what happened, there was speculation that Kinnick drowned after being knocked unconscious during the landing.

Kinnick's brother Ben, a Marine pilot, was killed 15 months later when he was shot down over the Pacific.

A half century after his death, Nile Kinnick remains a hero. Iowa's football stadium now bears his name, as does a park in Adel. His face is on the coin tossed by officials at the start of every Big Ten game.

"There was just an aura about him," Couppee said. "He didn't try to create it, it was just there. You really had the feeling you were in the presence of someone very special."

—RICK WARNER

The year was 1940 and Michigan tailback Tom Harmon had just led the Wolverines to a 40–0 victory against Big Ten archrival Ohio State at Ohio Stadium. In what was his final—and perhaps finest—college performance, Harmon ran for 139 yards and two touchdowns. He completed 11 of 12 passes for 151 yards and another two scores. He had four extra points and averaged 50 yards per punt. Doubling as a defensive back, Harmon intercepted three passes and returned one for a touchdown.

As he left the field Harmon heard an unexpected sound from the crowd of 73,000 Buckeye fans. It was applause ... for him, a Michigan man. In the rarest of tributes, Harmon received a standing ovation in Columbus. The audience knew that it had seen greatness that day.

Heisman Trophy voters knew it, too, which is why Harmon was the overwhelming choice when the ballot results were announced. The six-foot, 195-pound Harmon, powerful and fast (he ran the 100 in 9.8 seconds), carried every voting section of the country except the Southwest, which was partial to runner-up John Kimbrough, the Texas A&M fullback.

Born September 28, 1919, in Gary, Indiana, the bubble-gum chewing son of Louis and Rose Harmon dreamed of winning the award as early as his freshman year at Horace Mann High School. His boyhood idol was none other than Jay Berwanger, the first Heisman Trophy winner.

"I had so much respect for him," Harmon once said. "He had no help at Chicago. I wanted to become the player he was, a 60-minute man. I saw him in a newsreel, receiving the Heisman Trophy. I heard the announcer say that the trophy went to the outstanding college football player in the country. That stuck with me. I've always been goal-oriented, and from that day on, I had my eye on the Heisman."

It was in high school that Harmon might have earned the nickname Old 98 that stayed with him throughout his entire career, both as a player, an Air Force fighter pilot and a broadcaster.

The story goes that Harmon, who had won a local bubble-gum-blowing contest, showed up at the first day of practice with a wad of the stuff in his mouth. As coach Doug Kerr started talking, Harmon blew a giant-sized bubble that caught the attention of everyone, including a

1940

Tom Harmon

Greatness, Glory and a Bit of Luck

peeved Kerr, who told the freshman to immediately leave the field and return his uniform to the team manager.

"I'm not turning in my uniform," Harmon said. "I came out here to play football."

"Oh, you did, did you?" said Kerr. "We'll see about that."

So Kerr assigned Harmon to the kickoff return team, where the freshman promptly ran for a touchdown against the varsity. Kerr ordered another kickoff and again Harmon returned it for a score. There was no more talk about turning in his unform.

When Harmon went to choose his jersey for the first game, "there was only one left," he would say. "It was old, tattered, with holes in it."

Old 98.

By today's standards, Harmon's statistical accomplishments aren't overwhelming. In 1938, his first season on the Wolverine varsity, Harmon rushed for 398 yards and passed for another 310. The next season he gained 1,356 total yards, scored 14 touchdowns and 102 points to lead the nation and finished second in the Heisman balloting. In his senior year Harmon accounted for 1,346 total yards, 16 touchdowns and 117 points. As he had throughout his career, he punted, returned punts, returned kickoffs, played defensive back, kicked extra points and field goals—and, this time, won a Heisman.

For his career Harmon gained a total of 3,530 yards, which, for historical comparison, was nearly 1,700 yards fewer than Brigham Young quarterback Ty Detmer, the 1990 Heisman winner, had in a single season.

Yet Harmon's records were established in just 24 games, about half as many as a four-year Wolverine starter plays these days. In addition, freshmen weren't eligible, and Michigan was an infrequent participant in bowl games.

Against California on September 28, 1940—Harmon's birthday—the senior tailback was on his way to a third touchdown return when Harold Brennan, a former all–San Francisco end in 1929, dashed from the stands and tried tackling him at the two-yard line. Recalled Brennan, "The kid looks at me kind of funny and says, 'What the hell do you think you're doing?' And I say, 'I'm tackling you.' The next thing I know, two men have got me by the neck and doggone if it isn't two cops."

Like the Golden Bears themselves,

Harmon handled the kicking duties in addition to his roles as the team's primary rusher and passer.

1940 Tom Harmon

Brennan missed. Most everyone did. (Harmon later convinced the police to free the overzealous Cal fan.)

The Chicago Bears, the most powerful team of the day, made Harmon the No. 1 pick in the 1941 draft. But Harmon, a speech major, announced that he had no intention of playing professional football, planning instead to pursue a career in radio broadcasting. He joined a Detroit radio station and appeared in the movie *Harmon of Michigan*, which was a semi-flop, but earned him $25,000, enough to pay for a new home in Ann Arbor for his parents.

After the bombing of Pearl Harbor on December 7, 1941, Harmon enlisted in the Army Air Corps, where he got lucky twice. Flying over South America in April 1943, Harmon was the sole survivor when he and his crew were forced to bail out of their plane (named *Old 98*). He spent four days alone in a swampy jungle before he was found by friendly locals. After recovering from his injuries, Harmon was transferred to China, where he was shot down during an October 30 battle over Kiukiang. He suffered multiple burns during the dogfight but was rescued by Chinese guerrillas, who escorted him back to his base.

Shortly after returning to the United States, Harmon married Elyse Knox, a movie actress and model, at the same University of Michigan chapel where a special Mass had been said for him following his first air crash. Elyse's wedding dress was made from the silk of the parachute that saved Harmon's life in China.

To pay off a tax bill from his earlier movie fees, Harmon played two seasons for the Los Angeles Rams before returning to broadcasting, and for the next 20 years he covered almost every major sporting event.

On March 15, 1990 Harmon suffered a heart attack in Los Angeles. He died two days later, at age 70.

It was his son, Mark, the noted actor and former quarterback at USC (Harmon also had two daughters, Kelly and Christie), who one day asked about the Heisman Trophy that sat on a desk inside the house. The answer was vintage Tom Harmon.

"My dad's explanation was simple," recalled Mark. "Awarded once a year to the best college football player in the country ... and that he couldn't have accomplished any of it without his teammates. Those were the important moments for me ... the concept of teamwork, for sure, but the idea that this very great football player was also my father." —*GENE WOJCIECHOWSKI*

1941
Bruce Smith

The Game Breaker

On December 9, 1941, just two days after the Japanese bombed Pearl Harbor, Bruce Smith climbed the steps of the Downtown Athletic Club to receive the Heisman Trophy. Understandably, much of the talk that night would not be about football, but about the entry of the United States into World War II. In fact, the speeches were cut short so that those in attendance could listen to President Roosevelt's radio address from the White House.

This was fine with Smith, who was a most self-effacing young man. When he did speak that night, he gave most of the credit to his teammates and to his coach, Bernie Bierman, though everyone in the room knew that without number 54, the Golden Gophers would not have approached their awesome record of the past two seasons, when they went undefeated and won two national titles.

So great had been Smith's impact in key games that he earned the nickname the Game Breaker. As a junior he had run through a tough Ohio State defense, racking up 139 yards and scoring both touchdowns in Minnesota's 13–7 victory. As a senior he had watched the first quarter of the Iowa game from the sideline due to an injury, and without him the Gophers didn't get one first down. Smith limped onto the field in the second quarter, and though he touched the ball only seven times that day, he ran or passed for every Gopher touchdown in a 34–14 win.

It's too bad that Roosevelt was not there that night to hear Smith speak. "Those Far Eastern fellows may think that American boys are soft," he began, "but I have had, and even now have, plenty of evidence in black and blue to show that they are making a big mistake. I think that America will owe a great debt to the game of football when we finish this thing off. It keeps millions of American youngsters like myself hard and able to take it and come back for more."

Bruce Philip Smith was built to take it. A high school standout in football, basketball and golf, the Faribault,

His powerful frame notwithstanding, Smith was primarily a finesse runner, who left tacklers grasping at air.

1941 Bruce Smith

Minnesota, native stood six feet and weighed 200 pounds, with blond hair and blue eyes and rugged good looks. He chose to concentrate on football in college, and from 1939 to '41 his play in the Minnesota backfield dazzled fans.

Looking at him, one would assume that Smith would blast through defenders, but he was actually a finesse runner, capable of sharp cuts that left the opposition grasping at air. He did not have blinding speed, but he made up for it by possessing an uncanny feel for where his blockers were. As the tailback in Bierman's single-wing attack, Smith was also a great passer, kicker and receiver. It didn't take long for Bierman to hail Smith as "the greatest halfback I've ever seen play."

Of all the big plays Smith made, the exclamation point came against Michigan, in his junior year. In 1940 the Wolverines were led by senior Tom Harmon, their All-America running back. On his way to winning the Heisman Trophy, Harmon was determined to prove that Minnesota's victory the year before had been a fluke.

A heavy mist was falling in Minneapolis on November 2 as the two undefeated teams slugged it out in the mud. The Wolverines were moving the ball easily, forcing the Gophers back on their heels again and again. Michigan's lead was only 6–0, but on this dreary day, six points might as well have been 36, for unlike Michigan, Smith's squad seemed to be stuck in the mud.

Again the Wolverines bulldozed their way inside the Minnesota 10. But just when it seemed that the Wolverines were closing in for the kill, a Michigan pass was picked off in the end zone, and Minnesota took over on its own 20. Bierman, blessed with not one, but two outstanding backs in Smith and senior George Franck (who would finish third to Harmon in the Heisman race), decided to try something different. Smith went in at the wing position, while Franck lined up in Smith's tailback slot. Franck had tremendous speed, and everyone expected his number to be called. It was not. Smith took a handoff on a weakside reverse, catching the Wolverines off guard just long enough to slant off his left end and break into the secondary, dodging and feinting his way past no fewer than six defenders as he raced downfield.

The seventh was the safety, Harmon himself, but he never had a chance. Harmon later called Smith's 80-yard touchdown run "one of the finest the game of football has ever seen." The extra point was good, and Michigan suffered its only defeat of the season. The loss was especially galling to Harmon and his

Michigan teammates since it cost them both an undefeated season and the national championship, which went to Minnesota.

Harmon had graduated by the following year, but even without him the Wolverines were undefeated when the Minnesota game came round. Once again it was Smith who won the contest for the Gophers, breaking open a scoreless tie with a pass to set up the only touchdown in Minnesota's 7–0 victory. Once again it was Michigan's only loss that season.

Smith saved his greatest performance for the final game of his career. Playing against Wisconsin on a banged-up knee, Smith was a one-man marvel. He threw a 45-yard pass to set up his own 18-yard touchdown run; faked a pass, then ran 42 yards before lateraling to a teammate for the last five yards of the second touchdown play; set up the third touchdown by intercepting a pass and running it back 43 yards to the Badger 11; and then threw a farewell 20-yard touchdown pass before being helped off the field, leaving it to his inspired teammates to fill out the 41–6 victory. It was a perfect Hollywood ending to a brilliant career, and Hollywood coaxed him into starring in a movie based on his life, *Smith of Minnesota*.

It was not a time of make-believe, however, and Smith backed up his Heisman speech by enlisting in the Naval Reserves the following February. Determined to serve his country, he passed all his physicals despite having severely torn cartilage in his right knee. He received his fighter pilot's wings while continuing to dominate the game of football. He was named captain of the East squad in the 1942 East-West Shrine Game and the MVP in the College All-Star Game that same year.

After the war Smith joined the National Football League. He played four injury-plagued seasons with the Green Bay Packers and the Los Angeles Rams, where it was apparent that his numerous ailments had taken their toll. And so, at the age of 29, Smith left the game and became the first Heisman winner to have his college number retired. He was elected to the College Football Hall of Fame in 1972.

When Bruce Smith died of cancer on August 28, 1967, at the age of 47, he left behind a wife and four children. On September 28, 1970, Lucius Smith presented his son's Heisman Trophy to the University of Minnesota. Bruce Smith had always said it belonged to the 1940 and 1941 Badger teams.

—ANDREW L. THOMAS AND ROBERT MCG. THOMAS JR.

Frank Sinkwich

A Quirky Hero

You really had to have been there to fully appreciate the glory showered on Frank Sinkwich when he played for the University of Georgia. He was the antithesis of the sculpted giants you see carrying the football these days, some of whom are bigger than the tackles of Sinkwich's era. Sinkwich himself was stocky but short, described by one writer as "almost portly." Though just 180 pounds, he knew no fear and gained most of his yards between the tackles from the ancient single-wing formation.

"I run where they ain't," he was quoted as saying one time, which was hardly accurate even if it did come from his own mouth. To contradict his own description, he ran where they *were*.

A coach's dream, you might say, but there were eccentricities associated with such a talent that gave nightmares to Wally Butts, his coach at Georgia. Sinkwich once quit the team "to give more time to studies and the social life." The "social life" meant the lovely Adelaine Weatherly. When they slipped across the state line to South Carolina and got married, Butts was almost apoplectic. Another time Sinkwich told the coach his legs were bothering him so he thought he would have to give up the game. Butts sent him to a doctor in Atlanta, an old Bulldog tackle thoroughly briefed in advance, and the doctor came up with the magic diagnosis.

"They've been taping you wrong," the doctor said soothingly. Sinkwich reported back to the squad, said it was amazing how the new taping worked, and never missed a step.

After he quit the first time, in the off-season, Sinkwich moved out of the football dormitory and into a fraternity house. He found his reception so cool around the campus that he decided that his studies and social life weren't measuring up to expectations. He then told Butts he had changed his mind and wanted to come back.

"The players will have to vote on it," Butts told him.

Any player who might have even thought about voting against the return of Sinkwich would have been taken out and shot. He was welcomed back, first enduring a brutal turn scrimmaging as the third-string tailback, then quickly getting back on the path to the Heisman Memorial Trophy.

"Triple threat" is an unfamiliar concept to today's football fans, weaned on the specialized modern game.

The fearless Sinkwich was more than willing to bang away between the tackles.

Sinkwich was a true embodiment of that term: He ran, he passed, and he kicked. He also played defense, which was necessary in those one-platoon days. One of his teammates, Joe Geri, gave him a hearty testimonial, "Most people don't remember this," said Geri, "but he was a great defensive back." In a game against bitter rival Georgia Tech, Sinkwich knocked down three passes in a row at a critical point, preserving a close victory.

Anytime a running back is mentioned in the same breath as Jim Thorpe, Red Grange and Tom Harmon, everyone sits up and takes notice, and Sinkwich evoked such comparisons. National magazines sent photographers and writers to chase him around the campus. He was profiled in *Life* magazine and *The Saturday Evening Post*. He made every All-America team there was, and won several awards that don't exist anymore.

Still nothing drew quite as much attention to him as a break, a literal one.

In the second game of his junior season Sinkwich ran and passed South Carolina to death in a game as brutal as any old-timers can remember. Near the end he was driven out of bounds, and in the pileup, a knee caught him in the jaw and broke it. He was quick to say it was accidental. "There were plenty of fists and elbows flying, but my jaw was an accident."

Wasting little time, the Georgia trainer devised a sort of protective mask that covered half of Sinkwich's face, and his picture appeared across the country wearing his jaw guard. It just so happened that two weeks later Georgia was scheduled to play in New York City against Columbia, when the Lions still possessed a roar. Georgia won the game, and Sinkwich won the press, the jaw protector having as much to do with spreading his fame as his play.

Most of his individual records have been wiped out in these latter days of wildfire offense, lengthened games and rules cozying up to the offense. Still, Sinkwich's game against Texas Christian in the 1942 Orange Bowl ranks among the great postseason performances of all time. He gained a total of 382 yards that day; 248 yards and three touchdowns from passing and 134 yards and another touchdown on the ground.

He would put in two exciting seasons with the Detroit Lions and was the Most Valuable player in the NFL in 1944 before being drafted into the military. Sinkwich had accepted the Heisman Trophy dressed in a Marine Corps uniform, though not long after that he was discharged—it seems that his feet were too flat for the Marines. This time the Army Air Corps won him. The war was ending, but the commandant at Peterson Field in Colorado Springs, where Sinkwich was stationed, loved his football and kept his team in place into the regular season in 1945. Sinkwich tells the story of the end of his military career, which also led eventually to the end of his football career:

"I was about to be discharged, and on the following weekend I was supposed to be back playing for the Detroit Lions. The El Toro Marines happened to have an open date, so the general decided we ought to play them. I hadn't moved quite fast enough through the discharge line, so I was suited up and played.

"Elroy Hirsch caught a pass and I was tackling him when one of his blockers hit me from the side and tore up my knee. My last play in the service, and it left me with a limp."

When Sinkwich was healthy enough to try pro football again, he passed up the Lions for a contract with the New York Yankees of the upstart All-America Football Conference. It didn't work, and neither did another attempt, with Baltimore, also of the AAFC. His playing days were done.

Sinkwich made a pass at coaching, first with a minor league team in Erie, Pennsylvania, then at the University of Tampa. His record at Tampa wasn't bad, but conditions were. His team had to share the practice field with a bunch of roaring stock car racers. After two seasons Sinkwich returned to his college town like a homing pigeon and never left. The boy who had grown up in Youngstown, Ohio, found a permanent home in Georgia. He first became a partner in a furniture business, then landed a wine and beer distributorship and became a solid citizen of Athens. He was also elected to the College Football Hall of Fame.

Once he left the limelight, he stayed out of it, "a reluctant hero," the team chaplain called him. He was, however, one of the athletic department's most generous supporters. When the fund-raising campaign to build the Butts-Mehre Athletic Building began, he was the first donor, with a $100,000 check. He rarely made a public appearance and never spoke of his greatest runs, his greatest passes or his greatest games. They were history in Frank Sinkwich's mind.

He died in Athens at the age of 70 in October 1990, after a lingering illness.　　—*FURMAN BISHER*

1943

Angelo Bertelli

An Italian for the Irish

Angelo Bertelli was a man of many firsts. He placed first in the Heisman Trophy voting, although, with the nation embroiled in World War II, he played in only six of his team's 10 games, having been called to active duty by the Marine Corps on November 1. He was Notre Dame's first T formation quarterback—some say its best—and the first of the Fighting Irish to be a Heisman winner. As we know, he would not be the last.

Angelo Bortolo Bertelli, whose immigrant Italian parents spoke little English, came from West Springfield, Massachusetts. At Cathedral High School he was known as the Arm and, eventually, in the newspapers as the Springfield Rifle. He could throw the football, but as a teenager he preferred hockey and helped to sharpen the skates of the Springfield Chiefs, Eddie Shore's minor league team in that city.

Fellow Cathedral High graduate Milt Piepul, the Notre Dame captain in 1940, helped steer Bertelli to South Bend, although coach Elmer Layden had little interest in a tall, skinny 165-pound tailback with seemingly limited football skills. Bertelli was fourth string on the freshman team until he threw two touchdown passes in the annual freshman-varsity game.

Then Layden became the commissioner of the National Football League and Frank Leahy the new coach at Notre Dame. Leahy was either a genius or desperate when he nominated Bertelli to be his No. 1 tailback during spring practice in 1941. No one foresaw what was ahead, especially the dour Leahy, about whom Boston sportswriter Dave Egan wrote, "He automatically shuts his eyes in order that he may not see the silver lining to every cloud."

That fall the Irish won eight games, lost none and had one scoreless tie, against Army. Ranked third in the nation, they were the first undefeated team at South Bend since Knute Rockne's 1930 squad.

Bert, as his teammates called him, led

Bertelli was among the first of the talented quarterbacks of the modern T formation.

the nation in pass efficiency, with a .569 completion percentage. Helped by Notre Dame's record, by its renown and by All-America end Bob Dove's receptions, Bertelli wound up that year a surprising second in the Heisman voting, behind Bruce Smith, Minnesota's great halfback. The fourth-string freshman had again become the Springfield Rifle.

The following winter Leahy called Bertelli into his office and with his trademark exaggeration told him, "Bert, you are the finest passer and the worst runner I've ever coached." Behind the comment lay his decision to modify Notre Dame's quick-hitting box offense and adopt the modernized T formation made so attractive by Clark Shaughnessy with the Chicago Bears. Bertelli was to report to the gym and begin learning the footwork of the quarterback, lining up behind the center and handling the ball on every play.

Maybe Bertelli could not run much. He never tried to kick, and they often took him out when it came time to play defense. But he could make the football disappear and reappear as well as throw it, and the faking of the T quarterback came naturally to him.

Nevertheless, there were questions when the 1942 season began with a 7–7 tie against Wisconsin and a 13–7 loss to Georgia Tech. An exhausted Leahy became ill and went off to the Mayo Clinic in Rochester, Minnesota, with Ed McKeever left in charge. Leahy coached by telephone and the pieces came together as the Irish won seven of their next eight games. They ended the season with a 13–13 tie against the Great Lakes Naval Training Station, which fielded the first of its four World War II all-star teams.

By this time most male undergraduates had enlisted in some branch of the armed forces. Many football players, including Bertelli, were attracted to the Navy V-12 program, which kept them in an accelerated college program through the 1942 season and into the 1943 one, on campus in uniform and in a quasimilitary format. The V-12 term ended on November 1, 1943, and there were wholesale transfers and assignments.

Bertelli, by now a 22-year-old senior in the Marine Corps Reserve, was ordered along with several others to active duty. He boarded a train for the Marine base at Parris Island, South Carolina, and recalled later, "It was an awful, drizzly night. I was very upset. I had been looking forward to finally playing well against Army, and the next thing I knew I was in boot camp."

But what a season he had left behind! Notre Dame had routed all six of its opponents by a collective score of 261–31. Bertelli had completed almost 70% of his passes, 25 of 36 for 512 yards and 10 touchdowns with only four intercepted.

His country had called and away went Bertelli, to be succeeded by 18-year-old John Lujack, who would be the Heisman Trophy winner four years later. After 10 games Leahy's third Notre Dame team was poised at the threshold of an undefeated season when it went to suburban Chicago to play a tough Great Lakes squad.

Bertelli paced the recreation room at Parris Island as he listened to the radio broadcast of the game. Steve Lach, the former Duke star, completed a 46-yard touchdown pass with 30 seconds remaining, to beat the Irish 19–14. Still, Grantland Rice, writing in *The New York Sun*, called this team Notre Dame's best of all time.

As Bertelli left the rec hall a company clerk came up to him and handed him a telegram, too often the source of bad news during wartime. The message was that Bertelli had been voted the Heisman Trophy winner by the overwhelming margin of 648 points to 177 for Penn's Bob Odell.

He was only mildly elated. The sudden loss of Notre Dame's undefeated season diminished the thrill of the Heisman. The usual December awards ceremony had to be postponed until January because Bertelli could not get leave earlier. The war had priority.

A year later, in February 1945, he found himself in combat on Iwo Jima as a replacement platoon leader. He was awarded a Bronze Star for valor and a Purple Heart after being wounded.

After the war Bertelli, who was married and had a son, turned to pro football with the Los Angeles Dons of the All-America Football Conference. He suffered a knee injury in a preseason scrimmage and underwent surgery during each of the next three mostly inactive seasons with the Dons and the Chicago Rockets.

Bertelli then went into the retail liquor business in northern New Jersey. He was elected to the College Football Hall of Fame in 1972.

Bertelli's father had been killed by a hit-and-run driver when Bertelli was 17. In 1987 Bertelli told a *Sports Illustrated* interviewer, "It's fulfilling for me to feel that my father, who made such a struggle of it in a new country for his family, would have been proud of me. He never would have dreamed that a son of his would go to college, and that would have made him so happy. The Heisman, for him, would have just been a little something extra."

—*WILLIAM N. WALLACE*

Known as the Springfield Rifle, Angelo Bertelli, was the first of the fighting Irish to be named a Heisman winner.

The turbulent circumstances of a nation at war led Les Horvath to the Heisman Trophy.

After three seasons, which culminated in a national championship for Ohio State in 1942, Horvath thought his college football career was over.

A dental student, he was in the U.S. Army's specialized training program on campus and thus not eligible for varsity competition in 1943. But the wartime rules worked in his favor a year later, when he was granted an extra year of eligibility.

He came very close to not using it.

Horvath had been contacted by several professional teams considering his availability for the 1944 season. "I gave playing pro ball some serious thought," he said. "I was offered a contract by the Rams, who were playing in Cleveland in those days. They offered me something like $7,000, and I'd never seen $700 at that time, much less $7,000. It was pretty tempting. The money would have helped me start my dental practice."

Carroll Widdoes, who had taken over the Buckeyes that season after legendary coach Paul Brown was called into the service, did his best to convince Horvath to give college ball one more try.

"He and [longtime assistant] Ernie Godfrey told me they'd like me to come back because I would be a veteran and add some stability to the team," Horvath said. "I kind of hemmed and hawed about it.

"They finally came to me and told me they could understand that the money from the Rams was important and that I might not even make the Buckeye team anyway, because I'd been out of football for a year. I don't know if that was reverse psychology or what, but it was a challenge. I figured pro football could wait."

Widdoes knew what he was doing. Horvath, playing both quarterback and tailback, depending on whether his team was in a T or single wing formation, as well as defensive back, led Ohio State to a 9–0 record (its first unbeaten season in 24 years) and the Big Ten title.

The conference, however, denied the Buckeyes a trip to the Rose Bowl, which was a bitter pill for Horvath and his teammates to swallow at the time. "The school had promised us we would go to the Rose Bowl in spite of the Big Ten's decision not to send anybody," he said. "But when the Big Ten voted against us, our athletic director said we had to conform to the vote, and we didn't get to go."

Les Horvath

An Extra Year to Remember

But Horvath got a nice consolation prize: the Heisman Trophy, an honor that caught him totally off guard.

"I honestly didn't know I was even in the running for the trophy," said Horvath, who won by just 125 votes over Army's Glenn Davis. "I'd really never even heard of it. When they called me out of a chemistry class and told me I'd won it, I was shocked, stunned, actually. I still think it was a pure accident that I won."

At 5' 10" and 167 pounds, this Parma, Ohio, native was the smallest regular among the Buckeyes' starters that year. But he could do just about anything on a football field, and he was smart—so smart that he was more or less a playing coach during his Heisman season. Performing on both offense and defense, Horvath was in the lineup 401.5 minutes of a possible 540 in 1944. He carried the ball 163 times for 924 yards (a 5.7 average) and six touchdowns and completed 14 of 32 passes for 344 yards and six more TDs.

Half a century later, the thrill of that season remains with Horvath.

"We had a very unusual squad that year," he said. "We had four or five freshmen in our starting lineup every game. We were coming off a 3–6 season, too, so we really didn't expect to do that much to begin with, but week after week, those freshmen got better. They just didn't realize how good they really were."

Typically, Horvath downplayed his contributions to that magical season, which was often a tough one for him. He had to attend dental clinics every day before practice and frequently on Saturdays before games, too. He developed such severe problems with his legs from standing and running that the week before the Michigan game he hobbled to class.

His determination, skill and leadership were never more in evidence than in the Big Ten title game against Fritz Crisler's Wolverines. With Ohio State trailing 14–12 and just eight minutes remaining, Horvath took the Buckeyes on a 52-yard scoring drive. He capped it with a touchdown run, his second of the game, for an 18–14 victory. Ohio State ran the ball 73 times that day, and 33 of the rushes were by Horvath, who played every minute of the game.

Upon graduation from Ohio State, in 1945, with a degree in dentistry,

Wartime eligibility rules gave Horvath a chance to win the Heisman—and lead the Buckeyes to an unbeaten season.

1944 Les Horvath

Horvath entered the Navy, where, just as in college, he was a two-way threat. In the mornings he was a dental officer. In the afternoons he served as an assistant to Brown, his old college coach, with the Great Lakes Naval Station team. He continued coaching when he was transferred to Hawaii, winning the service championship there.

After his military duty ended, Horvath finally turned pro, joining the Los Angeles Rams for the 1947 and '48 seasons, and spending a year with the Cleveland Browns in 1949 before beginning a full-time dental practice in the Los Angeles area.

He was not exactly an instant success.

"I got the Rams' ticket mailing list and sent out notices that I was opening my dental office in that area," Horvath said, "but for six months I had only one patient a week. My first one was Joe Stydahar, who was an assistant coach with the Rams when I was with them. Before every game he always got sick to his stomach, and he told me that the reason he came to me was that he was scared of dentists and always got sick in their offices, too, but he knew I would understand."

Horvath practiced dentistry for 41 years, retiring in 1991 at the age of 70. He plays golf a couple of times a week now, often in charity tournaments. With his second wife, Ruby, he also enjoys socializing with the other Heisman Trophy winners. "You get a feeling of warmth between these fellas," he said. "They're all really nice people. I'm amazed at how Heisman people will go out of their way to do things for you."

The meaning of the Heisman Trophy wasn't always as clear as it is now.

Horvath's first wife, Shirley, who died in 1973, once asked him about the significance of the bronze trophy that was on their living room mantel. He tried to explain its history and importance. A few weeks later the Horvaths visited two couples, Tom and Elyse Harmon and Glenn and Harriet Davis, and both the Harmon and Davis homes had the same trophy prominently displayed.

"Les, you told me the Heisman Trophy was so exclusive," Shirley said. "Why, it looks to me as though everyone in Los Angeles has one."

He knew otherwise, of course. He realized how special it was, and still is.

"Over the years, people have always mentioned it, no matter where I go," he said. "It's almost as if my name has become Heisman Trophy winner Les Horvath, not just Les Horvath. The longer it's been since I won the trophy, the more importance it seems to have taken on. That's pretty satisfying."   —DWIGHT CHAPIN

1945

Doc Blanchard

Superman in Fatigues

Saturday afternoon radio broadcasts took on a special resonance in the fall of 1944: For a nation at war, the words "Blanchard through the line" meant that Army was on the move. There was no television to bring college football into millions of homes, but from 1944 to 1946 there wasn't a kid in America who didn't know exactly who Doc Blanchard was.

He was Army's Mr. Inside, the unstoppable, line-crashing fullback who, with Mr. Outside, the speedy Glenn Davis, formed the greatest tandem of running backs the game has ever seen. Together they set national rushing and scoring records, leading Army to consecutive national championships and three undefeated seasons.

Davis, who was the fastest player of his era, was the flashier of the two, but it was Blanchard who drew the awe of the wartime Notre Dame coach, Ed McKeever. After scouting an early-season Army game in 1944, he wired the ominous news back to South Bend: "HAVE JUST SEEN SUPERMAN IN THE FLESH. HE WEARS NO. 35 FOR ARMY AND GOES BY THE NAME OF BLANCHARD."

The Inside/Outside sobriquets were at once apt and deceptive. For just as Davis was more than a flyback, Blanchard was much more than a line crasher. Only in comparison to Davis could he be considered slow. He was a 10-second man in the 100-yard dash, remarkable for a 210-pound, six-footer. Even more remarkable, he was a sure-fingered pass catcher who would leap high between two defenders and bring down the ball with one hand. Just as deft on pass defense, he was the consummate two-way player, one who tackled the way he ran and ran the way he blocked, with full, driving force. He did all of Army's punting and kicked off, almost always to the end zone, sometimes between the goalposts.

As a combat pilot, Doc Blanchard would serve his country for 25 years with the same skill and distinction he brought to the football field.

To satisfy his voracious appetite and keep his place at the training table, Blanchard took up the shot put. Starting with modest tosses of 30 feet—not bad for a beginner at a time when few could reach 50 feet—he made astonishing progress, winning the 1945 IC4A championship, then setting a West Point record with a throw of 51'10.75".

The legend began early. A day after Felix Anthony Blanchard Jr. was born in McColl, South Carolina, on December 11, 1924, his father, a physician and former 240-pound fullback at Tulane, placed a football in his son's crib. His family planned to call him Anthony, but he looked so much like his father, he was soon Little Doc. Doc was the one with the satchel. Little Doc was the one with the football clutched close to his side.

As a fullback at his father's alma mater, St. Stanislaus, a boarding school in Bay St. Louis, Mississippi, Blanchard shattered school records and scored 165 points as a senior, leading the team to an undefeated season.

Heavily recruited, Blanchard chose North Carolina, where he played just one year, on the undefeated 1942 freshman team. With the draft looming, Blanchard was encouraged to join the Navy's campus V-12 program. He was declared five pounds overweight, and coach Jim Tatum gave up trying to help him sweat off the supposedly surplus weight. "He was all muscle and concrete," Tatum said. So Blanchard joined the Army instead, serving in a succession of posts before his father secured him an appointment to West Point. His father died a few weeks before Blanchard arrived at West Point, on July 2, 1944, so it was not as Little Doc but simply as Doc that he left his imprint on football history.

There are those who scoff at Army's wartime victories over teams whose best athletes had entered the military. There was surely some disparity as West Point outscored nine opponents 504–35 in 1944 (a 56–4 average) and 412–46 in 1945 (46–5), but that hardly detracted from the Touchdown Twins' achievements. Army, whose 1945 team is still widely regarded as the most powerful college team ever assembled, was so overstocked with talent that coach Earl (Red) Blaik once calculated that Blanchard and Davis averaged just 18 minutes a game through the first six games of the 1945 season.

Blanchard, for example, carried the ball just 61 times in 1944, but he was so impressive that he placed third in the Heisman voting. In 1945, when Blanchard led the nation with 19 touchdowns (to Davis's 18) and 115 points, he carried the ball only 101 times, averaging a remarkable 7.1 yards per carry and a touchdown per 5.3 carries.

This time Blanchard was the decisive Heisman winner, also capturing the Maxwell and Camp awards and becoming the first football player to win the Sullivan Award as the nation's outstanding amateur athlete. His chance to become the first repeat Heisman winner ended

in the first game of the 1946 season, when he tore two sets of knee ligaments. He was back in the lineup after two weeks, but he was not the same. He no longer kicked or scrimmaged, and as he put it, "I wasn't much good after that." Even so, he placed fourth in the Heisman vote.

After graduation, Blanchard and Davis made a movie, *The Spirit of West Point*, but were turned down when they sought additional leave to play professional football. Blanchard didn't argue. As a combat pilot he would serve his country for the next 25 years with the same skill and distinction he had brought to football. In 1959 he earned a citation for bravery after landing a burning plane rather than bailing out and endangering a nearby English village. In 1968, after flying 113 combat missions, 85 of them over North Vietnam, he was awarded the Distinguished Flying Cross.

He retired as a full colonel in 1971, served two years as commandant of the New Mexico Military Institute, then retired for good, settling in San Antonio, Texas, where he had met and married his wife, Jody King, in 1948, and with whom he had a son and two daughters.

His wife died in 1993, but for a man who has seen it all and done most of it, there are memories, maybe echoes. Ask him to name his greatest performance and Blanchard will say he guesses it was the 1944 Navy game, the showdown for the national championship.

It was touch and go until late in the third quarter when, with Army clinging to a 9—7 lead, Davis intercepted a pass on the Army 48. Then as a nation at war listened with rapt attention, it heard Blanchard's name called seven times in nine plays:

Blanchard around left end for 20 yards. Blanchard over left tackle for three. Davis around right end for three. Blanchard over the middle for five. Max Minor over left guard for a yard. Blanchard through the line for three. Blanchard through the line for four. Blanchard through the line for four. First down at the nine. Blanchard through the line. Touchdown.

After the game Blanchard told a cousin he had felt his father's presence: "He was there. I could feel him patting me on the back after every play and saying, 'Hit like your daddy did, son.'"

A ghost? Maybe. Or perhaps a ghostly echo, like the one that has been reverberating in aging American ears for half a century: Blanchard through the line.

—ROBERT MCG. THOMAS, JR.

Davis dated Elizabeth Taylor, then a teenager, whose movie career was just starting to blossom.

He will be linked forever as Mr. Outside to Felix (Doc) Blanchard's Mr. Inside. But, with a little luck and the shift of a few votes, Glenn Davis could have stood all alone, as the only three-time winner of the Heisman Trophy.

In 1944 and 1945, Davis led the nation by averaging an amazing 11.5 yards per rushing attempt, yet finished second in the Heisman voting each year, first to Ohio State's Les Horvath and then to Army teammate Blanchard.

In 1946, when he finally won the Heisman, Davis's average per carry fell to "only" 5.8, but by that point statistics didn't matter. Davis's rare abilities had been established for all time. "He's the best running back I've ever seen," said Columbia coach Lou Little. And Steve Owen, who was coach of the professional New York Giants at the time, said, "He's better than Red Grange. He's faster and he cuts better."

The superlatives have endured. Forty years after Little and Owen passed judgment, former University of Houston coach Bill Yeoman, who was a teammate of Blanchard and Davis's at West Point, said, "There are words to describe how good an athlete Doc Blanchard was. But there aren't words to describe how good Glenn Davis was. He's still the most phenomenal athlete I ever saw."

When Davis was at West Point, cadets were required to take a 10-event physical efficiency test called Master of the Sword. The record, before Davis arrived, had been 901.5 points out of a possible 1,000, with the average being not quite 550. He scored 962.5.

So it was little wonder that Davis, who had earned 13 letters at Bonita High School in La Verne, California, went on to win 10 more in college: four in football, three in baseball, two in track and one in basketball. Davis was so skilled a centerfielder for the Black Knights' baseball team that Branch Rickey, the Brooklyn Dodgers' president who had signed Jackie Robinson, made him a standing offer of $75,000, huge money in those days.

One memorable afternoon at West Point, Davis played the full nine innings of a baseball game, then, because Army was short of sprinters, rushed to compete in a track meet against Navy, even though he hadn't practiced a single day on the track or been in an outdoor meet. He won the 100-yard dash in 9.7 seconds, despite a bad start ("I could have run a 9.4 if I'd trained," he said), and estab-

Glenn Davis

"Better than Red Grange"

lished a meet and Academy record of 20.9 in the 220.

Davis, whom some still believe is the best athlete California ever produced, clearly could do anything. But football remained his main game.

Until sportswriter George Trevor of the old New York *Sun* gave Blanchard and Davis the lasting sobriquets of Mr. Inside and Mr. Outside, Davis usually was known as Junior, because he was born nine minutes after his twin brother, Ralph, in Claremont, California. Glenn and Ralph, a skilled shot-putter, entered the U.S. Military Academy together, in 1943. Glenn immediately did well on the football field for coach Earl (Red) Blaik, but not so well in the classroom.

"Coming from high school to West Point was a big jump," Davis said. "I wasn't prepared academically, and I played every sport besides." The routine of classes, football and study proved too much, and after flunking a math class, Davis was bounced from the academy and had to spend four months at a Southern California prep school before heading east again in 1944. "A certain amount of pride made me make up my mind that I wanted to go back to the academy," he said.

With Davis and Blanchard becoming perhaps the best one-two punch ever in college football, Army was almost invincible for the next three seasons. Only a 0–0 tie with Notre Dame in 1946 marred an otherwise unblemished 27-0-1 record. "I know what will stop Davis and Blanchard," Owen told some of his college coaching friends. "Graduation."

Blanchard finished 296th and Davis 305th in West Point's 1947 class of 310, but the corps of Cadets, well aware of their athletic exploits, cheered them mightily on graduation day. The two men, who excelled on defense as well as offense (Davis averaged 58 minutes a game in 1946), finished as the only three-time All-America backfield teammates.

Davis set an NCAA record of 8.26 yards per rush (2,957 yards in 358 carries) and scored 59 touchdowns, an average of almost one TD every nine plays. Rushing and passing, Davis accounted for 4,129 yards.

Although he was only 5' 9" and weighed just 170 pounds, Davis had unusual power to go with his tremendous speed and shiftiness. He

Possessed of astonishing speed, Davis averaged 11.5 yards per carry in the 1944 and '45 seasons.

The illustrious college career of Doc Blanchard and Glenn Davis very nearly ended in an ignominious loss to a vastly inferior Navy team. Arthur Daley was there to report the game—and to ponder the mysterious vagaries of football.

It's the biggest word in the English language even though it contains only two letters. That word is IF. If Navy had just a few more precious seconds of time, if Navy had just been able to run off one more play, if the crowd had not surged down to the fringe of the gridiron so that a Navy substitute who was rushed in to stop the clock could have been seen by the officials, if, if, if. The classic service struggle was balanced precariously on that tiny word.

That balancing operation almost was a Rube Goldberg structure, slightly on the incredible side. A Cadet eleven that had not been beaten in the three years of Blanchard and Davis and that had been recognized as the No. 1 team in the nation was fighting for its life in the shadow of the goalposts against a Midshipman combination that had lost seven straight and that was rated some 30 points inferior to its traditional foe.

It all seemed so ridiculous that no one in that vast crowd really had paid much attention to early Navy scores. All they had accomplished was to contribute heartwarming reactions at Annapolis gallantry and spirit. This still looked to be West Point's game right up to the third Middie tally in the final quarter. But then the perspective changed—violently.

Navy had a chance. It wasn't too strong a chance, but it was strong enough to electrify the customers. And when Captain Tom Hamilton's spirited youngsters came storming down at the end to throw the fans into a frenzy, the impossible actually began to seem possible. For just a few feverish moments it looked as though Navy would perpetrate the greatest upset of a generation. But Army held. The clock helped, of course, but that's the way this game is played. Sixty minutes is the allotted time and not one second more. Thus did Army win, 21–18.

The hatchet men undoubtedly will swing into action now and attempt to decapitate the Cadets. They will resurrect the old arguments that the West Point record was

achieved for the past three years by shooting down clay pigeons as represented by kids and 4Fs. Yet the 1946 Kaydets had none of the depth of their more illustrious predecessors. It was one team. The others were two teams deep—and more.

That false premise was shouted when Notre Dame waged a scoreless tie with Army. It will be repeated again now. Whom did Navy lick? the scoffers will ask. They won't stop to realize what an utterly unpredictable and screwy game football is. Granted that Notre Dame walloped the Midshipmen, 28–0, with one hand tied behind its back.

Still, Navy scored thrice against Army and the Fighting Irish not at all. How can that be explained away?

Football history is filled with instances of spirited teams up-ending or almost up-ending odds-on favorites. No one has to knock down Army in order to build up Navy. The Annapolis performance speaks for itself. On that one afternoon the Midshipmen were superb and enough credit cannot be piled on the team, on Tom Hamilton and Rip Miller, and on everyone who had a part in contributing to Navy glory.

With rare exceptions, no team can score unless it has possession of the ball. The Middies always seemed to have the ball. A statistical breakdown reveals that the Black Knights from West Point ran off only 44 plays, the Blue Knights from the Severn the astonishing number of 86 plays, or almost twice as many.

Army gulped off the yardage in huge chunks. Navy ground it out painstakingly. It almost seemed as though the Middies were always making first downs by inches. Yet that's how they contrived to keep possession. Let's get statistical again for just a moment, because the figures are quite illuminating. For their three touchdowns the Cadets traveled 182 yards in 14 plays, while the more laborious Midshipmen covered 194 yards in 41 plays. Notice the difference?

Even when the boys from the Severn registered their first tally to make the count 7–6, Army supporters didn't raise an eyebrow. In effect, they applauded politely and remarked condescendingly: "Well done, old chap. It's nice to see Navy make such a bold fight of it." Actually, though,

would break tackles if he had to, but his wonderful change-of-pace agility usually left opponents flat-footed and thoroughly flustered. "Every time Davis touched the ball," said Gene Rossides, who played against him for Columbia, "it would be like an electric current going through the defending team."

Sadly for Davis, the current short-circuited shortly after he left the academy. While he and Blanchard were filming *The Spirit of West Point*, an eminently forgettable movie, Davis, who had never been seriously hurt in a real game, twisted his right knee and sustained both tendon and ligament damage. "It was the end of me," said Davis.

they weren't worried. Nor were they concerned any more when the second touchdown came. It was the third which scared the daylights out of them.

Prior to that third one Glenn Davis and Doc Blanchard had dominated the proceedings so completely that it appeared as though one or the other of them could cross the goal line any time he pleased. Junior scored the first, Doc the second, and they combined on a pass play for the third. They scored three out of the first four times Army had the ball, a fumble spoiling the initial venture.

It was in the last quarter that Navy took fire. The Middie tackling became more robust and vicious, their blocking sharper and their running harder. Army never could get unwound after that and never could get into scoring position again. The key play of the game came when the Cadets gambled for a first down from their own 35 and Navy held. So the Middies swooped those final 35 yards for the touchdown which put them three scant points behind.

The most bewildering part of the entire episode is that Navy still was three scant points behind at the final gun. Yet the impression appears to have been given that the Midshipman moral victory was an actual one. So perhaps the fairer thing to do would be to give a little credit to Messrs. Blanchard and Davis for engineering the three touchdowns which made the Army success possible. [Davis (upper left), Blanchard (35), Bob Waterfield (7) and Tom Harmon (98) are shown above in a shot from *Yankee Rebel*, a film in which the four stars appeared together.]

As the greatest pair of backs ever to decorate our collegiate scene, they at least deserve that salute as a farewell gesture. So long, Doc. So long, Glenn. It was delightful to have you with us.

Well, it was not quite the end, but it was certainly the beginning of the end for Davis as a football player. He reinjured the knee while practicing for the College All-Star Game and hurt it again while playing in another charity game. A few weeks later he underwent surgery.

After leaving West Point both Blanchard and Davis received lucrative offers to play pro football, including $130,000 apiece for three-year deals with the San Francisco 49ers. Both applied for extended leaves to play with the 49ers, with the blessing of Major General Maxwell Taylor, the West Point superintendent. "We told him that if the Army would give us a leave of absence each year to play pro football, we would sign an agreement to stay 20 years in the service," Davis said. "He went to the War Department, then came back and told us we had a deal."

But the issue quickly became a political football after it was picked up by the press, and the War Department ultimately denied the players' requests.

So it was three years, including a year spent as an infantry officer in Korea, before Davis could complete his military commitment and try pro ball. He was nearly 26 when he joined the Los Angeles Rams in 1950.

"Laying off that long a time, it was almost impossible to come back," he said. "As a running back, you have to use your legs, and for three years I didn't really train. I was a better player my senior year in high school than I was with the Rams." But there was a bit of glamour to those early years. For a few months, Davis dated Elizabeth Taylor, then a teenager whose film career was just starting to blossom. Gossip columnists reported that they were engaged, but Davis said that wasn't so. In 1951 he was married for a short time to actress Terry Moore.

Davis played mainly on heart his two seasons with the Rams. Still, he made the Pro Bowl after his rookie year, in which he led the Rams with a 4.7-yard rushing average and caught 42 passes. But after injuries mounted during his second season, Davis retired and went into the petroleum business in Texas. Then he gave that up for one last shot at football glory, a brief and unsuccessful comeback stint with the Rams in 1953.

After he and Moore were divorced, Davis wed Harriet Lancaster, with whom he has two children. For more than 30 years he was director of special events for *The Los Angeles Times*, running a large number of charity events. Golf has become an enduring athletic passion since his retirement in 1987. He lives, conveniently, just off the 6th tee at La Quinta Country Club in Palm Springs, California.

Years out of the headlines, the naturally shy Davis has become more comfortable with his celebrity. But the accomplishment he values most doesn't involve any of the prodigious things he did with a football.

"The thing I'm proudest of," he said, "is graduating from West Point." —*DWIGHT CHAPIN*

John Lujack

Fitted to the T

Johnny Lujack, the man regarded by many as the greatest football player in Notre Dame history, actually blushes when he hears such talk. Or, at least he would blush if it weren't for that deep suntan painstakingly honed by years of forging an eight handicap on the golf courses in and around Indian Wells, California, where he spends five months a year.

It has been nearly a half century since Lujack became a Notre Dame legend and won the 1947 Heisman Trophy. He has sold his auto dealership in Davenport, Iowa, and dedicated himself to mastering the game of golf, an effort in which he says with characteristic modesty that he has made "very little headway." But Lujack never forgets his illustrious career as a Notre Dame quarterback. His fans won't let him. Neither will they allow him to downplay his puzzling yet remarkable four-year professional career with the Chicago Bears, which ended abruptly in 1952 when he decided that "you can't win a battle against George Halas [the Bears' owner-coach]."

Lujack is remembered as an exemplary T formation college football quarterback, one of coach Frank Leahy's favorite pupils and technicians. But the play with which he is most often associated, the one which will forever be a part of Notre Dame and college football lore, was his game-saving tackle against an undefeated Army squad in 1946.

The man Lujack brought down was none other than the great Doc Blanchard, who burst through the line to find only Lujack between himself and the goal line. Lujack made a smashing tackle to preserve a 0–0 tie and maintain Notre Dame's unbeaten record.

"People still bring up that tackle," Lujack said recently with a chuckle. "I really couldn't understand all the fuss. They said Blanchard couldn't be stopped, one-on-one, in the open field. I simply pinned him against the sideline and dropped him with a routine tackle.

"I saw Blanchard a few years later,

Lujack went to South Bend with just $20 but left with two national titles and an army of fans.

and he asked me if I remembered that tackle I made. I said, 'I sure do.' He said, 'You know, you scared the hell out of me. I thought I had killed you.' "

Lujack insists he was no hero on the day of that historic tie. "It was the worst game I ever played," he has said. "Everybody was tense because it was Notre Dame versus Army. I'm glad nobody remembers the other three tackles I made. They were on Arnold Tucker. Know why I had to tackle him? He had intercepted three of my passes. Some hero!"

Red Smith, the respected *New York Herald Tribune* sports columnist, didn't agree with Lujack's self-appraisal in the tie against Army. Smith wrote that Lujack, playing the full 60 minutes on a tender ankle, "called every Notre Dame play, threw every Notre Dame pass, kicked every Notre Dame punt, ran the ball with speed and malevolence, and tackled with hideous violence."

The son of a railroad boilermaker in Connellsville, Pennsylvania, Lujack quarterbacked Notre Dame to national titles in 1943, 1946 and 1947. In his Heisman year, 1947, he threw for 777 yards and nine touchdowns. In his three years as a starter the Irish were 20-1-1 and Lujack passed for 2,080 yards and 19 TDs. Even though football was his No. 1 priority and coach Frank Leahy frowned on other sports as extracurricular nonsense, Lujack became the only man to letter in four varsity sports—baseball, track, basketball and football—in one year at Notre Dame.

Lujack had his sights set on Notre Dame throughout an outstanding high school career in which he starred in three sports. He received offers from 13 major colleges, and his congressman got him an appointment to West Point. But Lujack wanted to play for Leahy, despite Leahy's reputation for toughness and lack of affection for his players.

"I think he liked me," Lujack reminisced. "I know a lot of players he liked. He was the greatest coach I ever played for ... a great man, a great motivator.... His toughness was his way of getting the most out of us.... Evidently he saw something in me that I wasn't able to see in myself."

"I never had any money at Notre Dame," Lujack once told columnist David Condon of *The Chicago Tribune*. "When I got to Notre Dame I had only the suit of clothes I was wearing and a traveler's check for $20. I cashed the traveler's check, locked $15 in my old Gladstone bag, and put $5 in my pocket. I walked around the campus for eight hours telling myself I was the richest guy in the world. I didn't believe there was anyone alive who could have more than $5 in his pocket."

Lujack achieved sudden national fame as an 18-year-

old sophomore when he succeeded Angelo Bertelli after the sixth game of the 1943 season, when Bertelli was called into the Marines. With Lujack at the controls the Irish wiped out previously unbeaten Army 26–0, then followed with victories over Northwestern and Iowa Pre-Flight to capture the national title. Later, looking back, Lujack said, "I really think 18 years old is too young to play college football."

A single wing tailback in high school, Lujack received a quick introduction as an Irish freshman to the intricacies of the T formation. "When the freshmen got the ball I played tailback [in practice] if we were scheduled against a single wing team that week," he recalled. "If we were going to play a T team, I played quarterback."

When the Marine Corps summoned Bertelli, Lujack easily made the transformation to first-string T formation quarterback. He never again started at running back, though he rushed for 438 yards and two touchdowns on 81 carries. And when the Irish were on defense, Lujack was either a safety or halfback in Notre Dame's basic 5-3-2-1 alignment.

In 1944 Lujack's Navy V-12 class was called up, and he

Coliseum that Lujack had won the Heisman Trophy. Lujack beat out such illustrious contenders as Michigan's Bob Chappuis, SMU's Doak Walker and Mississippi's Charley Conerly to become the second of seven Notre Dame players to win the coveted award.

Lujack downplayed the honor with characteristic modesty. "Winning each game was my primary concern," he said. "Winning any individual award is icing on the cake.... I'm lucky that I went to Notre Dame. I never saw a time when there was any jealousy at Notre Dame. There never was a time that I went for an individual award."

For a short time—four seasons, to be exact—Lujack enjoyed a pro career that was often spectacular, sometimes prosaic and always unpredictable. The Chicago Bears of the National Football League acquired the rights to Lujack. Halas, who was forced to open his treasury because of the war with the upstart All-America Football Conference, gave Lujack an unheard-of four-year contract at $18,750 a year.

"I was All-Pro my first year as a defensive back and All-Pro my third year as a quarterback, but I think my second year was my best," said Lujack, who was signed as a back-up to aging Sid Luckman.

Lujack intercepted eight passes in 1948. He also played every first series on offense that season while the immortal Luckman sized up the defense; Lujack then turned the ball over to Luckman. In 1949 Lujack took over the QB job and passed for 2,658 yards and 23 TDs. In the season finale, against the Chicago Cardinals, Lujack threw for six touchdowns and 468 yards.

Halas had initially counted on either Lujack or Bobby Layne, the Texan who went on to become a legend in Detroit and Pittsburgh, to replace Luckman when he retired in 1950. But Halas traded Layne to the New York Bulldogs in 1949, and Lujack looked like a prize until he hurt his right shoulder during his third season. And suddenly the Bears, who had seemed so rich in quarterbacks, were scraping the bottom of the barrel.

Great things come in twos: Chicago Bear quarterbacks Lujack (32) and Luckman confer on the sideline.

Lujack went back to Notre Dame to join Leahy's staff after the 1951 season. "Halas and I never talked money," Lujack said recently. "I wanted to be traded. Halas wanted four first-team Los Angeles Rams for me.... My shoulder never really got a chance to heal, so I became more of a runner than a passer. There were pressures from my family to quit after four seasons. I have no regrets. It was wonderful while it lasted."

—COOPER ROLLOW

found himself skippering a sub chaser in the English Channel. Lujack returned to Notre Dame for the season of 1946 with his junior and senior years still ahead of him, as did Leahy, who had also gone into the service after the 1943 football campaign.

"The military enabled me to grow as a person," Lujack said. "It also made me more mature athletically."

After Lujack led Notre Dame to a 38–7 thrashing of Southern Cal on December 6, 1947, to stretch the Irish's latest unbeaten streak to 12, the announcement came to the Notre Dame locker room at the Los Angeles

1948
Doak Walker

A Soft-Spoken Miracle Worker

In Southwest Conference football's boom days of the late 1940s, everyone knew what the large block *M* stood for on Doak Walker's Southern Methodist University letter sweater.

Miracles.

Great plays seemed routine for this 5'11", 168-pound halfback with a neck like a bull, the grace of a ballroom dancer and the cool cunning of a riverboat gambler. The Mustangs were never out of a game if Doak was in it. A natural leader as well as a natural athlete, he thrived on tough games and challenging competition.

Ewell Doak Walker Jr., son of a onetime high school coach who later became the assistant superintendent of Dallas schools, was also modest, friendly, generous and bright. Any way you viewed him, he truly was an all-American.

His father had called the shot the day his son was born, January 1, 1927. A beaming Ewell Walker was asked if he wanted his baby son to grow up to be president. "No," said Doak's dad. "He's going to be an All-American football player."

And he was—three times—in 1947, '48 and '49, as a sophomore, junior and senior at SMU. Doak and the Mustangs so completely captured the hearts of fans eager to embrace new heroes in the first years after World War II, that crowds soon overflowed SMU's cozy campus stadium, prompting the school to move its home games to the 47,000-seat Cotton Bowl. By Doak's senior season, the historic stadium on the grounds of the State Fair of Texas had been expanded twice, to seat 75,000, and was hailed as the House That Walker Built.

Doak ran, passed, punted, kicked, caught and played defense with the best, but above all he was the thinking man's football player. His mind seemed to be a couple of moves ahead of his opponents', perhaps because he always remembered his dad's advice.

"Football is a chess game," his father told Doak when he taught him to play chess at age six. "You must get your opponent out of position. When you have two strong men

Walker, as effective in the NFL as he was in college, swept for five yards against the New York Yankees in 1950.

who are physically even, the man who makes the fewest mistakes will win."

As a sophomore at Highland Park High School, Doak met a flamboyant quarterback named Bobby Layne, and a rare friendship began. They enjoyed some wonderful times as teammates, first in high school and later with the NFL champion Detroit Lions. A few months before Layne died, in 1986, he was able to celebrate his old friend's election to the Pro Football Hall of Fame, an honor many felt was long over-due for a man who, in an abbreviated five-year pro career, was Rookie of the Year, a two-time NFL scoring leader and an All-Pro four times.

The Walker legend almost began at the University of

Texas instead of at SMU, where Walker became such a widely beloved figure. In the late stages of World War II, he and Layne enlisted in the Merchant Marine, Doak just out of high school and Bobby fresh from his first college season at Texas. By October 1945, with the war over and their services as radio operators no longer needed, they received discharges in New Orleans on a Friday and planned to be in Austin on Monday to enroll at UT, just in time to be eligible for the remainder of the football season. But SMU, which had hired their old Highland Park coach, Rusty Russell, as backfield coach that season, was in town to play Tulane, and they stayed over to watch the game on Saturday. They checked into the same hotel as the Mustangs.

Texas backfield coach Blair Cherry, in New Orleans to scout SMU, came to the hotel to welcome Walker to the Texas program and congratulate him on his decision to join Layne in a Longhorn uniform. But while Cherry was on an elevator going up to Walker's room, Walker was on another elevator heading down to a lobby jammed with SMU fans. Cherry never caught up with Walker before the game, and afterward Walker boarded the same train to Dallas as the SMU team.

Russell used the long ride to visit with Walker and ask him to reconsider his choice of a college. He followed up on Sunday evening in Dallas by visiting with Walker and his parents in their home. On Monday morning Walker enrolled in SMU. That afternoon he became a member of the starting backfield for that Saturday's game with, iron-ically, Texas.

SMU led 7–6, thanks to Walker's darting touchdown run, until Layne threw a long scoring pass in the final two minutes to give Texas a 12–7 victory. The old friends would meet once more as rivals. In 1947, when Walker returned to SMU after spending the '46 season in the Army, the Mustangs beat Texas 14–13 before a sold-out Cotton Bowl crowd of 47,000. The Mustangs, with a dazzling array of wingback and spread formations, finished with a 9-0-1 record, then played a thrilling 13–13 tie with Penn State in the Cotton Bowl Classic on New Year's Day—the 21st birthday of their freshly minted All-America halfback.

SMU finished undefeated that season because Walker gave one of his greatest performances in the regular-season finale against archrival TCU in Fort Worth. The Frogs jumped into an early lead, and TCU tackle Harold Kilman, a Golden Gloves heavyweight champion, started a steady line of chatter with Walker.

1948 Doak Walker

Walker thought ahead, just as his father had told him he should in those long-ago chess games.

As he raced past SMU head coach Matty Bell, Walker yelled, "Get the Old Man ready!" The Old Man was passing specialist Gil Johnson, a balding, gimpy-kneed war veteran who threw strikes under pressure. On the next play Johnson connected with Walker on the TCU nine-yard line, then the Mustangs scored with the last seconds ticking off the clock. The game ended in a 19–19 tie when an exhausted Walker missed the extra point, sending a surprising message to America that he was only human.

Walker's statistics that bright November day were nonetheless almost superhuman. He accounted for 471 total yards, including kickoff returns of 77 and 57 yards, a 61-yard TD run, and he completed 10 of 14 passes. He also returned punts, caught passes and played defensive safety superbly.

One year later, just a few days before Walker was voted the Heisman Trophy winner for 1948, he shocked TCU again. The Frogs had taken a 7–0 lead late in the fourth quarter, and the ensuing kickoff had left SMU 99 yards from the end zone. In came Johnson again, who teamed with Walker to get the Mustangs past midfield. Walker came to the sideline for a quick breather just as Johnson passed for another first down, on the TCU 30. Only a few seconds remained. Offensive specialist Russell had designed a play for such a situation, but in the excitement none of the coaches remembered the name of the play. Bell quickly called his All-American to his side.

"Doak, what's the name of the play where we throw a pass off a naked reverse?" Bell asked. "The Sally Rand," Walker replied calmly.

"That's it!" Bell yelled, shoving Walker toward the field. "Go in there and call it!"

On New Year's day in '49 Walker (in raincoat) was forced to sit out SMU's Cotton Bowl matchup against Oregon.

On the next snap Johnson took the ball, faked a handoff to Walker, swinging left, and the entire TCU defense followed him. Then Johnson carried out his fake a few steps, bootlegging the ball toward the right sideline before he fired a pass to a wide-open receiver in the end zone. Walker kicked the extra point, and the Mustangs happily chalked up another incredible comeback.

This was too much for frustrated Frog coach Dutch Meyer. He jerked off his pearl-gray Western hat, held it high for a moment, then slammed it on the ground in a fury and jumped on it.

Doak Walker, soft-spoken miracle worker, could do that to you.

—SAM BLAIR

When TCU went ahead 12–0, Kilman had to gloat. "You can't come back now, Doak," he said. But Walker calmly replied, "We'll be back, don't worry."

The Mustangs fought back and took a 13–12 lead, but TCU scored again for a 19–13 lead with 1:40 left to play.

"You can't do it now, Doak," Kilman said.

"Yes, we can," Walker answered and promptly returned the kickoff 57 yards to put SMU deep in TCU territory. And while he ran by the SMU sideline on his return,

Leon Hart

Bigger than Life

Kyle Rote, the former Southern Methodist halfback, remembers Leon Hart as being eight feet tall and weighing 350 pounds. Pro scouts considered Hart the most irresistible football force since Minnesota's Bronko Nagurski. Coach Frank Leahy regarded his monster Notre Dame end as one of the most "destructive" pass receivers of all time.

Hyperbole? Perhaps, but only slightly. Hart, the co-captain of the 1949 Fighting Irish national championship team, was, indeed, a huge man. At 6'5" and 260 pounds, he was the largest player ever to win the Heisman Memorial Trophy. Hart had it all—towering size, finesse and unbelievable speed for a player of his dimensions. Notre Dame never lost a game during his four years at South Bend.

Without hesitation Hart calls Leahy "the greatest man I ever met. I was afraid of him. So was everyone. But we worshiped the ground he walked on. He would tell us, 'I want the 11 most savage men to play for me.' So we growled coming out of the huddle.

"Leahy used to tell us, 'Lads, you're not to miss practice unless your parents died or you died.' He wanted to get my afternoon labs changed because I couldn't get to practice some days until very late. But the university wouldn't hear of it. You were at Notre Dame to study.

"I was walking in one day after practice," Hart continued, "and Leahy said, 'Leon, how do you feel?' I said, 'I feel tired.' He said, 'Take 10 laps.'

"The next day after practice Leahy said, 'Leon, how do you feel?' I remembered the day before, so I said, 'I feel great.' He said, 'Take 10 laps.'

"The very next day Leahy said, 'Leon, how do you feel?' I looked at him and said, 'Coach, how do you want me to feel?' He laughed and let me go in."

The Fighting Irish went 36-0-2 and won three national titles during Hart's four years. Hart was the first to point out that he was surrounded by such All-Americans as quarterbacks Johnny Lujack and Bob Williams, fullback Emil (Red) Sitko, tackles George Connor, Ziggy Czarobski and Jim Martin, guards John Mastrangelo and Marty Wendell and center George Strohmeyer.

Hart was not always a giant. Born and brought up in Turtle Creek, Pennsylvania, a mill town near Pittsburgh, he was a puny child who only began to indicate his future bulk as a teenager. By the age of 14 Hart had shot up to 5'11". Three years later he was 6' 2", 225 pounds, an honor roll senior and the most widely sought-after football end and basketball center in the Pittsburgh area.

He visited many campuses but said he wasn't wooed by any one particular person at Notre Dame. "Notre Dame did a lousy job of recruiting me," Hart said. "But when you want to go someplace, you go. Notre Dame—the school itself—is the best recruiter, not football."

Hart may have assumed that nobody at Notre Dame cared about acquiring his services, but Moose Krause, Leahy's line coach who later became a fixture as athletic director, wanted to ensure that the big end from Turtle Creek wound up in South Bend. When Hart arrived one evening for a recruiting visit, he called Krause from the train station, asking Krause to pick him up.

It was pouring rain, and Krause's wife objected. "No football player," Mrs. Krause declared, "is worth pneumonia." "You only say that because you've never seen Hart," Krause retorted, scampering out the door.

Notre Dame was loaded with talent after World War II, but Leahy quickly found room for Hart, who earned the first of his four varsity letters as a freshman member of the 1946 national championship team. In 1947, as the Irish cruised to a 9–0 record for their second straight national title, Hart added blocking and defensive rushing to his repertoire and made All-America as a sophomore.

The Irish were 9–0 during Hart's junior year when they traveled to the West Coast for a season finale with Southern Cal. Early in the second quarter, after fumbling the ball away six times, including the opening kickoff, Notre Dame had possession at the USC 45-yard line. Quarterback Frank Tripucka tossed a short pass to Hart, who blasted at least half of the Trojan team out of his way on his way to the end zone.

"It was," exuded Leahy, "the most destructive run I've ever seen. Eight Southern California lads had their arms around Leon at various times, but he just ran over them and left them for dead."

The game wound up in a 14–14 tie, which cost the Irish the national championship (won that year by Michigan). But Notre Dame still had a 28-game unbeaten streak. In 1949, Hart's senior season, the big man led the Irish to victory in their first nine games. As in the season before,

One of only two ends to win the Heisman, Hart never tasted defeat during his career at Notre Dame.

The day before Herschel Walker's coronation as
1982's Heisman winner, George Vescey spent some
time with Leon Hart and Larry Kelley, discussing the many
changes in the game they once dominated.

Leon Hart and Larry Kelley admit it. Every season they scan the newspapers and the television for a massive brute of a lineman who cannot be denied the Heisman Trophy, given to the outstanding college football player.

Yet every year the Heisman Trophy goes to either a quarterback or a running back, not to a player who works in the trenches, as Leon Hart and Larry Kelley once did. This year's award seems sure to go to Herschel Walker of Georgia, at long last, in tomorrow night's televised ceremonies.

Even Hart [pictured at right with Detroit Lions coach Bob McMillin] and Kelley were not pure linemen, the kind of incredible hulks who are not allowed to touch a ball unless it happens to flop on the ground in front of them. They won the Heisman as offensive ends—Kelley for Yale in 1936 and Hart for Notre Dame in 1949—and they excelled at catching the ball and running over people.

But they also played defensive end when many athletes still played both ways and they earned the right to identify with today's tackles and guards and centers who must be content with the Outland Trophy for the best college lineman.

Theirs was a time of the complete player. Hart, who later played end, and occasionally fullback, for the Detroit Lions as a professional, says college football should still emphasize "effort and stamina as well as ability." He adds: "Today you ask a guy if he plays football and he says, 'No, I play left linebacker.'"

Kelley, who never played pro ball and is now retired in Pensacola, Florida, says: "Fair or unfair, the game has changed. When we played both ways, I could intercept passes as a combination defensive end and weakside linebacker."

Hart, who owns several manufacturing companies in Birmingham, Michigan, says: "Specialization killed it. There's no way you can be part of statistics. Maybe a defensive lineman can record a few sacks, but who keeps track of how many good blocks you make on offense?" The two former linemen gave their views this week while visiting New York for the Heisman ceremonies, where they will appear in Bud Greenspan's film about the award.

The film shows more respect for linemen than the Heisman voting usually does. Kyle Rote of Southern Methodist University, the 1950 runner-up to Vic Janowicz of Ohio State, recalls the defensive ability of Leon Hart in the famous near-upset of Notre Dame in 1949 when a Dallas newspaper ran the headline: SMU WINS—20 TO 27.

And Charlie (Choo Choo) Justice of North Carolina, the runner-up for the Heisman in 1948 and 1949, pays homage to linemen everywhere when he recalls how he outran his All-America blocking guard in an intraservice game in Bainbridge, Maryland, in 1943.

After he was tackled, Justice recalls, "As I started to get up, I felt something grab at the seat of my britches and on the nape of the neck and the shoulder pads. He turned me around to his face and he says, 'You little high school so-and-so, you think you're the greatest runner in the world, don't you? So let me tell you something. I love to block as well as you love to run, and you just made a fool out of me out here in front of all these people. And if you ever do that again, I'll kill you.'"

Neither Larry Kelley nor Leon Hart recalls that kind of lineman's rage, but both have their own pride in often having played 60 minutes.

"I watched a game last year when Alabama ran in 70 players by halftime," Hart says. "The game used to belong to the players on the field. Now it's a puppet show, a chess game. The quarterback is not a field general anymore."

Kelley says: "When we played you couldn't even send in a play with a substitute. The new player had to stand outside the huddle with the referee until the signal was called."

Hart says: "The one change I would make that would restore football to what it was is the old rule that if you left the game, you could not come back in until the next quarter. I think free substitution is the cancer of the sport. I've been preaching this for years."

As the president of his class in 1950, Hart says he frequently has contact with football officials. He says, "They argue that more people play football today, but I'm not sure. As time goes on, athletes are polarized. The big colleges stock up and other colleges drop the sport. Detroit, Marquette, Villanova. I question whether more people are playing football."

Hart, who was one of the biggest college players of his time, at 6'5" inches and 260 pounds, says regretfully that platoon football has downgraded the value of stamina in smaller men and driven them into other games, notably soccer.

"I had to laugh the other night when Cosell said the offense better stay on the field a while because the defense

was just on for five straight minutes. Five minutes!" Hart says with a rumbling laugh.

Hart, who was graduated in four years with a degree in mechanical engineering, and Kelley, who was graduated in four years with a history degree, fear that the stockpiling of athletes leads to abuses of redshirting and lack of degrees.

"Are players getting a good education today at some of the schools?" Hart asks. "I doubt it. I say colleges should not think of themselves as farm systems for the professionals."

The two linemen insist that players would prefer to play both ways if the rules were changed. Hart says: "You'd be surprised how good sportsmanship would result from the chance to retaliate. You wouldn't take a cheap shot at a guy if you knew he'd be playing opposite you for 60 minutes."

For all their concerns, Kelley and Hart are still close to football. They were disappointed when Hugh Green of Pittsburgh, a defensive end, finished a distant second to George Rogers of South Carolina in the 1980 Heisman voting. But they hold out hope that a lineman can be judged as the outstanding player in a game or even a season.

"I saw a pro game on Thanksgiving that proved it," says Kelley. "Lawrence Taylor of the Giants turned the Detroit game around at linebacker. He was fantastic."

If a linebacker can do it, so can an interior lineman, Hart and Kelley insist. And they plan to keep rooting until the Heisman Trophy once again goes to somebody down in the trenches.

the gods had willed a thrilling finish for Notre Dame, but this one had a happy ending. With Hart playing fullback for much of the finale against SMU, the Irish won 27–20, for their third national championship of the postwar era.

"You are my greatest team," an emotional Leahy said in the locker room after the game. "God bless you, everyone."

Hart, whose modest Irish career stats (13 TDs, 49 pass receptions for 742 yards) belie his iron-man contribution to the team, in 1949 became the third Notre Dame Heisman winner, following quarterbacks Angelo Bertelli (1943) and John Lujack (1947).

Hart's roommate in South Bend was Bill Wightkin, a gifted Irish end with a hearty appreciation for Leon's size.

For a time, recalled Wightkin, who was built along more modest lines than Hart, big Leon borrowed his clothes. When stopped on a train trip to Southern Cal, Wightkin said. "He stretched my new sport shirt around his size 18.5 neck, went into the diner, sneezed, and popped the top button across the aisle onto a lady's plate. He was terribly embarrassed, and he's kept his neck out of my shirts ever since."

Hart endured a somewhat turbulent eight-year professional relationship with the Detroit Lions, who drafted the big end as a bonus pick after the 1949 season. During his tenure with the Lions, the team won three National Football League crowns. Hart's best season was 1951, when he caught 35 passes for 544 yards and 12 touchdowns and added two interceptions to make All-Pro on both offense and defense.

But Hart, who formed his own manufacturing company in the Detroit area after his Lion career ended in 1958, was never truly happy as a pro. He didn't dominate opponents as he had at Notre Dame, and he had a basic philosophical disagreement with Bobby Layne, the Lions' colorful quarterback. Layne wanted to drink, play football, then drink some more. Hart, though certainly not antisocial, merely wanted to play football.

All the controversy left Hart embittered with pro football. Years after he hung up his helmet, he declared, "I loved to play football, but pro football tore it out of me.... Pro football is a business, and you're the laborer."

Hart may have been right about the professional game, but for four years he made college football a labor of love for himself and his teammates.   —COOPER ROLLOW

1950

Vic Janowicz

Mr. Unbelievable

The Vic Janowicz story is about the fulfillment of the American dream. Born on February 26, 1930, in Elyria, Ohio, Janowicz was the eighth out of nine children born to Polish immigrant parents. To them, every day of life in America was an achievement, any additional honors a treasure.

At Elyria High School, Vic not only earned membership in the National Honor Society but was also the greatest athlete Elyria has ever known. He earned all-state honors in football, basketball and baseball and captained all three sports during his junior and senior years.

When he graduated from high school, in 1948, Vic had tryouts with two major league baseball teams—the Detroit Tigers and the Cincinnati Reds. All offered him minor league contracts, but he turned them down. Sixty colleges contacted him, making him the most heavily recruited athlete in the country.

But Ohio State was particularly eager to sign Janowicz. The school was a member of the Big Ten, and in 1948 that conference did not have athletic scholarships. But Ohio State did have the Frontliners, a group of Columbus businessmen who helped recruit football players and sometimes offered them jobs.

John Galbreath, who headed one of the nation's largest construction and real estate companies, was a Frontliner, one of the most powerful men in this powerful group. The Galbreath firm had already started a construction job in the Elyria area, and Galbreath offered Vic a part-time job while he was in school and a guaranteed job after graduation. The offer would be good whether or not Vic made the football team.

With the means now to attend Ohio State, Janowicz enrolled in the fall of 1948. Because freshmen were not eligible for varsity sports, it was another year before he joined coach Wes Fesler's team. Fesler's offense was blessed with a group of experienced running backs, so he placed Janowicz in the defensive back-

On his way to the 1950 Heisman Trophy, Janowicz swept around end for five yards against Pittsburgh.

field. That season Ohio State won a Big Ten co-championship. In the Rose Bowl on January 2, 1950, Janowicz intercepted two passes. He ran one back for 41 yards, and Ohio State beat California 17–14.

Fesler was one of the last coaches to use the single wing. In 1950 he made Janowicz the tailback. Vic ran, passed, punted, placekicked and played defense, putting in 50 minutes every game. He was the catalyst of the Buckeye offense, a shifty runner. "It was like when I played tag as a kid," Janowicz said. "I didn't want anybody to catch me."

The Buckeyes opened the season with a loss to SMU, 32–27, in which Janowicz scored 15 points. Ohio State then reeled off six straight victories, and Vic was a dazzler. Against Pittsburgh on October 7, he threw six passes and completed six. Four were for touchdowns as the Buckeyes

won 41–7. They nailed Northwestern 32–0 and Minnesota 48–0, a game in which Janowicz kicked a 90-yard punt.

Janowicz remembers the Iowa game three weeks later because it was played on Father's Day for Ohio State, and his father was in the stands. Vic wanted to make his dad proud.

Janowicz kicked off, sending the ball clear past the end zone. Iowa took the ball on its own 20 and fumbled. Janowicz recovered. Ohio State lined up, and Janowicz ran for a touchdown. Janowicz kicked the extra point.

Janowicz kicked off again. Iowa tried three plays and punted. Janowicz returned the punt 61 yards for a touchdown. Janowicz kicked the extra point

The game was hardly two minutes old, and the scoreboard read Ohio State 14, Iowa 0. Or, as I wrote in my story for *The Cedar Rapids Gazette* that day, "Janowicz 14,

Iowa 0."

For the rest of the day Janowicz threw four touchdown passes and kicked eight extra points. Ohio State won 83–21, and Janowicz accounted for 46 points.

Ohio State seemed headed for the Big Ten championship but faltered, losing to Illinois and Michigan. The Michigan game, on November 25, was played in Arctic conditions. A blizzard had hit Columbus on Friday night and continued all day Saturday.

The temperature at game time was 3°. But there were 50,000 fans in the stands, a tribute to football fever in Columbus. Right away Janowicz kicked a 27-yard field goal against the stout wind and Ohio State led 3–0.

It was a game in which Ohio State made three first downs, Michigan none. Ohio State completed three passes, Michigan none. But Michigan blocked two Ohio State punts, scored a safety on one, a touchdown on the other and won 9–3.

As a result, Ohio State lost the Big Ten championship, and Michigan went to the Rose Bowl. Feeling the heat of intense criticism, Fesler decided to resign as coach.

Despite his team's collapse, Janowicz swept the postseason awards. The first was the Silver Football, a trophy awarded by *The Chicago Tribune* for the Big Ten's best player. Janowicz was also named the nation's Player of the Year by *The Sporting News* and UPI, and was a unanimous All-America halfback selection.

Then came the Heisman Trophy. It was Janowicz in a landslide, with 633 points over the 280 garnered by runner-up Kyle Rote of Southern Methodist.

Vic Janowicz topped any and all other competitors. He was the only one who could do so many things so well. In 1967 the Big Ten would publish its history and refer to Janowicz in 1950 as "Mr. Unbelievable."

The 1951 season, however, would be different. The Buckeyes had a new coach, Woody Hayes, and he put in the modern T formation. In two games, victories over Northwestern 3–0 and Pittsburgh 16–14, Janowicz delivered the winning play, a field goal. But the new Buckeye formula was different from 1950's. Janowicz had a lesser role and was injured for part of the season. He did not repeat his 1950 accomplishments.

But he was named to play in the East-West Shrine Game. The East coach, Biggie Munn, moved Janowicz to fullback. He was the star of the game and was voted the Most Valuable Player. In the Hula Bowl in Honolulu, a team of college all-stars was matched against a lineup of Hawaii players plus pro stars. This time they made Janowicz a quarterback, and he earned another Most Valuable Player trophy.

He was then out of sports for a year while serving in the Army. About the time of his discharge on December 4, 1952, Branch Rickey, the general manager of the Pittsburgh Pirates, announced the signing of Janowicz to a baseball contract.

Janowicz was with the Pittsburgh Pirates for the 1953 and '54 seasons. He was in 83 games as a catcher, third baseman or pinch hitter. He batted .214 and was released in the fall of 1954. He then jumped immediately into pro football with the Washington Redskins, making him one of the few men of his time to play both major league baseball and football in the same calendar year.

In 1955 Janowicz led the National Football League in scoring up to the last week of the season, when he yielded the title to Doak Walker of the Detroit Lions.

The next year he seemed headed for greatness. He sparkled in exhibition games. Then in August 1956, tragedy struck. He was critically injured in an auto accident while in California. Doctors said he would never play football again.

Janowicz's recovery was slow. While he was recuperating at his in-laws' home in Chicago, Ohio State came to town to play Northwestern and Hayes stopped in to see Janowicz. Seeing that Vic was struggling, Woody decided to take him back to Columbus on the team plane and lined him up with a series of doctors there. Though Janowicz eventually made a full recovery, he did not play football again.

He went on to a career in broadcasting, covering the Ohio State games on radio for three years. Janowicz works today as an administrative assistant to the state auditor of Ohio. Honors still come his way. The late Wes Fesler wrote an article in *The Saturday Evening Post* titled "The Greatest Player I Ever Coached—Vic Janowicz." Elyria—his hometown—has built the Vic Janowicz Ballpark. On February 14, 1992, a crowd of 1,500 jammed a Columbus hotel banquet room for a tribute to Janowicz as "Ohio State's Greatest Athlete of the Last 50 Years."

Vic will always remember this date: December 12, 1950. That is when he was presented the Heisman Trophy by the Downtown Athletic Club, and his father was there. The D.A.C. clubhouse is located in lower Manhattan. From its upper floors one can see the New York harbor and its centerpieces, the Statue of Liberty and Ellis Island. On that day Vic's father saw Ellis Island and remembered. That's where he first came when he arrived in America in 1913. And now, 37 years later, he watched as his son received a great American honor.

It happened. Only in America.   —PAT HARMON

Dick Kazmaier

A Tiger, Burning Bright

After Dick Kazmaier graduated, an informal decree took hold that no other Princeton athlete in any sport was to wear his uniform number, 42. Such a noble institution was not into deifying an athlete, or even retiring a number, and so 42 was just quietly put aside—until Bill Bradley showed up a decade later. Bradley wore number 42 with a distinction that equaled his predecessor's and went on to highly visible careers in the National Basketball Association and the United States Senate.

Kazmaier was certainly famous in his era. He appeared on the cover of *Time* magazine on November 19, 1951. He was also the subject of a controversy concocted by Joe Williams, the sports editor of the Scripps Howard newspapers, which played a major role in college football through its annual sponsorship of the Coach of the Year award.

Kazmaier's most formidable—and perhaps only—rival for the Heisman Trophy that fall was Hank Lauricella of Tennessee, who, like Kazmaier, was a single-wing, triple-threat tailback. Scripps Howard had a paper in Knoxville, two in Memphis and one in New York, the flagship *World-Telegram & Sun*, so Williams saw good reason to promote a comparison between Kazmaier and Lauricella to determine which was the more worthy. He would impanel a blue-ribbon jury and let them decide.

The courthouse was Mama Leone's restaurant on West 48th Street in New York City. The jurists included Chick Meehan, a former coach at Syracuse, New York University and Manhattan; Earl (Red) Blaik of Army; Lou Little of Columbia; Harvey Harman of Rutgers; Steve Owen of the New York Giants; and Jack Lavelle, a scout for the Giants, Notre Dame and other clients. Vince Lombardi, an assistant at Army, was there to run the projector because film would be the evidence.

Host Gene Leone laid on a sumptuous feast and the wine flowed. Following dinner the film presentation began: small poorly lit figures pranced on a black-and-white screen while cigar and cigarette smoke curled above the projector light. The room became quite warm, and heads drooped as Lombardi closed and opened can after can of game film. Finally the jury voted and chose Kazmaier in politely close balloting.

The Heisman voting was not close, the slim senior from Maumee, Ohio, gaining 1,777 points to 424 for Lauricella, one of the largest margins in Heisman history.

Kazmaier had a lot going for him: the *Time* cover story; Princeton's No. 6 ranking in the Associated Press poll (Tennessee was No. 1); the Tigers' two straight undefeated seasons and a 22-game winning streak, plus some television coverage that had included Dick's most celebrated game.

The latter took place in Princeton's Palmer Stadium before a capacity crowd of 49,000 on October 26, 1951. The Big Red of Cornell also entered the game undefeated. Although the Ivy League did not become a formal league with a round-robin schedule until 1956, it was stated that this match would produce an Ivy champion and perhaps an Eastern one, too.

There was no contest as Princeton won 53–15. However, the enormity of the rout and the performance of Kazmaier made this a game to recall. The Princeton tailback completed 15 of 17 pass attempts for 236 yards and three touchdowns, two of which were 33- and 45-yard plays. He ran with the ball 17 times, twice for touchdowns—one of them on a 51-yard dash to the end zone. He averaged seven yards per carry. Allison Danzig, who covered the game for *The New York Times*, noted that Kazmaier's performance was "one of the greatest passing exhibitions seen on any gridiron since the introduction of the pass in 1906."

The game the following Saturday, at Brown, had far less importance, yet his coach, Charlie Caldwell, called it Kazmaier's finest. "We were heavily favored," wrote Caldwell a year later in *The Saturday Evening Post*. "Then the weather turned terrible. In the rain and mud, Kaz couldn't pass. So he gained 267 yards on the ground and was the primary factor in our 12–0 victory."

In his collegiate career Kazmaier played in 27 games of which 24 were victories. He gained 1,964 yards rushing, passed for 2,393; scored 20 touchdowns and passed for 35 more. In his Heisman year he was the nation's leader in completion percentage, .626; touchdown passes, 22; and in total offense, 1,827 yards.

Kazmaier also had Caldwell, a brilliant coach who made the traditional single wing offense so multifaceted that it could easily compete with the "modern" T formation. Kazmaier said of Caldwell, who died of cancer in 1957, "He had a lot of deceptions, a lot of variations. By the end of our junior year, every passing

Kazmaier threw for 2,393 yards and 35 touchdowns—22 of them as a senior—during his stellar Princeton career.

Just days after Dick Kazmaier's dominant performance against a highly regarded Cornell squad, Arthur Daley presented this trenchant analysis of the man who would win the Heisman Trophy that year.

Princeton received a million-dollar legacy from a non-Princetonian the other day, but it is doubtful if the Sons of Old Nassau appreciate it a fraction as much as another unexpected gift they had dumped into their collective lap a few years ago. This one can't be measured in dollars and cents. It isn't impressive if measured in avoirdupois, but it's a gift beyond valuation, the 171 pounds which adds up to Dick Kazmaier.

Kazmaier [pictured at right being carried off the field after his final collegiate performance] is the finest college backfield performer these eyes have seen in many a moon. He is one of those old-fashioned, triple-threat backs that almost have gone out of style. He is an exquisite runner with blinding speed and uncanny change of pace. Only Frank Merriwell in his fictional prime had days that could compare with the one Dandy Dick had against Cornell last Saturday.

The entire Big Red team combined to gain 98 yards rushing. Kazmaier gained 126. All the Ithaca passers gained 112 yards. Kazmaier clicked on 15 of 17 passes for 236 yards. But it was even more an artistic success than a statistical one. The little fellow had to be seen to be believed, and even then he strained credulity.

Goggle-eyed observers threw caution to the winds, stated flatly that he was the best back in Princeton history and then were aghast at their temerity. Princeton history, you see, encompasses the entire history of football because the Tigers started the Great Autumnal Madness with the help of Rutgers in 1869. Stubbornly they stuck to their original estimate, though.

Dandy Dick is a surprise package. As far as Nassau was concerned he was the man nobody wanted. The director of admissions at Princeton, C. William Edwards, interviewed the youngster and was unprophetic in his written report. He still has the card which says: "Fine boy. Excellent record. Has played football and other sports in high school. But too small to play college football."

Coach Charlie Caldwell first looked at the then 155-pounder and sighed. Kazmaier would never do. So Charlie persisted in searching elsewhere on the squad for a tailback to engineer his streamlined single wing attack. He searched and he searched before the realization hit him. The man he wanted had been there all along and Caldwell was on his way to become Coach of the Year in 1950.

It's possible that Caldwell will get the same honors again, because the current team represents a more impressive coaching job. The Tigers lost six of the 11 men from last year's defensive platoon and 10 of 11 from the offensive squad. Lone holdover is Kazmaier, but as the realistic Caldwell says with a grin:

"Dick makes a great coach out of me."

Yet Kazmaier might not have reached Nassau if Princeton authorities had a policy other than the careful screening they use on applicants for admission. They strive to spread their students over a broad geographic base, taking them from big schools and little ones in an effort to strike a representative cross-section. Kazmaier, the Maumee (Ohio) schoolboy, just happened to fit the precise category, geographically and otherwise. That he should wind up as a sure-shot All-America is an accident of his own manufacture.

Dandy Dick loves football with such a passion that he enjoys even spring practice, a dread and disagreeable chore for most gridiron performers. He also is unusual in that he's so meticulous. Other players carelessly toss their equipment into their lockers. Kazmaier not only puts everything precisely in its place but hangs up his ankle wrappings. He also is unusual in his inquisitiveness.

The ordinary player accepts the commands of his coach without question. Not Kazmaier, though. He has

play started from a running formation. I took a step to the side and started moving. I took the same steps, went the same direction to start a passing play as I did for a run. The defense had no time to decide what we were going to do."

This was heady stuff in 1951, for Caldwell had created an innovative run–pass option offense far ahead of its time. For that Cornell game the coach gave Kazmaier a new series. The balanced line became unbalanced, a guard overshifting to make a strong side, and the wingback was placed as flanker on the weak side against the 6-2-2-1 defense that was the standard for its time.

This shift, said Caldwell, "put an almost intolerable burden on the secondary defense unless Cornell changed to a five-man line." When coach Lefty James did shift to a

senior year Kazmaier had grown to 5'10" and 171 pounds.

He always had the athletic ability, the background and the attitude. His father had been captain of the Toledo University team and two of his uncles were football coaches. Kazmaier made football look effortless. Holland Donan, his teammate and an All-America tackle, said, "Although he didn't look fast, he was fast. You could never make a solid tackle on him. Give him a step and he was gone."

Russ McNeil, the fullback Kazmaier's senior year, said, "He had absolute concentration, very intense." George Stevens, the quarterback and his roommate for three years, said, "There was no mystery to Dick Kazmaier—

to know the whys and wherefores of everything he does, a hound for detail.

"Why do I take that extra step?" he'll ask Caldwell. "Where do I take it, and why do I take it just there?"

Once he has an intelligent understanding of each maneuver, he can execute it far better. Admittedly this is a rare approach to the game, but it must be admired.

In this era of salaried amateur collegians it is ironic to report that Kazmaier holds an inconsequential $300 scholarship award that can't begin to pay his way through Princeton. And just after he was named to the All-America team picked by the Associated Press last year, the unimpressed college authorities notified him that his marks had sloughed off two-tenths of a point and that his scholarship had been forfeited. He regained it the next term.

If Kazmaier isn't the best college halfback in the country, he'll do until a better one comes along.

dedication, durability. He was a precisionist, a perfectionist. He worked until it became second nature to him."

Kazmaier took the acclaim calmly. He often said that his interests at Princeton were first, his friends; second, his studies (he was a psychology major); and third, football.

Although he was drafted by the Chicago Bears after graduation, Kazmaier spurned pro football for the Harvard Business School. He played his last game for the East All-Stars against the West in the annual Shrine game at San Francisco. Years later he said, "That was one great game [East 15, West 14]. Our backfield consisted of myself, Al Dorow of Michigan State, my teammate Dick Pivirotto and Vic Janowicz of Ohio State. The West had Ed Brown and Ollie Matson of San Francisco, Frank Gifford of Southern California and Hugh McElhenny of Washington. That's three pro Hall of Famers."

Kazmaier became a successful businessman and the father of six daughters. He has had a long association with the National Football Foundation and its College Hall of Fame, of which he is a member, and has served as the foundation's president. In this capacity he has often been a spokesman for academic and athletic integrity in college football and a supporter of reform measures by university presidents, which he believes might return the sport to the purer era he once graced.   —*WILLIAM N. WALLACE*

five-man front, the blocking angles opened up for the Tigers, and Kazmaier ran right through the Big Red. "Best back I've ever seen," said James later.

When Caldwell took his first look at Kazmaier in the fall of 1948 he saw not a Heisman Trophy candidate but a 155-pound freshman. "I felt sure he was too scrawny to play college football," Caldwell later recalled. By his

Billy Vessels is the first Heisman winner of the modern era. Not because of his size, although at six feet and 185 pounds, Vessels was as big as a linebacker in his day. No, Vessels is the first modern recipient of the Heisman because of *how* he won.

He won because of television. The nation saw him play at his best. His performance against Notre Dame late in his senior season captivated the Heisman voters.

"Billy was a remarkable athlete," his coach, the late Bud Wilkinson, once said. "He was the first player that I had ever been around who was the fastest player on the field and also the toughest. Those two things don't normally go together."

Vessels earned his toughness as a child in Cleveland, Oklahoma, a small town (pop. 2,064) adjacent to the Osage Indian Reservation. He came from a hardscrabble background but thrived thanks to the concern of others. Everyone in Cleveland lent a hand in raising him. The boys at the barbershop timed young Billy's daily dash around the block, and the local preacher took him fishing—as long as he saw Billy in church twice a week.

Following World War II, when his father, a mechanic, took a job at an Air Force base in Oklahoma City, Billy remained in Cleveland. To support himself Billy worked for the local druggist, in the feed store and in the bank. "You learn maturity," Vessels later said of his high school days, when he essentially raised himself.

Vessels became a football star at Cleveland High. In one game he carried the ball five times, scoring touchdowns of 97, 93, 90, 76 and three yards. Not bad for having his right wrist in a cast.

Every schoolboy in Oklahoma wanted to play for the Sooners and the dashing young Wilkinson, who had taken over as head coach in 1947 at the age of 31. Wilkinson didn't inspire his players through fear, as did his counterpart at Kentucky, Paul Bryant. Wilkinson seemed so earnest, so good, that his players would do anything for him. Said one of his assistants, Sam Lyle, "He's the guy you wished you had for a father."

That rang especially true for Vessels. In his freshman year the Sooners went 11–0 and finished No. 2 in the nation to Notre Dame. Even though freshmen were ineligible at the time, Vessels had trouble adjusting to the

Vessels was the first Heisman winner to benefit from the bright spotlight of national TV coverage.

Billy Vessels

The Sensational Sooner

rigors of academia and nearly flunked out. What saved him was a conversation with Wilkinson, who impressed upon him the importance of his studies. "It was," Vessels later said, "like a message from God."

Vessels survived to reach his sophomore season. He didn't start, though Wilkinson usually put him into the game early in the first quarter. He established himself almost immediately, when the third-ranked Sooners traveled to Dallas to play their archrival, fourth-ranked Texas.

A crowd of 76,000, the largest in the history of the recently expanded Cotton Bowl, watched as Vessels entered the game on the Sooners' second possession. He gained 19 yards on his first carry and finished the drive with a two-yard touchdown run.

But after that initial score, the Longhorns shut down the Sooners and were leading 13–7 late in the fourth quarter when punter Billy Porter mishandled a snap. Oklahoma recovered on the Texas 11-yard line. On second down Vessels broke a tackle and ran in for the winning touchdown with 3:46 to play.

Vessels closed the season by rushing for a school-record 208 yards against Nebraska. He finished the year with 870 rushing yards and 15 touchdowns for the No. 1 Sooners.

It was a good thing the wire services awarded the national championship before the bowls. Bryant's Kentucky Wildcats upset Oklahoma 13–7 in the Orange Bowl, ending the Sooners' winning streak at 31 games. Vessels accounted for Oklahoma's lone score, throwing a 17-yard touchdown pass in the fourth quarter. He also rushed for 68 yards on 17 carries. All of which set up 1951 as a season loaded with potential.

But instead of dominating the field as a junior, Vessels was given a valuable lesson about the fleeting quality of fame. Against Texas he suffered a knee injury and was carried off the field on a stretcher. He would not play again that year. "The low point in my life," Vessels said. "You think you can't be replaced, and a week later you're forgotten."

Though his knee healed well, Vessels gave no clue as his senior season approached that he would be the most outstanding player in the nation. Then again, no one anticipated the boost he would get from television.

Before that season TV had not had much impact on college football. But that began to change in 1952, the first season the NCAA contracted to televise the sport nationally. That year NBC paid $4 million for the rights to nine games. Twenty-five million people, the largest audience of the season, tuned in on November 8, 1952, when No. 4 Oklahoma played at No. 10 Notre Dame.

Until that game the national spotlight had shone not only on Vessels but also on backs such as Johnny Lattner of Notre Dame, Don McAuliffe of Michigan State and Paul Giel of Minnesota. Against Notre Dame, however, Vessels outshone Lattner and became the star of the season. He did everything but beat the Irish. He rushed 17 times for 195 yards. He scored on runs of 62 and 46 yards, and scored the Sooners' third touchdown with a 28-yard reception. He intercepted a pass. But late in the fourth quarter, with Oklahoma trailing 27–21, Vessels fumbled at the Notre Dame 20. The Irish recovered.

With tears streaming down his face after the game, Vessels told Wilkinson, "Remember, coach, when I was a freshman and you told me it was the team that counted, not the individual? I know what you mean now."

Two days before Thanksgiving, Sooner publicist Harold Keith went to the locker room to inform Vessels that he had won the Heisman.

"What's the Heisman?" Vessels asked.

He would learn. But the honor Vessels cherished most came from back home. "Some of my Indian friends wanted to throw a stomp-dance for me right after I got home from the Heisman presentation," Vessels told *Miami Herald* columnist Edwin Pope. "For the longest time they couldn't find a place for the stomp-dance, but they finally got a town hall and we had a time."

Vessels ignored the entreaties of the Baltimore Colts of the NFL, choosing instead to play in the Canadian Football League, the first Heisman winner to do so. After one season with the Edmonton Eskimos, in which he won the Schenley Award, given to the CFL's most valuable player, Vessels returned home to enter the Army. He injured a knee while in the service, yet when he mustered out, the Colts called again. He played one forgettable season, then decided, at the age of 25, that he'd had enough.

Vessels moved to the Miami area, where he became successful in the real estate business. When President John Kennedy sounded the alarm about physical fitness, Vessels served as a director of the national program. In 1974 the National Football Foundation elected him to the College Football Hall of Fame.

He had come a long way from Cleveland, Oklahoma.

—*Ivan Maisel*

John Lattner

A Player of Great Promise

In the months leading up to his sophomore year at Notre Dame, Johnny Lattner was a caldron of conflicting emotions. Excitement was part of the mix, since he was about to play his first season of football for the Irish. But at the same time Lattner's father was dying of cancer. As the season drew near, Lattner went to visit his dad, taking with him Notre Dame's starting quarterback, Johnny Mazur. In a promise inspired by Knute Rockne's "Win one for the Gipper" plea, Mazur told Lattner's father, "Your son will score for Notre Dame in his first varsity game."

That game came against Indiana. Lattner played defense in the first half, never once getting to play on the offensive side of the ball. However, in the third quarter Notre Dame moved the ball down to Indiana's two-yard line. Frank Leahy looked down his bench and told Lattner to go into the game.

The rest of the story was straight out of Hollywood. As Lattner entered the huddle, Mazur told him, "This one is for your dad." On the next play Lattner barreled into the end zone, carrying two tacklers with him.

A new star had been born at Notre Dame.

Lattner was never known for his blazing speed, overpowering strength or fancy moves. He was regarded as "the Eddie Stanky of football," a player without much flash but with one valuable asset: "All he does is beat you."

Lattner did that and more at Notre Dame. He was the key player on the Irish's 9-0-1 squad of 1953. On both offense and defense, Lattner did it all. In one of the closest races in Heisman history, Lattner edged Minnesota's Paul Giel by 56 votes.

Lattner was the storybook Heisman winner. He played both offense and defense, drank all his milk and was modest to a fault. After winning the award, Lattner said, "I don't think I was that good.... Giel was a better offensive back than I was—no ifs, ands or buts about it. He could run and cut

Lattner modestly insisted he was the beneficiary of football's brief return to a single platoon system.

better than I could, and he was a better passer."

So how did a player who didn't even lead his own team in rushing, passing or scoring win the Heisman Trophy?

"I think if you would evaluate John's athletic ability," Leahy said, "you would find a lad on our squad who is a better runner, another who is a better blocker, another who is a better tackler, and another lad who is a better passer. However, you would find no one on our squad, or any other squad, who has the ability to do all these things as well as John Lattner."

"I was there at the right time," Lattner said.

Indeed, he was, for in 1953 college football went back to single-platoon football after experimenting with the two-platoon format. One writer described the change: "Gone is the recently familiar mob scene of 22 players rushing onto the field as 22 others trotted off each time the ball changed hands." Gone for 1953, but not for long as the two-platoon game eventually returned.

The brief departure, though, was a blessing for Lattner. Even during the two-platoon days, Lattner played on both sides of the ball. As a junior he was unanimously

94

selected as an All-America on both offense and defense. When the single platoon came back in vogue, Lattner stood out that much more. He played 421 of a possible 600 minutes, scored nine touchdowns, accounted for 855 yards of offense, intercepted four passes, had 424 yards on kickoff and punt returns and had a 35-yard punting average. In short, he did everything, and that is why he won the Heisman.

"If it was the two-platoon system, I never would have won," Lattner said.

Leahy called Lattner Notre Dame's best all-around player since Johnny Lujack, the 1947 Heisman winner. "The thing both boys like to do most is tackle, a sure sign of a football player," Leahy said.

Lattner agreed. "If you make a good tackle, it peps you up. You get a good feeling, and you're ready to go to town. If you make a mistake on offense, like fumbling, you get a chance to make up for it by tackling."

If Lattner had a flaw, it was that he fumbled too much. He once said glumly, "I broke the school record for fumbles." Nobody, though, could accuse him of not trying to rectify that fault. For a time he could be seen walking around campus carrying a football with a handle taped to it.

And when he did manage to hold on to the ball, he was hardly the kind of runner who made the highlight films. "John's greatness isn't that he's spectacular, it's that he's consistent," said Notre Dame tackle Joe Bush. "It isn't, 'There goes John Lattner for 99 yards and a touchdown.' It's 'There's Lattner for five yards. There's Lattner for seven yards. There's Lattner falling on a fumble. There's Lattner intercepting a pass.' "

However, when Notre Dame needed a big run, Lattner delivered. In a win over Penn he had runs of 92 and 56 yards.

Lattner was destined for Notre Dame. He grew up in a crowded three-room apartment above Mofield's Meat Market on Madison Street in Chicago's west side, a neighborhood full of hardworking Irish and Germans. When he was 10 years old his father gave him a football helmet, and Lattner began training. His mother remembers that her son once went on a cod-liver oil binge, drinking 17 pints of it in a single week. "Do you know who his idol was in those days?" Mrs. Lattner said. "It was Superman."

Lattner was himself something of a Superman at Fenwick High School in Oak Park, a Chicago suburb. Known as Big John to his teammates, Lattner averaged 18 yards per carry. He became the first Illinois player to make all-state at two different positions. He played for the high school championship in front of a crowd of 67,000 peo-

ple.

Naturally, Lattner became a prized recruit. The offers came from all over the country, but Notre Dame was an easy choice. "I came down that driveway and I saw that Golden Dome with the statue of the Blessed Mother, all lighted up, and it was one of the biggest thrills of my life," he said. "I got kind of choked up, and I was awful glad I came here."

The feeling only intensified when Lattner saw the movie *Knute Rockne—All-American* on his first night at Notre Dame. "I got a big bang out of it. I was ready to kill anybody who said a word against Notre Dame. I still am," he said.

Even when Lattner became a star, he didn't change. He was unfailingly modest. He never wore any of his All-American sweaters. And he was considerate, too. An All-American in 1952 and 1953, Lattner was the only member of the Associated Press teams to send a letter of thanks to Ted Smits, the sports editor of the AP.

But his professional prospects weren't stellar. The scouting report read, "Not enough speed" and warned against "wasting an early draft pick on Lattner." However, Pittsburgh Steeler owner Art Rooney decided to chuck the scouting reports and picked Lattner in the first round. His faith was rewarded. Lattner earned All-Pro honors in his first year, rushing 69 times for 237 yards and five touchdowns.

Lattner then joined the Air Force, where he suffered a knee injury while playing in a service football game. He made a couple of comeback attempts before retiring in 1958. Afterward Lattner enjoyed a long career in the restaurant business in Chicago. He kept his Heisman Trophy on display at his steakhouse, and when the place burned down, melting his trophy, he asked for and was given a replacement. Lattner is now an executive for a printing company and has been active in fund-raising for many charities.

Lattner is remembered fondly at Notre Dame, though his own memories of his career there differ from those of most Notre Dame fans. "I'd fumble the ball or make some mistakes on defense," he said. "But the ball used to bounce my way a lot. I'd screw up, but Leahy would keep me in the game, and I'd eventually do something well."

Yes, Lattner did many things well. In 1953, Lattner *was* Notre Dame.

—ED SHERMAN

1954
Alan Ameche

A Stampede of One

Lee-no. Lee-no. Lee-no-Lee-no-Lee-no.

For a nation whose immigrants are greeted by a Statue of Liberty offering succor to the outcasts of the world, America can be strangely cruel to its recent arrivals. Even those born here to Old World parents can feel the sting of being different.

For Lino Dante Ameche, who was born in Kenosha, Wisconsin, on June 1, 1933, the sting was pronounced. Taken abroad when he was a toddler, he spent his pre-school years in Italy. When he returned to start school in the blue-collar factory town of his birth, he spoke no English.

That, coupled with his funny, foreign name, made him an instant object of ridicule among some of his schoolmates. It didn't help that Lino grew up not so much on the wrong side of the tracks as practically on the tracks, near a freight yard, a junkyard and a coal yard.

For all his childhood poverty and the ridicule, Lino had a couple of things going for him. One was America itself, a land of real opportunity despite its occasional cruelties. Another was his adored brother, Lindo, five years older and five years wiser.

Rigging up makeshift barbells from paint cans filled with concrete, Lindo encouraged Lino to build up his body as armor against the schoolyard taunts. As a diversion, Lindo also introduced Lino to classical music, which became a lifelong passion. Then, to remove the immediate object of the teasing, he took him to the Kenosha federal building, where for 50 cents apiece they exercised their common-law right to choose their own names.

Lindo became Lynn, and Lino became Alan, who, it became increasingly clear over the next four decades, would bring honor to any name.

The boy who became Alan (the Horse) Ameche first earned his reputation by setting collegiate rushing records as a pile-driving Wisconsin fullback and winning the

The big Horse was almost impossible to bring down, as he galloped around and over would-be tacklers.

1954 Heisman Trophy. He then went on to an acclaimed six-year professional career with the Baltimore Colts and followed that with a highly successful business career. After retiring as a wealthy man, he shifted his attention to philanthropy and community service.

When he died after undergoing heart surgery in August 1988, at the age of 55, it would be hard to deny that Lino had done himself and his nation proud.

His brother's body building strategy had worked. By the time Ameche was a high school junior, his classmates were still chanting his given name, but no longer in derision. For Lino had grown into a star athlete, a 10.2 sprinter in

the 100-yard dash and a champion shot-putter (50'2⅜").

As a junior Ameche led his conference in scoring. As a senior in 1950 he became the state's most famous athlete, leading his team to an undefeated season while averaging 8.1 yards a carry and scoring a conference- record 108 points. More than 40 years later, in August 1993, a panel of coaches polled by *The Milwaukee Journal* selected Ameche as the state's alltime greatest high school player.

After that sensational season the only question was which college to pick, a choice that was quickly narrowed to Notre Dame and the University of Wisconsin. During a visit to Kenosha, Notre Dame coach Frank Leahy won

over Ameche's mother and persuaded the youth's second cousin, the actor Don Ameche, to call him on behalf of Notre Dame even though the actor, a Kenosha native, had attended law school at Wisconsin.

Ameche's girlfriend, Yvonne Molinaro, also favored Notre Dame because, as she candidly explained in an interview in the spring of 1994, "There weren't any girls at Notre Dame."

But Notre Dame, which even agreed to accept two of Ameche's high school teammates, never had a chance, and not because Wisconsin agreed to take seven teammates. The decision had been made two years earlier when

Ameche spent a weekend with his brother at Wisconsin and came home raving about the beauty of the Wisconsin campus, about the Wisconsin fight song and especially about the Wisconsin music room. As Yvonne later recalled it, "He said they had every phonograph record in the world there, and you could play them as loud as you wanted to."

Arriving in Madison in 1951, Ameche showed immediate promise. When the freshman coach, George Lanphear, saw his hard-charging, knees-high running style, he said he ran like a horse. A nickname and a legend were born.

Although freshmen were then eligible for varsity football in the Big Ten, Ameche was assigned to the junior varsity. But not for long. After hammering the line and making several long gains in the jayvee opener against Iowa, he was yanked from the game and told to report to the varsity.

The next day, in the varsity opener against Marquette, he didn't get in until the next to last play, gaining one yard on a single carry. Two games later he was the starting fullback, displacing the team captain, John Hammond, who played out his senior season on defense.

Over the next four years, Ameche ran roughshod over all opposition, winning accolades and setting school, conference and collegiate records.

Ameche, who led Wisconsin to a 26-8-3 record, never missed a game in his four seasons, often playing hurt, but never complaining. When new restrictions on substitutions forced him to become a two-way player his junior year, he made the difficult adjustment, becoming a competent linebacker, an experience he said made him a better runner. Because he regularly played almost 60 minutes a game, Ameche soon became known as the Iron Horse.

His amiability and sensitivity made Ameche one of the most popular figures on campus. So much so that when she visited him during his freshman year, Yvonne was said to be miffed at all the adoring attention her boyfriend received from Wisconsin coeds, 11 of whom, it was once reported, called for him while she was waiting for him in his boarding house parlor.

Yvonne doesn't remember it that way. "I'd like to think it was the other way around," she said. Whoever was receiving what attention from whom, the matter was settled on Thanksgiving Day in Ameche's sophomore year when he and Yvonne were married. By the time he was a senior, they had two children, their first of six.

Ameche also excelled in the classroom, overcoming the handicap of his early school days when he spoke no English. He got into the habit of spending hours on his studies, and at Wisconsin earned high enough grades to win him recognition as an Academic All-America. The early handicap, he said, was an advantage since he had learned to work harder.

The W might well have stood for wins, since Ameche led the Badgers to 26 of them over his three seasons. Ameche, whose best game netted 205 yards, never had one of those really big, "Heisman" games, but he did have 16 100-yard games, and under his sure, steady running, the yards piled up until his career output, 3,212 yards, established a new collegiate record.

Modest about his accomplishments, he said he hadn't even known that as a junior he'd finished in the top five in the Heisman voting. When he won in 1954 he said what the honor meant most to him was that he would get to meet his idol, Doc Blanchard, the 1945 winner.

Passed over by his home state Green Bay Packers because he was judged too slow to run off tackle in the pros, Ameche was drafted in the first round by the Baltimore Colts. On his first play from scrimmage, against the Chicago Bears, he ran 79 yards for a touchdown and went on to lead the league in rushing as a rookie. Over the next six seasons he gained a total of 4,045 yards, scored 44 touchdowns, was named an All-Pro four times and provided an important counterpunch to quarterback John Unitas's acclaimed passing game.

For all that, he is perhaps best known for a single, electrifying moment in football history, his one-yard touchdown run on December 28, 1958, that secured the Colts' overtime championship victory over the New York Giants in what has been called the greatest football game ever played.

"It's probably the shortest run I ever made," he said later, "and yet it's the most remembered."

Ameche's career ended when he injured an Achilles tendon in December 1960. He and some associates then started a series of Baltimore restaurants known as Ameche's, which later grew to a chain of 550 fast-food restaurants named Gino's, for Ameche's Colt teammate Gino Marchetti. The chain was sold to the Marriott Corporation in 1982, by which point Ameche had gone on to other things, including opening a series of indoor tennis clubs in the Philadelphia area and even, at one point, becoming a sports agent. That endeavor lasted only six months, when Ameche, whose initial Colt contract had been for $15,000, became disillusioned. "I was trying to play by the rules," he said, "but I was working against guys who break all the rules."

Ameche was inducted into the National Football Foundation's College Football Hall of Fame in 1975 and donated his Heisman Trophy to the University of Wisconsin in 1984. In his last years he broadened his philanthropic and civic work, serving as, among other things, a director of the Philadelphia Orchestra and corporate chairman of the United Negro College Fund.

After Ameche's death in 1988 his friends created the Alan Ameche Foundation, which is devoted to two of his major interests, children and education. It provides scholarships to more than 30 children in the Philadelphia area, based not on athletic ability or academic achievement but on the sole basis of need. It is a particularly fitting memorial, a reminder of Ameche's early days, when his brother provided the kind of unqualified support that now goes to other Linos of the world.

—*ROBERT McG. THOMAS JR.*

His full name is Howard Albert Cassady, but only the register of deeds in Columbus, Ohio, would recognize him by that fancy moniker. To the rest of planet Earth, and especially to the world of sports, he is simply Hopalong Cassady, a legendary football player with a nickname courtesy of a caption writer on a Columbus newspaper. His friends call him Hop.

He is, however, not the only famous Hopalong. In another arena, far removed from the gridiron, there was Hopalong Cassidy, the clean-cut cowboy dandy of the movies who triumphed over evil in any form.

Hoppy was perhaps the nation's most popular cowboy and Hop one of college football's best halfbacks in the 1950s. Actor William Boyd, who played the kindly, white-haired Cassidy both on TV and in the movies, was born in Cambridge, Ohio, a Buckeye like Howard Cassady, the big-play buster on coach Woody Hayes's first successful team at Ohio State.

The two Hopalongs, bonded by their common nicknames, enjoyed a mutual admiration society. When Ohio State played in the Rose Bowl after the 1954 season, Hoppy the cowboy drove over to Pasadena from Hollywood (he didn't trust his horse on those notorious Los Angeles freeways) to watch a few Buckeye practices.

"I had some pictures taken with him," Hop the halfback recalled with a chuckle. "I'm wearing his guns, and he's carrying the football. He signed one picture, 'From one Hopalong to another.'"

Cassady, it was said, was too small, too slow and too weak to play football. But he became a game breaker, scoring 37 touchdowns in 36 Buckeye games, and after Cassady was named a landslide winner of the Heisman Trophy in 1955, Hayes called him "the greatest player of this century."

Cassady stood only 5' 10" and weighed less than 180 pounds. But he was a solidly built, thick-chested, red-headed Irishman with a 17-inch neck and no fear of mortal combat. He was a terror on defense; not once did a rival quarterback complete a pass over him in four years of Big Ten action.

According to Hayes, Hopalong knew better than to trust mere instinct, using his ample intelligence instead.

Hopalong gained 2,466 yards rushing for an average of 5.6 yards per carry during his college career. But he insisted there were no secrets to his running style.

1955
Hopalong Cassady

A Buckeye Buckaroo

"I just grab the ball and go," he said.

Not so, according to Hayes. "There is a good reason why Cassady comes through so consistently in the clutch. Hopalong makes the *right* move instead of the *instinctive* move. There's a tremendous difference between the two. Take the way Hopalong runs off tackle, for instance. Once he gets through the hole, he slashes straight ahead, which is the right move, instead of slanting out toward the sidelines, which is the instinctive move. By going straight ahead, Hop crosses those first seven yards beyond the line of scrimmage a step or two quicker than a back who instinctively slants out.

"That's tremendously important because most of the tackles are made somewhere in those first seven yards. Hop doesn't waste a second in that danger zone. That's the big difference between a back like Cassady and an ordinary back. Your ordinary back learns the right move in practice, but under big game pressure he reverts to his old habits and makes the instinctive move," the venerable Buckeye coach once theorized.

Cassady, who grew up in a tough, working-class neighborhood, climbed over a fence to see his first Ohio State football game. He rarely missed a Buckeye home game again, often sneaking by the stadium guards without a ticket. "Someday I'm going to play for Ohio State," vowed Hopalong.

The first time Hayes and Cassady met, the 155-pound freshman asked the salty old coach if Hayes thought he was heavy enough to play. "You are if you're good enough," Woody said.

After Cassady dazzled Buckeye fans by scoring three touchdowns in the season opener against Indiana, Hayes said, "I guess you're heavy enough."

An electrifying player with a quick change of pace, Hopalong became a fan favorite. Hop's dip of a hip could fake a rival defensive back out of Ohio Stadium. Hayes must have had Cassady in mind when he drew up his famous "three yards and a cloud of dust" offense, although Hop often gained much more.

He was also astounding on pass defense. In 1954 Cassady returned an interception 88 yards for a touchdown to break open a close game and beat a strong Wisconsin team led by Alan Ameche, 31–14.

Cassady excelled as well in baseball. He hit .327 as an outfielder to help Ohio State win the Big Ten baseball championship during the spring of 1955, after leading Ohio State to a 20–7 victory over Southern Cal in the Rose Bowl on New Year's Day.

The fall of that year was a season for the archives, fine enough to make even Wayne Woodrow Hayes blush with pride, as Cassady scored 15 touchdowns and boosted his four-year point total to 222, highest in Ohio State history.

Cassady's final game before the hometown fans deserves a special place in Buckeye lore. In the final quarter Cassady dived over from the three-yard line for his third touchdown of the day, and Ohio State players celebrated their 20–10 victory over Iowa by hoisting him onto their shoulders in the gray dusk as fans cheered and wept.

"It was O.K.," Hop said with characteristic modesty. "But I wish they hadn't done it. I asked them not to before the game."

The one thing that Hayes hadn't done in his five years at Ohio State was beat Michigan at Ann Arbor. Hopalong helped Woody accomplish this elusive goal in the 1955 season finale as the two teams once again battled for all the Big Ten marbles. A crowd of 97,369 attended the game in Michigan's mammoth bowl. As usual, Ohio State, playing as if the forward pass had not been invented, left it up to Cassady, who climaxed his fabulous college career by slashing through the veteran Michigan line 28 times for 146 yards to spark the Buckeyes' 17–0 victory and assure their second straight Big Ten title.

"The remarkable thing about Hop," said Hayes, "is that he does it and does it and does it, and then does it again."

Cassady kept on doing his thing for eight years as a pro in the National Football League, mainly with the Detroit Lions. The NFL's highest paid rookie after the Lions made him their top draft pick in 1956, Cassady developed into a nifty pass receiver after a college career in which he had seldom seen the football in the air except on defense. He was a vital member of the 1957 Lion team that routed the Cleveland Browns 59–14 for the NFL championship. After brief stints with Cleveland and Philadelphia, Cassady finished his pro career in Detroit in 1963, coming out of retirement to play in an injury-riddled defensive secondary.

He hooked up with an old friend, George Steinbrenner, in 1973 and moved to Tampa to work for Steinbrenner's shipbuilding company. In 1976 Cassady went to work as a physical fitness director in the New York Yankees' farm system and is one of the few employees Steinbrenner has never fired.   —COOPER ROLLOW

Paul Hornung

The Golden Boy

They called Paul Hornung the Golden Boy, and it was easy to see why.

It wasn't just his wavy blond hair or the fact that he played for Notre Dame under the Golden Dome. Most of all it was the golden touch he had—on the football field, in the classroom and with the ladies. He was handsome enough to be lured by Hollywood, tough and talented enough to be one of the best players of his era and smart enough to become a millionaire after his football career ended.

He wasn't some sanitized version of the all-American boy. Hornung liked to drink and gamble and stay out late, habits that occasionally got him into trouble. But his greatest love was football. "I would rather score a touchdown on any particular day than make love to the prettiest girl in the United States," he once said.

Hornung scored a lot of touchdowns in his career. He won the Heisman Trophy despite playing on an awful team, led the NFL in scoring three straight seasons, captured two league Most Valuable Player awards and helped the Green Bay Packers become a dynasty in the 1960s.

Hornung wasn't the best runner, passer, receiver or kicker in college or the pros. But he could do all of them well, making him—in the words of no less an authority than Vince Lombardi—"the most versatile man who ever played the game."

Paul Vernon Hornungs' introduction to sports began in Louisville, Kentucky, where he was raised by his mother after his parents separated. Early on it was apparent that Hornung was a special athlete. At 13 he was playing with 18-year-olds on an American Legion baseball team that reached the national playoffs. He went on to become a three-sport star at Flaget High, leading the football team to a state championship, setting a tournament scoring record in basketball and, despite a serious lack of control, pitching a no-hitter in baseball. "I gave up so

In 1960 Hornung scored a still-standing NFL record of 176 points in spite of playing in only 12 games. Hornung breaks tackles of Bubba Smith, Gino Marchetti and Ordel Brasse.

lose a no-hitter by the score of 13–12," he said.

Kentucky coach Bear Bryant tried to recruit the home state hero. But Hornung signed with Notre Dame because of the school's winning tradition and because his mother, a devout Catholic, wanted him to go there.

Hornung didn't become a starter at Notre Dame until his junior season. He played on the freshman squad his first year and was a backup fullback as a sophomore in 1954, when All-America quarterback Ralph Guglielmi

led the Fighting Irish to a 9–1 record and No. 4 finish in the polls.

In 1955, with Guglielmi gone, Hornung took over as the starting quarterback and had a standout season. He threw and ran for 1,215 yards and 15 touchdowns, kicked five extra points and two field goals and intercepted five passes.

The Irish won eight of 10 games that year, including a comeback victory over Iowa that highlighted Hornung's all-around skills. With Notre Dame trailing 14–7 in the fourth quarter, he returned a kickoff 23 yards, then completed three of four passes, including a scrambling 17-yard touchdown strike to Jim Morse.

After booting the tying extra point, Hornung kicked off, raced downfield and tackled the Iowa runner on the two-yard line. But he wasn't done yet. When Notre Dame got the ball back, Hornung led the Irish into scoring position and kicked the winning 28-yard field goal.

There weren't many moments like that during Hornung's senior season. Depleted by graduation and injuries, the Irish slumped to 2–8, the worst record in the school's history. "I knew it was going to be a tough season, but I didn't think it was going to be that bad," Hornung said.

Without Hornung, Notre Dame would have been even worse. Although he played in pain much of the time after dislocating a thumb in the fourth game, Hornung finished second nationally in total offense, with 1,337 yards, and led the Irish in almost every category. In his last home game he scored every point for the Irish, rushing for three touchdowns and kicking three PAT's in a 21–14 win over North Carolina.

No player from a losing team had ever won the Heisman Trophy, so Hornung was stunned when he won the award by a narrow margin over Tennessee's Johnny Majors and Oklahoma's Tommy McDonald. After getting the news Notre Dame publicist Charlie Callahan summoned Hornung to his office. When he arrived Callahan handed him the phone and said, "Here, tell your mother you just won the Heisman Trophy."

"I couldn't believe it when they told me I'd won it," he said at the time. "I didn't think I was even up for consideration."

With wavy blond hair and blue eyes, Hornung achieved matinee idol status in both South Bend and Green Bay. Hornung's versatility was a drawback in his early years with the Packers, who weren't sure where to play him. In his first two seasons in Green Bay, Hornung played quarterback, halfback and fullback on terrible teams that won a total of four games. The problem was solved when Lombardi arrived in 1959. He immediately made Hornung his starting halfback, teaming him with powerful Jim Taylor to form the NFL's best backfield. Lombardi also changed the attitude of the Packers, transforming them into the most disciplined, hardest-working team in the league. "From his first meeting with the team, all of us knew life had changed," Hornung wrote in 1962. "Here was a tough son-of-a-buck who knew what he was doing and meant what he said."

Hornung and the Packers thrived under Lombardi. In 1959 the Golden Boy led the NFL in scoring with 94 points, and Green Bay improved to 7–5. The next season was even better. Hornung set an NFL record, with 176 points, was named the league's Most Valuable Player and led the Packers to the NFL championship game, where they lost to the Philadelphia Eagles.

In just 12 games Hornung scored 15 touchdowns, made 15 of 28 field goal attempts and was 41 for 41 on extra points. No one since has scored more points in a season, even though teams now play 16 regular-season games. "Inside the 10-yard line, he was probably the finest football player I've ever seen," said Green Bay teammate Bob Long.

In 1961 Hornung again won the league's scoring title and Most Valuable Player award and helped the Packers win their first NFL championship in 17 years. Unable to practice during the week because of military service, Hornung still scored 19 points as Green Bay routed New York 37–0 in the championship game.

Hornung was serious about winning, but he liked to have fun when he played. After scoring a touchdown against the Bears, he spotted a pretty, young woman in the stands and tossed the ball to her. During a downpour in a game against San Francisco, he belly flopped into the end zone like a seal splashing in the ocean.

The Packers won their second straight championship in 1962, but Hornung missed the following season after he and Detroit lineman Alex Karras were suspended for gambling on NFL games. Although commissioner Pete Rozelle said there was no evidence either player bet against his own team, both were banned for 11 months.

Hornung rejoined the Packers in 1964 and scored 107 points, but he was never the same player again. He did enjoy a few moments of glory the following season, scoring five touchdowns against Baltimore and rushing for 105 yards and a touchdown to help Green Bay beat Cleveland for the NFL championship. But injuries hampered him in 1966, and he had to watch from the sidelines as the Packers defeated Kansas City in the first Super Bowl. Hornung was taken by New Orleans in the expansion draft after the season, but he decided to retire.

Hornung got into broadcasting and real estate after his football career ended. In the early 1980s the NCAA tried to prevent him from announcing college games because of his earlier gambling suspension and his playboy image. But Hornung sued the NCAA and won.

He was later inducted into the college and pro football halls of fame.

—*Rick Warner*

1957
John David Crow

The Bear's Prized Cub

Like Bear Bryant, his legendary coach, John David Crow was a backwoods boy who made it really big in college football.

So big that for his superlative senior season at Texas A&M in 1957, he won the Heisman Memorial Trophy, an award which will be toasted forever in Aggieland. It also had a special place in Bryant's heart. Surprisingly, Crow was Bryant's only Heisman winner in his historic 38-year head coaching career at Maryland, Kentucky, Texas A&M and Alabama.

Just as Bryant had been during his own athletic career, Crow was a large, rugged athlete who thrived on competition. Unlike Bryant, who played opposite pass receiver Don Hutson on Alabama's 1935 Rose Bowl champions, the 6'2", 218-pound A&M halfback was blessed with game-breaking speed. But both were drawling, personable men who were proud of the work ethic they learned early in life growing up in small rural communities. Bryant was from Moro Bottom, Arkansas, and Crow from Springhill, Louisiana, which he said was so far back in the woods "that they have to pipe in sunshine."

Elmer Smith knew the way to Springhill, though, and the A&M assistant coach spent three months in a little motel there in the spring of 1954 on orders from Bryant, who made signing Crow the number one priority in his first recruiting year at A&M. Smith had coached Crow's older brother at a small Arkansas college, and he was on friendly terms with the Crow family. Even so, he came close to wearing out his welcome. As Smith once recalled, "John David got so disgusted with me hanging around so much, he said, 'Coach, I don't know whether I'll be able to finish high school or not.'"

On signing day, however, Smith's down-home personality and familiarity with the Crow family paid off for the Aggies. According to Southwest Conference rules during this era, no coaches could have a letter of intent in their possession until 8 a.m. on signing day, and Bryant knew, of course, that SMU and TCU recruiters, who would be coming from Dallas and Fort Worth—a good two hours closer to Springhill than College Station—would be wasting no time in getting to Springhill to sign Crow as soon as they could leave their schools with a letter of intent. So he told Smith to stay in Springhill until early that morning, then drive to the Shreveport airport, where a letter of intent ready for Crow's signature would be delivered to him. Smith then sped back to Springhill and signed Crow an hour before the rival coaches arrived by airplane—a first in recruiting-warfare tactics.

Throughout an intense recruiting season, Crow said he always liked the idea of playing at A&M because of Smith. "I didn't know Coach Bryant.... But I knew Elmer and knew him to be an honest, decent man. Elmer Smith recruited me, and Elmer Smith is the reason I came to Texas A&M."

John David soon knew Bryant very well. The Aggies' new coach realized the future of his program rested with his talented freshman team, so he worked them long and hard that fall.

"I remember a long, long scrimmage we had one day," Crow said. "Afterward I was sitting in a metal folding chair under the shower when the manager came in and yelled, 'Put 'em back on!' I said, 'What? You're crazy!' He said, 'Nope. The Man said put 'em back on.' We did and went back outside. Coach Bryant told us to grab a knee, but I knew if I went down to one knee, I'd never get up. Then he started telling us what we were going to accomplish.

"I looked at him, framed by the tunnel at the north end of the stadium, and listened. I don't recall what he said, but I said to myself, 'By god, you might kill me, but you're not going to run me off!'

"And he almost did. I woke up three hours later in the infirmary, holding an orange drink, with my wife, Carolyn, standing at the side of the bed and Coach Bryant standing down at the end. I'd had a heat stroke.

"Coach Bryant looked at me and said, 'John, why didn't you tell me you were tired?'"

Crow survived and thrived. As a sophomore in 1955, he was instrumental in A&M improving to 7-2-1 from the 1–9 record of the scrawny '54 varsity. Folks were calling him the best all-around back in the Southwest Conference since Doak Walker, sweet words to Crow, who had idolized Walker in junior high school.

His junior season the Aggies finished 9-0-1 and were unbeaten in the SWC but were denied the host school's spot in the Cotton Bowl Classic on New Year's Day in Dallas because of recruiting violations. Instead Crow and his teammates savored their victories over their two toughest SWC rivals: 7–6 over TCU at College Station in

Crow, the only Heisman winner Bryant coached in his long career, shared the Bear's intensity.

a rainstorm that reached hurricane proportions, and 19–13 over Baylor at Waco the next Saturday.

Against TCU, the Aggies held the visitors to a 6–0 lead in the fourth quarter after staving off a half-dozen other scoring threats. Then just as the sun came out, the Aggies got possession on their 20 after Don Watson's end zone interception. Crow bolted 21 yards to ignite A&M's best drive of the day, and soon Watson raced 37 yards to the TCU 20. Crow banged it to the eight, then caught Watson's option pass on the goal line for the touchdown. Lloyd Taylor kicked the extra point, and the Aggies survived a wild, wet, weird afternoon.

One week later came a Baylor game that Bryant always called "the bloodiest, meanest and toughest game I've ever seen." Again the Aggies came from behind to win in the fourth quarter. On fourth down Crow said, "Give me the cockeyed ball, and I'll put it in there." Well, they gave him the ball, and he put it in there from about six yards out.

As a senior in 1957, Crow made championship plays all year long on offense and defense, and the Aggies, less explosive and talented than the 1956 team, were 8–0 and ranked No. 1 nationally when they went to Houston to play Rice on November 16. The morning of the game *The Houston Post* ran a story speculating that Bryant would be going to Alabama in 1958, a move he confirmed less than a week later. By then the Aggies had lost by one point to Rice, 7–6; by two to Texas, 9–7; and instead of taking a perfect record to the Cotton Bowl Classic, they settled for a trip to the Gator Bowl, where they lost to Tennessee 3–0.

It was a down time for A&M football, but Crow picked it up when he won the Heisman, outscoring Alex Karras, Iowa's star lineman, by almost 500 points in the national voting. Bryant campaigned hard for his Aggie star to win the Heisman. "John David is the greatest athlete who ever lived, for my money," Bryant said. "He had a burning desire for the team to win. If he doesn't get the Heisman, they ought to quit giving it."

In his final act at A&M, Bryant sent Elmer Smith, the faithful assistant who landed Crow for A&M, to New York to celebrate with John David and his family at the awards dinner. Smith beamed as Crow stood at the dais, ran his hand down the handsome black-and-gold trophy and made perhaps the shortest acceptance speech in Heisman history.

"It all seems like a dream," Crow said, "and I want to sit down before I make a racket that might wake me up." —*SAM BLAIR*

Pete Dawkins

A Star Man and More

Pete Dawkins was extraordinary, but he didn't look it as a skinny six-footer entering the United States Military Academy in the summer of 1955. But four years and numerous accolades later, Dawkins embodied the all-American image on and off the field of play. He was the first Heisman Memorial Trophy winner also to be a Rhodes scholar. These were but two achievements in a life overflowing with striking personal accomplishments.

He was 36 in 1975 when he became the youngest man to be inducted into the College Football Hall of Fame. He was also the youngest brigadier general in the United States Army when given his star rank in 1984.

This brilliant young man from Royal Oak, Michigan, was not only captain of the undefeated Army team in 1958 when he won the Heisman Trophy but was also the highest-ranking member of the student body as first captain of the corps of Cadets for the 1958–59 academic year when he served as president of his senior class. He never played hockey before going to West Point but became an all-East defenseman on the Army hockey team. He played a half dozen musical instruments and sang in the West Point choir.

Dawkins was such an exceptional young man at the military academy that there may never be one like him again. He was a "star man," meaning he was in the top 5% of his class academically. Dawkins was the 53rd first captain at West Point to also be a star man. Only 11 of those 53 were also class presidents. And only two have been captain of the football team. Dawkins, however, is still the only Cadet to be all four: star man, first captain, class president and football captain.

He finished his West Point career by graduating 10th in the class of '59 before going to Oxford on a Rhodes scholarship. During his two years at Oxford, Dawkins successfully played rugby and cricket and rowed crew even though he had never taken part in any of those sports before going to England.

Not much could stop Dawkins, who achieved a stunning sweep of West Point's academic and athletic honors.

Tours of duty in Vietnam and Korea plus assignments at the Pentagon and the White House were but a few of his Army postings while he also earned a Ph.D. in international politics from Princeton in 1970.

Dawkins lived up to what was written about him by his classmates in the 1959 United States Military Academy yearbook: "We have stood in awe of this man. We were not completely sagacious, but we knew a great leader, a great friend, a great man."

Nevertheless Dawkins nearly missed out on it all after being struck with a moderate case of polio when he was 11. Even though doctors told Pete he would never play football, the youngster was determined. Instead of wearing one of those heavy metal braces so common to polio sufferers in those days, Dawkins went through rigid therapy regimens of exercises and weights to correct a slightly curved spine and regain muscle strength. It worked, and he played quarterback at the Cranbrook School, a prep school near Detroit.

But when he reached West Point his arm wasn't strong enough. He couldn't throw a major college pass with enough zip and distance. But he could make twisting, swerving, leaping runs into the end zone from about anywhere on a gridiron. Ergo, Dawkins at halfback.

Then came the 1958 season, one of the most notable in Army's football history. Dawkins became the third Army player to win the Heisman Trophy. Colonel (Red) Blaik, who had been at Army for 18 years and had coached Doc Blanchard and Glenn Davis, the first two Army Heisman winners, in 1945 and 1946, retired at the end of the 1958 season. But before bowing out Blaik had his fifth undefeated season at West Point and created a football curiosity that was dropped after his departure. This was the "lonely end," a wideout receiver who did not return to the Army huddle between plays. He just trotted back to a wide set after each play.

Partly because of the novelty of the lonely end, and partly because Army had another fine running back in Bob Anderson, Army's opponents could not devote enough attention to Dawkins to slow him down very much. In fact, in the season opener, Dawkins gained 113 yards, a quarter of his season's rushing yardage, and scored four touchdowns, a third of his 1958 total, in a 45–8 triumph over South Carolina. The Gamecocks paid too much attention to that wideout, Bill Carpenter, who did little that day but serve as a decoy.

Dawkins had a total of 428 yards rushing, 491 yards pass catching and scored a dozen touchdowns in 1958. Thirty years later those numbers wouldn't get a player a mention in the Heisman race. But in 1958,

While at Oxford, Dawkins added cricket, rugby and rowing to his repertoire of athletic pursuits.

when they played offense and defense, Dawkins was the flashiest running and receiving back in football, in addition to being a good safety. He was also one of the smartest men ever to play the game.

However, he outsmarted himself once, in the fifth game of the season, when Army played Pittsburgh on a wet field. Hobbled by a pulled hamstring muscle, Dawkins stood on the sideline watching as Pitt tried to rally from a 14–0 deficit in the second half. Certain that Pitt's quarterback, Bill Kaliden, would be able to throw over his Army replacement at safety, Dawkins convinced the coach to let him go in. Kaliden, of course, knew the circumstances of Dawkins's injury and immediately threw a bomb over Dawkins's head. John Flara caught the ball and went in to complete a 43-yard touchdown play. Pitt then went on to catch Army for a 14–14 tie, the only nonvictory for the Cadets that season.

Dawkins's biggest play of the year came in the final minute against Rice as the teams were deadlocked at 7 and Army had the ball on its own 36 after blocking a Rice field goal attempt. On most of Army's early pass plays Dawkins noticed that the Rice cornerbacks were favoring him to the outside. He told Joe Caldwell, Army's quarterback, "I'll fake a move outside, then head down the middle. You throw that sucker as far as you can."

It worked for 64 yards and the winning touchdown.

Years after that wonderful 1958 season, Dawkins assessed his own football talents by comparisons. "I was never a strong inside runner. Anderson did most of the inside running. I ran mostly outside. I didn't have the blinding speed of the Herschel Walkers, but I had good speed and good balance. If I had decided to play professional football instead of staying in the military, I probably would have been a receiver. I was more like a Fred Biletnikoff, who was unimpressive in almost any statistic but success. He wasn't bigger, stronger or faster than the others. He just happened to get free, catch the ball and score touchdowns better than anyone else. I was that sort of garbage player."

Dawkins did, however, occasionally have to accept defeat.

Five years after retiring from the Army, Dawkins was the 1988 Republican candidate for the U.S. Senate running against the incumbent Democrat, Frank Lautenberg. In a sometimes vicious battle, Lautenberg won even though New Jersey went for Republican George Bush for president that election day.

Dawkins decided to put his political ambitions behind him. In 1991 he became chairman of Primerica Financial Services, the life insurance unit of The Travelers Inc.

These days Dawkins's Senate defeat is just a dim memory. His record of service to his country, however, is one that still stands brightly: a thoughtful, modern soldier who earned the Distinguished Service Medal, the Legion of Merit, two Bronze Stars for Valor and three Gallantry Crosses, Vietnam's decoration for bravery.

A soldier, scholar and athlete, Dawkins was an Army hero while still an undergraduate. Pete Dawkins had the qualities and résumé that Army Cadets, for generations to come, will see as the most worthy of goals.

—*GORDON S. WHITE JR.*

1959
Billy Cannon

His Tricks Were a Treat

Halloween 1959 was a miserable night for football in Baton Rouge—warm, damp and hazy. Moisture was fairly oozing out of the air, and as the game unfolded, so was the gloom for fans of No. 1–ranked Louisiana State. Third-ranked Mississippi was hanging on grimly to a 3–0 lead, and it was beginning to dawn on the crowd of 67,500 and a national television audience that, after winning the 1958 national championship, Paul Dietzel's undefeated Tigers were approaching the end of their winning streak.

The night had been especially miserable for LSU's acclaimed halfback, Billy Cannon. The hero of many a Tiger triumph, he had fumbled in the first quarter to set up Ole Miss's field goal. Later, LSU's most promising drive had come to an end on a fourth-and-nine gamble when Cannon was thrown for a loss.

Even Cannon's one flash of brilliance had fizzled. At the start of the third quarter he had intercepted a pass, but the play not only failed to produce a score—a field goal attempt was blocked—it also prompted Mississippi coach Johnny Vaught to decide it was time to dig in his heels. Vaught ordered his team to punt on first down the next three times Ole Miss got the ball. As Cannon waited for yet another punt, the Tiger faithful must have wondered if their hero had run out of magic.

Cannon was born in Philadelphia, Mississippi, on August 2, 1937. When he was four his family moved to Baton Rouge, where his father worked in a defense plant until an accident forced him to give up factory work and become a janitor at LSU. Though Cannon grew up just outside the north gate and sold soda and peanuts in Tiger Stadium, it seemed doubtful he would ever play there. In junior high he was so small that the team didn't have shoes to fit him, as Peter Finney tells it in his book, *Fighting Tigers*. Cannon deliberately flunked his final exams so he would have an extra year to grow before entering high school.

Even so, in his first year at Istrouma High he weighed only 138 pounds and didn't play much. The next year he bulked up to 175 and made all-state. From that season on he was a huge star in Baton Rouge. Cannon made five touchdowns in a single half against Baton Rouge High and racked up 229 points to help Istrouma go undefeated in his senior season.

After that sensational season, Cannon, who grew into a 6' 1", 208-pounder, was welcomed to LSU, where he became known for his prodigious speed and strength. In weightlifting he could lift close to the Olympic records for his weight class. After he ran 100 yards in 9.4 seconds, then put the shot 54' 4.5", fans joked that he was either the world's fastest shot-putter or its strongest sprinter.

Despite the fact that the local hero was to make his varsity debut, the stadium was half empty for the Tigers' home opener, against Rice. But after Cannon ran for touchdowns of 53 and 73 yards, tickets for the remainder of the home schedule became prized items in Baton Rouge. A full stadium was guaranteed the following week when Cannon broke a 7–7 tie at Texas Tech, turning a short pass into a 59-yard touchdown romp, and then, after Texas Tech had gone ahead 14–13, returning the kickoff 97 yards for another touchdown.

But even with further heroics by Cannon, who emerged as a five-threat man—running, passing, receiving, returning kicks and punts and even punting—LSU finished the season with a 5–5 record. Dietzel and Cannon were just warming up. The following season Cannon was even more dazzling, finishing third in the Heisman voting and leading the 11–0 Tigers to the national championship.

Though no stranger to heroics, Cannon was almost certainly not thinking about a runback as he waited for that punt on Halloween night 1959. When he saw the ball hit and skid past the 20, he fully intended to let it go, mindful of Dietzel's firm rule that punts were not to be fielded inside the 15.

Then, perhaps with a goblin assist, the ball took a surprise high bounce straight into Cannon's hands at the 11, and all rules were off. Accepting fate, he took off and carried the ball 89 yards down the right sideline into football history. He was hit at the knees at the 19 and at the shoulders at the 20, but by the 30 the tackler had slid down to his ankles, and after a block at the 40 Cannon was gone, passing a distraught Vaught at midfield. When Cannon reached the end zone, the crowd and the Heisman were his.

Indeed, Cannon, who swamped his closest rival, Richie Lucas of Penn State, by a vote of 1,929 to 613, did not so much receive the 1959 Heisman as snatch it, a gesture he literally repeated when Vice President Richard Nixon fumbled the trophy

Wet but happy, Cannon basked in the glow of his sensational 89-yard punt return against Ole Miss.

1959 Billy Cannon

and Cannon lunged to the rescue.

LSU finished the regular season with a 9–1 record. Then Mississippi avenged the 7–3 Halloween defeat with a 21–0 victory over LSU in the Sugar Bowl, but by then Cannon, who was held to eight yards on six carries, was distracted. Over Thanksgiving weekend he had secretly signed a three-year, $50,000 contract proffered by Pete Rozelle, the youthful general manager of the Los Angeles Rams. Then, a few weeks later, in Baton Rouge, he secretly signed a three-year, $100,000 contract with the Houston Oilers of the new American Football League. When the matter came to court the next June, a federal judge rejected the Rams' contract, accusing Rozelle of having taken advantage of "a provincial lad untutored and unwise in the ways of the business world."

Whatever the justice of the ruling, Cannon became professional football's first six-figure athlete and promptly proved he was worth every penny, making All-Pro his first season and getting named most valuable player of the AFL championship game. The next year he led the league in rushing, with 948 yards, and was again the most valuable player of the championship game.

After being traded to the Oakland Raiders for three players in 1964, he was switched to tight end, catching 32 passes for 10 touchdowns in 1967. Cannon retired after the 1970 season. In his 11 pro seasons Cannon gained 2,455 yards rushing, 3,656 yards as a receiver and 1,882 yards on kick returns while scoring 392 points.

After football, Cannon set up a lucrative orthodontic practice in Baton Rouge, where he was regarded as a god. But he had a darker side, which became shockingly manifest in 1983 when he was charged with masterminding a $6 million counterfeiting scheme. The prosecutor said Cannon was a heavy gambler, but Cannon, who pleaded guilty and served more than three years of a five-year sentence, has made it a point not to discuss his crime. "I made a tragic mistake," he said. "What else can I say? I assume full responsibility. I paid my debt to society."

He has resumed his orthodontic practice, and with nudging from LSU coach Curley Hallman has been gradually coaxed back into the Tiger family.

There are, no doubt, some who will never forgive him, but then there are many who will never forget that one transforming moment on a soggy field on a humid Halloween night when goblins were loose in Tiger Stadium and a youngster wearing No. 20 for LSU raced down the sidelines and into immortality.

—*ROBERT McG. THOMAS JR.*

1960
Joe Bellino

15 Minutes in the Sun

If any Heisman winner fits Andy Warhol's prediction that everyone will be famous for 15 minutes it is Joe Bellino, who ran like a rocket for Navy in that 1960 season when the Midshipmen soared briefly from mediocrity to excellence. The Middies won nine of 10 games against the likes of Boston College, Notre Dame, Southern Methodist and Washington and were ranked fourth best in the nation before losing to Missouri in the Orange Bowl, 21–14. Little Joe—he was 5'9", 181 pounds, but with legs like chopped tree trunks—set Naval Academy records for most points in a season (110), most rushing yards (824), most carries (168) and most points in one game (24, against Virginia).

Glory of that magnitude was a new experience for Bellino, and something he would never experience again. In his junior season he was an unheralded back on a team with a 5-4-1 record. As an injury-plagued sophomore he gained only 266 yards. In 1965, following graduation and four years of service as a deck officer overseas, Bellino tried pro football with the Boston Patriots, whose offense featured a big power back, Jim Nance. Bellino lasted for three seasons, but his legs never really got going, a shame considering that he possessed excellent speed.

But that fleeting autumn of 1960 belonged to Little Joe. Years later Bellino would acknowledge that in some ways he was lucky to have had such success. "[Navy coach] Wayne Hardin believed if he had a runner, he'd build the offense around a running game," said Bellino. "If he had a passer, he'd build a passing game. I shudder to think what would have happened if Roger Staubach and I had been in the same backfield." Staubach, of course, reached Annapolis the year after Bellino graduated and won the Heisman in 1963.

Football's most exciting role is that of the breakaway halfback and Bellino filled it well. His assets were his legs. "Anyone who hit me there was out of luck," he once said. "I was a scatterback. My first step was at top

In one season of greatness, Bellino gained 824 rushing yards and led the Middies to a 9–1 record.

1960 Joe Bellino

speed. I could hit the hole as fast as anyone, and *then* get outside. I could move laterally without losing speed."

Such a comment may sound naive today when lateral movement is standard among top-level running backs, a standard established by the Walter Payton types. But football is an evolutionary sport, one played by ever larger and faster athletes on a field that has had the same dimensions since 1912. Indeed, in a 1987 interview Bellino, now an auto-lease marketing executive in the Boston area, spoke as a casual television viewer of football. He said, "I don't know how I ever played this game."

Hardin, however, knew what to do with talent. It was obvious that Bellino's talent was for running, so, in the absence of a true passer, Hardin had him run, again and again. Said Hardin, a bright young coach who used over-statement to make his point, "Our goal is to run him 70 or 80 times a game so he can break out once or twice."

Bellino would also stop and throw a pass. He did this twice for touchdowns, which was enough to put fear in the foes' minds as they hatched their defensive plots.

Bellino also had soft hands and ran good patterns. Of his 18 touchdowns that season, four came as a receiver, the last against Missouri in the Orange Bowl on a spectacular play, a short pass and a long darting run through and around defenders.

Quick kick? Sure, for an average of 47.1 yards. He also had five punt returns at an average of almost 20 yards and 11 kickoff returns for 240 more yards.

Defense? Even though this was the two-platoon era again in college football, Bellino was on the field for Navy in the final and crucial moments of the Army game that fall.

The Middies preserved a 17–12 lead near the end of the game thanks to Bellino's goal line interception. Years later he was able to reconstruct the last 10 plays of that game, one of which had been a fumble of his own at the Navy 17. "But I came back and intercepted the pass, and we held on. I went from goat to hero in a very short time."

Army-Navy was a super bowl before there was a Super Bowl. Each year 100,000 rabid fans jammed into Municipal Stadium at the south end of Broad Street in Philadelphia next to the Navy Yard. Bellino was brighter than ever in these games. In 1959 he scored three touchdowns, a new Navy record, in the 43–12 rout of Army. His TD total for three Army games was five.

Bellino's hometown was Winchester, Massachusetts, an old mill town outside Boston, and his parents were Italian immigrants from Sicily. His father, Michael, worked in a factory that made gelatin and routinely laid off its workers when orders were slow.

Joe Bellino picked up 58 yards through the Army line in a 17 to 12 victory over Army in 1960.

Joe and his two older brothers were all built small. Their mother, Sarah, explained the family genes to Shirley Povich of the *Washington Post*. Povich wrote, "She drew up her skirt discreetly to reveal the Joe Bellino–type calves and said, 'Look, Joe's legs.' "

Bellino, a terrific high school halfback, sifted through dozens of college offers before choosing the Naval Academy. But it wasn't a straight line from Winchester to Annapolis. There were other temptations. Bellino was also a terrific high school baseball player, and it was reported—Boston sportswriting leaning perhaps on its old curse of exaggeration—that Little Joe had offers of $50,000 to $75,000 to sign with the Red Sox or some other team.

He later denied such grand offers but did play baseball for Navy, first as a catcher who maintained a pretty good batting average. There was a gap, a season missed in favor of hitting the books, and then a thud to an outfield posi-

tion and a modest .272 average at the plate in his senior season. The major league scouts faded away.

To complete the transition from Winchester to Annapolis, Bellino had to overcome mathematics, a problem that has forever been the burden of the service academy recruit, jock or not.

He spent a year improving his math skills at Columbian Prep in Washington, D.C., a small school that had on its football schedule the annual game against the Navy Plebes, the freshman team over at Annapolis. Columbian had never beaten the Plebes.

In the 1956 game Columbian came out with the usual 17 players while Navy had 62 in uniform. But two for Columbian were extraordinary: Bellino and the end, Frank Dattilo, who came from the Bellino's Winchester neighborhood, the Plains, and whose Italian parents were, like Joe's, similarly ignorant of football.

Before those four baffled parents, down from Winchester on a visit, Dattilo blocked and Bellino ran and Columbian Prep won 34—33. Little Joe soon became a

whiz at math, and Annapolis drew closer.

Years later, when Bellino was himself the parent of a five-year-old son, he said, "Little John is going to learn all about that Heisman on the shelf in the corner of the living room when he asks.

"It is important to tell a child that you've got to try hard and something good will come. I can tell my son that if you try hard, this is going to happen to you. Because I tried hard. And I was given the highest honor ever given to a football player."

—*WILLIAM N. WALLACE*

When Ernie Davis was eight years old, he tried out for a Midget League baseball team in Uniontown, Pennsylvania. He made the squad but missed the season-opening parade through town because there weren't enough uniforms to go around. "It was my first big disappointment in sports," he said.

There weren't many more after that.

Davis went on to become a high school basketball and football star in Elmira, New York, before attending Syracuse University, where he broke Jim Brown's rushing records, led the Orangemen to a national championship and became the first black player to win the Heisman Memorial Trophy.

Davis's greatest performance may have come in the 1960 Cotton Bowl, where Syracuse beat Texas 23–14 to complete an 11–0 season. Playing with a pulled hamstring, Davis scored two touchdowns—one on a bowl-record, 87-yard pass play—set up another TD with an interception and scored twice on two-point conversions.

"I think Ernie had more talent than even he knew," said teammate Ger Schwedes. "He was shy and one of the most humble people I've ever met. But he was big and strong, with great speed. He could cut, he had finesse, but he had all the power of a fullback when he needed it."

Everyone predicted stardom for Davis in the pros, but the 6'2", 210-pound halfback never got a chance to play in the NFL. Seven months after signing a $90,000 contract with the Cleveland Browns—at the time, the largest rookie contract in NFL history—Davis was diagnosed with leukemia. He died of the blood disease on May 18, 1963.

People always admired Davis, who was as gentle off the field as he was tough on it. "Ernie was just like a puppy dog, friendly and warm and kind," said his college coach, Ben Schwartzwalder. "He had that spontaneous goodness about him. He radiated enthusiasm.... Oh, he'd knock you down, but then he'd run back and pick you up. We never had a kid so thoughtful and polite."

Blessed with power, speed, agility: Is there any doubt that Davis would have enjoyed a brilliant pro career?

As a young child Davis was raised by his grandparents. His father died in an accident before Ernie was born, and his mother, poor and alone, couldn't take care of him. So he was sent to live in Uniontown, where his grandfather was a coal miner. There Davis devel-

Ernie Davis

Still Someone Special

oped a love of sports and dreamed of becoming a famous athlete like Stan Musial or Johnny Lujack, who grew up in the same area.

But Davis didn't blossom as an athlete until he moved to Elmira and rejoined his mother when he was 11. He won 11 varsity letters at Elmira Free Academy, where he was an all-state basketball and football player. He averaged 7.4 yards per carry in football, but many thought he was even better in basketball, where he set scoring records and led his team to 52 straight victories. "He was a great jumper and rebounder. And he could shoot, too," said Jim Flynn, his high school basketball coach.

As soon as Davis arrived at Syracuse, he was compared with Brown, who had set the school's career rushing and scoring records a few years earlier. Expectations were high, but Davis exceeded them.

As a sophomore, wearing the same number 44 jersey as Brown, the "Elmira Express" gained 686 yards and scored 10 touchdowns as Syracuse won its first national title. The Orangemen weren't quite as successful the next two years, going 7–2 in 1960 and 8–3 in 1961, but Davis continued to excel, gaining over 800 yards in both his junior and senior seasons and being named an All-America both years. He finished his career as the leading rusher (2,386 yards) and scorer (220 points) in Syracuse history.

Davis won the 1961 Heisman in a close vote over Ohio State's Bob Ferguson. While in New York to accept the trophy, he briefly met President John Kennedy at the Waldorf-Astoria Hotel. "It was a big thrill for me," Davis said. "I never thought I'd get the honor of shaking hands with him."

Ten days later Davis led Syracuse to a 15–14 comeback victory over Miami in the Liberty Bowl. He rushed for 140 yards and a touchdown as the Orangemen rallied from a 14–0 halftime deficit. Davis also made a big defensive play, batting away a long pass near the Syracuse goal line to preserve the victory. "We goofed around in the first half. Then Ernie took over," Schwartzwalder explained.

After the season ended, Davis was hotly pursued by the National Football League, the American Football League and pro teams in Canada. He finally signed with the Browns, who obtained him in a trade from Washington after the Redskins made Davis the No. 1 pick in the NFL draft.

Cleveland fans couldn't wait to see Davis in the same

This story was originally published in The Saturday Evening Post *on March 30, 1963. Less than seven weeks later, on May 18, Ernie Davis passed away. He was 23 years old.*

One day last fall I was standing outside a movie theater in downtown Cleveland when a stranger asked me, "Are you Ernie Davis?"

I didn't want any fuss. I said I wasn't.

"You're lucky you're not," the man said. "Ernie Davis has leukemia. He won't live six months."

I turned and walked away. There was nothing I could say. For all I knew the man could have been right. I knew something was seriously wrong.

This thing happened so suddenly. One July day I was practicing football with the College All-Stars, going through final drills for a game against the Green Bay Packers. The next day I was in a hospital. For many weeks I was to be in that hospital, and others, without knowing why.

I was never in pain and I never felt sick. That was the hardest part. I would lie there feeling good and strong, as if I should be able to leave and do what I wanted to do, which was play football for the Cleveland Browns, but I couldn't leave. Nobody knows much about leukemia. It's supposed to be a cancer of the blood. All I know is it hasn't made me feel sick.

What I remember most from last summer is waking up early in the morning and staring at hospital walls. There was nothing to do except think. At first, that was the worst part of it. It was a very lonely time.

In the beginning I had no idea what was wrong. Then I started getting letters from friends all over the country. They were trying to cheer me, but they wrote they had heard I had this or that, all the serious illnesses, right down the line.

During all that time I didn't press the doctors to tell me what was wrong. Even now I am not sure why I didn't. The little things I heard people say, the uncertainties, were hard to live with. At the same time I think that down deep inside I was afraid of what the answer would be. So I put off asking the question.

The waiting ended on October 4. Dr. Austin Weisberger, the specialist who was treating me, asked me to come to his office, as he had often done before. Dr. Vic Ippolito, the Browns' team physician, was there when I arrived.

We talked a few moments, and then Dr. Weisberger said, "Ernie, we think you are ready now to be told what your illness is."

I guess you always wonder what you would feel at a time like this. You might think something dramatic would happen, like a lot of things suddenly shooting through your mind. All I know is that it just wasn't that way with me. My mind had been conditioned by all the weeks of waiting.

The doctors talked to me very gently. They said my physical condition was excellent, that I had responded remarkably to treatment and that I had every reason to be encouraged.

. Then Dr. Weisberger mentioned the word "leukemia" for the first time.

It's a word that jumps out at you, a frightening word. I can't imagine what my reaction would have been if they had told me during my first days in the hospital. Now there was only the first shock, and that was all. For a long time I had realized leukemia was one of the possibilities.

The doctors explained that my condition was "in a complete state of remission," that my blood count was as good as anybody else's. They told me to try not to worry. And, best of all, they said I could start practicing football. There was, they said, no reason I couldn't play.

When I left the office, I felt I had heard the worst. It was bad enough, but now I knew what I was battling and that there was something to look forward to: football. That's what I thought when I was told I had leukemia.

Someplace along the line you have to come to an understanding with yourself, and I had reached mine a long time before, when I was still in this hospital. Either you fight or you give up. For a time I was so despondent I would just lie there, not even wanting to move. One day I got hold of myself. I decided I would face up to whatever I had and try to beat it. I still feel that way.

Some people say I am unlucky. I don't believe it. And I don't want to sound as if I am particularly brave or unusual. Sometimes I still get down, and sometimes I feel sorry for myself. Nobody is just one thing all the time.

But when I look back I can't call myself unlucky. My 23rd birthday was December 14. In those years I have had more than most people get in a lifetime. I think everybody wants some kind of recognition, something that will pick them out of a crowd and make people admire them.

There has been so much for me. I was the first Negro to win the Heisman award as the best collegiate football player in the nation. I made All-America teams. I led the graduation parade last June at Syracuse University, as the senior who had contributed most to the university, scholastically and athletically. From the time I started in sports I always was the player who got the limelight, who had the nice stories written about him.

All this I gained merely by doing what I liked to do most. I worked to improve myself in sports, but the ability had to be there to begin with. That was a gift to me that made all the rest possible. That is why I can't say I have been unlucky.

During those weeks in a hospital bed I had plenty of time to look back over the happy years. Little things from far back seemed so clear, as if what occurred when you were trying to get someplace stayed with you better than what happened after you arrived. Games that had seemed so very big at Syracuse University sort of blurred together, and yet I could easily remember every detail of a Midget League baseball parade.

I was living in Uniontown, Pennsylvania, and to understand why the parade was so important you would have to know about my neighborhood. Some great athletes had come from around there. Stan Musial was from Donora and John Lujack from Connellsville, both nearby, and the Big Ten and Notre Dame always recruited players from our district. Sandy Stephens and Bill Munsey, who went on to become football stars at the University of Minnesota, were on the same playground with me. We pretty much lived on the playgrounds. Sports were the only recreation we had.

When I was eight, the Midget League was organized, and Sandy Stephens and I tried out for a team named the Bensons, which was backed by a local clothing store. We wouldn't settle for anything else because the Bensons had the best uniforms, ones like the Dodgers wore, and we had never had real uniforms. We walked four or five miles to each tryout, and then back again.

The age limit was eight to 12, so I barely qualified, and a lot of kids were out for the Bensons, but I was tall and could hit the ball a long way if they tossed it up easy.

The Bensons had only 15 uniforms, and my special goal was to be wearing one when the Midget League paraded through town to open the season. At the last tryout the coach told me I was the 15th man on the team. I could just imagine the looks on my buddies' faces when I came by in that uniform.

I arrived early the day of the parade. For some reason the coach couldn't make it, and there was a mixup in passing out the uniforms. I didn't get one. I couldn't believe it. I kept standing around, trying not to cry. Finally the parade took off. I can still see the way they looked, marching up the street, marching up and out of sight without me.

It was my first big disappointment in sports. Not many have hurt that much and, while it seems amusing now, I still can understand how I felt. Nothing seemed as important to us as succeeding in athletics. We wanted to play so badly that season, Sandy and I kept walking the eight or 10 miles to and from practice, and we never did get in more than a couple of innings late in the games. (continued on page 126)

I lived with my grandmother in Uniontown until I was 11. My mother was separated from my father, whom I never knew and who was killed in an accident. My mother had moved on

backfield with Jim Brown, who had won five straight NFL rushing titles. But the perfect pairing never took place. While practicing in Chicago for the College All-Stars' game against the NFL champion Green Bay Packers that summer, Davis's face became swollen. Doctors at the hospital ran tests and discovered that Davis had leukemia. They told Browns owner Art Modell but withheld the news from Davis, who only knew that he had some type of blood disorder.

But Davis started to hear the rumors.

Doctors finally told Davis the truth in October. By that time the disease was in remission and Davis thought he might be able to play for the Browns. But after consulting with a Cleveland hematologist, coach Paul Brown refused to let Davis practice. Davis stayed in shape after the 1962 season by playing basketball and still harbored hopes of resuming his football career. However, the disease recurred in March and his condition worsened. Davis checked into Lakeside Hospital in Cleveland on May 16 and died two days later.

Although Davis never played a down for the Browns, almost the entire team came to his funeral in Elmira, where 1,600 people packed the First Baptist Church and another 3,000 paid their respects in a nearby park. The day before, mourners had filed by his open coffin for 12 hours at a recreation center where he had played as a kid.

Later, the city paid tribute to Davis by naming his high school and a nearby park after him. In 1988, on the 25th anniversary of his death, a life-size bronze statue of Davis was dedicated in front of the school.

Every year his high school football coach, Marty Harrigan, places flowers on Davis's grave at Woodlawn Cemetery. The headstone reads: "Ernie Davis. Heisman Trophy 1961."

"A lot of star athletes today are thought of as heroes," Harrigan said. "They are ballyhooed, then they retire, and you don't ever hear about them again. The opposite is true of Ernie Davis. He was a great player, a hero. And as time goes by, all these years later, Ernie Davis is still someone special."

The Browns and the NFL obviously agree. Cleveland retired Davis's jersey number, 45, even though he never wore it on the field.

"When you talk about Ernie Davis, you're treading on hallowed ground," Schwartzwalder said when Davis died. "We always thought he had a halo around him, and now we know he has." —*RICK WARNER*

to Elmira, New York, and when I turned 11 I moved there. I liked Elmira, especially the way it had sports programs organized for kids.

I was one of the few freshmen ever to play a varsity sport at Elmira Free Academy, and I remember my first game because of an unusual circumstance. I played varsity basketball with a broken wrist in a cast.

I had broken my left wrist in the first minute of my first game of junior varsity football, which was the last time I was sidelined with an injury. I went out for the basketball team anyway, and the coach took one look at the cast and said I couldn't play. However, I kept hanging around, and finally he gave in.

I didn't start the first game, but midway in the opening quarter the coach sent me in. I wasn't any scared little kid. At 15, I was already six feet and 175 pounds, and I had been playing organized sports since kindergarten. I scored 22 points that day, and from then on I was a regular.

The honors started coming fast. We had good teams; in fact our basketball team set a state record by winning 52 straight, and I got used to being the big guy. I was an end and then a halfback in football, and I made all-state and high school All-America in football and basketball, both my junior and senior years.

Almost from the beginning at Syracuse University I found I had drawn a tough role. I would pick up the papers, even when I was still a freshman in 1958, and see myself referred to as "another Jim Brown." Jim, the great fullback with the Cleveland Browns, had played his final season at Syracuse in 1956. When I entered Syracuse I knew this much: I wasn't another Jim Brown. I wasn't that good.

But I don't think they were disappointed with me at Syracuse. I broke 10 of Jim's records, including the ones for rushing, total yardage and scoring. I was a regular halfback from the start as a sophomore on a team that went undefeated and won over the University of Texas in the Cotton Bowl, and in one game that year I scored two touchdowns against West Virginia. I led the team in rushing all three years and made All-America as a senior.

So I had every reason to expect a good offer to play pro football. I had no idea how good it would be.

On December 29, 1961, in San Francisco, where I was practicing for the East-West Shrine Game, I sat down in a room full of reporters and photographers and signed a contract that was called the largest ever given to a football rookie up to that time. At the table with me were Anthony DeFilippo, my lawyer and friend from Elmira, and Arthur Modell, owner of the Cleveland Browns. The contract would net me a $15,000

bonus and $65,000 over three years. While the photographers were shooting pictures, a reporter asked me what I had in my pockets. I pulled out 16 cents.

That was a happy day to look back on, and there seemed to be no end to the success and good fortune coming my way. But sometimes you see a football game in which one team gets every break, then all of a sudden everything goes the other way. It happened to me, and change came almost from the start of 1962.

There certainly was no hint of problems ahead when I returned to classes at Syracuse in January. But then my college life began to change. I would go to classes, and when I returned there would be messages for me to call this person or that person, from all over the country. I would sit down at night to study and there would be more calls. They all wanted me to appear at banquets, to speak or accept awards. I began to realize what it meant to be the Heisman winner and an All-America.

I found myself leaving college almost every Friday and not getting back to campus until Sunday, traveling all over the East and Midwest. Finally, I reached a point where I decided I had to get some time to sit down, relax and enjoy myself. I stopped making appearances in April. Even then, after graduation in June, I still felt worn down.

I was scheduled to report for practice for the All-American Bowl Game, which was in Buffalo, June 29. I would have liked to skip it, but I didn't think I could without stirring up a fuss. The game turned out to be a personal disappointment, even though our Eastern team won. I was used mostly as a blocker and got to carry the ball very little.

After that I reported to Hiram, Ohio, on July 8, for the Browns' preliminary training camp, and from there I went directly to Evanston, Illinois, to join the College All-Stars for their game against the Packers on Friday, August 3.

Things still were not going well. Two wisdom teeth which started bothering me in Buffalo had become worse. I also had contracted trench mouth. I went into the hospital to have the teeth pulled and missed the first three days of All-Star practice. Even after I rejoined the team, my mouth was very sore. I hadn't enjoyed a meal for a month.

Surprisingly enough, I was in good football condition, and when I told the doctors this after going into the hospital, they had a hard time believing me. My wind was up and I could run a long time without tiring. The week before the All-Star Game I was our leading rusher in a scrimmage against the Chicago Bears.

Then, on the Tuesday before the All-Star Game, I woke up

and found the side of my face had blown up where a tooth had been pulled. A trainer sent me to the Evanston hospital. Even then I was certain I would play against the Packers. Of course I did not. Instead, I was started on the long ordeal that took me to Marymount Hospital in Cleveland and the National Institutes of Health in Bethesda, Maryland, and left me with the questions for which there would be no answer for so long.

I left Dr. Weisberger's office the day I learned I had leukemia and stepped into the October sunshine. Everything looked brighter. Even knowing what I did, I felt relieved. I felt almost free and easy, as if something that had been pressing down on me for weeks had suddenly been lifted.

The public announcement of my illness was made the next day, along with the news that I was to start working out. The plan was for me to undergo an individual conditioning program for three or four weeks. After that I was supposed to start practicing with the team. The Browns still had 11 games to play. I hoped to be ready for the last part of the season.

It helped merely being around the players again. They acted as if nothing had happened. They never questioned my illness. I was always perfectly at ease with them, and thoughts of my problems didn't enter my head. I was living in an apartment with John Brown, a tackle who had been in my class at Syracuse, and Charley Scales, a halfback. The only lonely times were the weekends when the team played out of town.

Each day the Browns practiced I was there working out by myself, running and throwing the ball. Weeks went by, and my condition kept improving. After a month I felt I was as ready as I ever could be without actual competition. Still nobody said anything to me, and I was not practicing with the team.

When only three games remained, Mr. Modell called me in. He told me as kindly as he could that it had been decided that I would not be allowed to play at all for the Browns during 1962.

That wasn't the end of it. In January, Mr. Modell replaced Paul Brown as coach, and that really stirred things up. A lot of the stories said that a disagreement over playing me had been a big factor. I think that part was blown up out of proportion. The Browns had been through a generally disappointing season. I do know, however, that Paul Brown personally didn't think that I should play, even though the doctors did, and that was why I never got to practice with the team. Maybe he thought I couldn't make up for all the lost time. Maybe he had other reasons. Whatever his reasons were he never told me.

But I certainly hold no ill will toward him. I can understand he had plenty of other problems. In the few dealings we had, he treated me very well.

Now all this is in the past and, as far as I am concerned, forgotten. I am keeping fit playing with the Browns' basketball

team. I am looking toward the future. I have been promised that, if the doctors still approve, I will be with the Browns when training camp opens in July.

I have no big ideas that I could start right out being an outstanding halfback in the National Football League. Pro defenses are so much tougher. A running back like myself has a lot to learn, things like timing, knowing the holes and the opposing teams' personnel. Even Paul Hornung and Jim Taylor didn't do too much during their first seasons at Green Bay. Jim Brown, of course, was great from the start, but he is the exception to everything.

I know some people have wondered whether it would be fair to the other teams to let me play, whether the opposing players would be reluctant to tackle me as hard as they would somebody else. I am sure it wouldn't make any difference. In the heat of the contest they would forget there ever had been anything wrong with me. If I felt differently I wouldn't play.

As I sit in my house in Cleveland now and look out the window, it seems a long time until July. But I have become accustomed to waiting.

I remember the night at the Evanston hospital when they told me I couldn't play in the All-Star Game. Mr. Modell, who has been a good friend to me, came to my room and I guess I sort of broke down and shed some tears and got very emotional. I thought I had either the mumps or mononucleosis and that I might have to wait a couple of months to play football. That seemed like the end of the world.

It is hard to explain how I feel about football. The money isn't too important, because the Browns have promised to pay me even if I never play again. A lot of things go into it: the excitement, the physical contact, the skill, the crowds.

But the big thing to me in football has always been the competitiveness. Sometimes when the game is close and the play is roughest you forget the crowd and the noise, and it is just you against somebody else to see who is the better man. This is what I liked and took pride in the way I could do and, after all the waiting, I want a chance to do again.

For me 1962 was a long year, and I hope I never have to go

through another like it. I think I have faced up to my problems and now I am looking ahead and trying to prepare for my future as if nothing had happened.

The late John F. Kennedy congratulates the late Earnie Davis on being the winner of the 1961 Heisman Memorial Trophy.

Terry Baker led Oregon State to the Final Four in basketball and pitched his high school baseball team to the state championship. He was president of his college fraternity and an honors student in mechanical engineering who went on to become a successful lawyer. It was in football, however, that Baker made his biggest mark.

The Renaissance Quarterback

Baker didn't even play freshman football, preferring to concentrate instead on basketball, baseball and his studies. But once he joined the team, there was no stopping him. By the time he left Oregon State, the lanky 6'3", 190-pound quarterback had gained more yards passing and running than anyone in NCAA history except Drake's Johnny Bright.

As a senior Baker led the Beavers to a 9–2 record, became the first player from the West Coast to win the Heisman Memorial Trophy and was named *Sports Illustrated*'s Sportsman of the Year. He ended his college career in storybook fashion, racing 99 yards on a frozen field in Philadelphia for the only score in Oregon State's 6–0 victory over Villanova in the 1962 Liberty Bowl.

"At that moment," *Sports Illustrated*'s Alfred Wright wrote, "Terry Baker … did exactly what he had done whenever his team had been in trouble during the three years of his varsity football career. Like a James Bond in shoulder pads, he called on himself to transmute imminent peril into triumph."

Many players were stronger and quicker than Baker, but no one had a better knack for the big play. It was a trait that Baker displayed in his very first basketball game at Jefferson High School in Portland, Oregon. Baker, who entered the contest after the starting guard fouled out, made the winning shot in overtime. "He shot with about three guys hanging on him," his brother Gary recalled. "It was the first time he ever played in a varsity sport at Jefferson. It was his first shot and his first basket, and it won the game."

Terry and his two older brothers were raised by their mother after their father walked out. "We were always in poor financial shape," Terry said. "As long as I can remember, my mother did nothing but work, work, work to take care of us. Even so, she always wanted us to keep up our athletics."

In high school Terry was all-state in baseball, basketball and football. Oregon State basketball coach Slats Gill recruited him hard, but football coach Tommy Prothro wasn't interested because he thought Baker "didn't like to get hit." So Baker ended up on a basketball scholarship at Oregon State, where he led the team in scoring as a freshman.

When basketball season ended, Terry joined the baseball team. But there were so many rainouts that he got bored and decided to give spring football a try. He was an instant success. As a sophomore, he set a school record for total offense with 1,473 yards even though he alternated at single-wing tailback with junior Don Kasso.

Prothro was so impressed that the following season he switched to the T formation to showcase Baker's versatility as a runner and passer. The team struggled with the transition, finishing with a 5–5 record, but Baker ended up among the national leaders in total offense and was called "the best athlete in college" in a *Sports Illustrated* cover story. "In an era of specialization, when few college graduates have time or energy to devote themselves to more than one campus activity, Terry Baker … is that rare thing—the all-around man," the story said.

Baker proved it again during his junior basketball season, when he and seven-footer Mel Counts led the Beavers to the West Regional final in the NCAA tournament. Although they lost to UCLA in the regional championship game, Baker was named to the all-regional team.

Baker started his Heisman-winning senior season with a flourish. In Oregon State's opener he threw three touchdown passes and ran for three scores in a thrilling 39–35 victory over Iowa State. With his team trailing 35–33 in the final minute, Baker threw a 43-yard TD pass to tight end Jerry Neil. After the game Iowa State coach Clay Stapleton called Baker "one of the truly great quarterbacks in college football history. He can beat you with his passes, and he can beat you with his runs."

The following week Baker had his worst game of the year, accounting for only 109 yards in a 28–8 loss to Iowa. But that was an aberration in an otherwise superb season. With Baker leading the way, Oregon State won six of its next seven games before closing the regular season against Oregon in Corvallis, where the Beavers hadn't beaten their archrivals since 1946.

Oregon led 17–6 at halftime, but Baker led a dramatic rally in the second half. He capped the comeback

The week before he won the Heisman, Baker led the Beavers to a dramatic comeback victory over Oregon.

with a fourth-quarter touchdown pass that gave Oregon State a 20–17 victory. When the game ended, the Beavers carried Baker off the field on their shoulders.

Three days later Baker won the Heisman Trophy, edging LSU's Jerry Stovall by 89 points. His reaction was typically low-key. "No kidding," he said. "That's great. I'm a very lucky boy."

Baker's statistics spoke louder than he did. He led the nation in total offense with 2,276 yards and 15 touchdown passes. He also ran for nine scores, passed or ran for a dozen two-point conversions and punted 33 times for a 37.4 average. He finished his career with 4,979 yards, second at the time to Bright's record of 5,903.

Baker received the Heisman during a whirlwind, six-day visit to New York, during which he appeared on the *Ed Sullivan Show* and met Attorney General Robert Kennedy. He then flew back to Corvallis to take final exams and practice for the Liberty Bowl in Philadelphia, where frigid conditions limited the crowd to 17,048 and forced the Beavers to wear tennis shoes on the slippery field. Asked to describe his 99-yard dash, Baker said, "Some guys ice skated by me, but that was it."

When Baker got back to Oregon, he was so sore he could barely walk. But he immediately began practicing with the basketball team and a few days later led Oregon State in scoring in his season debut against West Virginia. The Beavers went 22–9 that year and advanced to the Final Four, where they lost in the semifinals to eventual champion Cincinnati. Baker averaged 13.4 points as a senior but decided his athletic future was in football.

The Los Angeles Rams made Baker the No. 1 pick in the NFL draft. However, his pro career was short and uneventful. Unimpressed with his arm, the Rams tried to convert Baker into a running back and later a receiver. Finally, after three seasons, he was released. Baker played one more year, with the Edmonton Eskimos of the Canadian Football League, before retiring.

Fortunately Baker was prepared for life after football. He had attended law school at Southern Cal while playing for the Rams and was admitted to the Oregon bar in 1968. Today he is an attorney in Portland who doesn't dwell on his days as a sports hero. His Heisman Trophy sits in a display case at Oregon State, and there's no athletic memorabilia in his office. Still, he is often reminded of his glory days. "I'll get a call in the middle of the night from some guy in a bar who's arguing about what year I won the Heisman," Baker said.

In Oregon few people have to ask. More than three decades after winning the Heisman, Terry Baker's 1962 season is still a magical memory.   —RICK WARNER

Roger Staubach

A Rollercoaster Year

Among the dinner guests at the White House one summer evening in 1963 was Admiral Charles Kirkpatrick, the superintendent of the U.S. Naval Academy. During the reception beforehand, President John Kennedy was recalling the fun they had sitting together for the first half of the previous Army-Navy football game.

"Say, Admiral," he asked, cocking his right arm as if to throw a football, "do you still have that man?"

"Yes, sir, we sure do!" Admiral Kirkpatrick confirmed proudly.

The superintendent was one of many at Annapolis eagerly anticipating another exciting season from Roger Staubach, the Middies' 6' 2", 190-pound quarterback from Cincinnati's Purcell High School. As a sophomore, in 1962, Staubach had closed with a brilliant game against Army, and now he was surrounded by some of the finest talent in Navy history.

Staubach more than delivered (just as he would later in his Pro Football Hall of Fame career with the Dallas Cowboys). He exceeded all expectations, with a flashing, daring style, completing 107 of 161 pass attempts for 1,474 yards and seven touchdowns. The Heisman race was something of a runaway, with Staubach easily outpointing Georgia Tech quarterback Billy Lothridge, 1,860 to 504 points. With Staubach leading the way, the Middies earned a No. 2 national ranking, finishing the season 9–2.

The *Time* magazine All-America team, picking players based on their professional potential, picked Staubach No. 1 and quoted Pittsburgh Steelers coach Buddy Parker: "For his position, the best college player I've ever seen."

And *Los Angeles Times* columnist Jim Murray wrote, "Staubach has gotten every award but the *Good Housekeeping* seal this season. He can run, pass, catch, kick, cook and sew, to hear the Naval Academy tell it; he plays basketball, baseball, football and would be a threat in any contest up to and

Staubach, a runaway winner of the Heisman in '63, was a class act both on and off the field.

Like every other American, Staubach found it difficult to concentrate in the harrowing fall of 1963.

including the Pillsbury bake-off. If you could bottle him, you'd get rich."

As the Middies' daring, scrambling quarterback in 1963, Staubach was a true maestro. He was superb all season, even in a bruising, bitter 32–28 loss to SMU in the Cotton Bowl at Dallas on a Friday night in October. It was Navy's only regular-season loss as they prepared for the climactic Army game scheduled for Philadelphia on November 30. If the Middies beat their archrivals, they would be invited to return to Dallas and challenge No. 1 Texas in the Cotton Bowl Classic on New Year's Day.

Both service academies traditionally had an open date the previous weekend, allowing them two weeks to build

up to their showdown, but all the anticipation and all the excitement suddenly disappeared on Friday, November 22.

"I was stretched out on my bed, half asleep and half awake, just resting a few minutes before I went to thermodynamics class," Staubach said. "I heard some commotion in the hall, which was unusual in the middle of the day … so I got up and walked out.

"The hall was filled with a strange emotional electricity. Guys were running back and forth yelling. I said, 'Hey, what's going on?'

"Someone yelled, 'The President has been shot!'"

In a state of shock Staubach started off to class. As he crossed the campus, everybody was calling back and forth about President Kennedy, but no one knew anything def-

128

inite about his condition.

"Everyone in thermodynamics class just sat and stared," Staubach said. "The professor was off somewhere listening to a radio. Finally he came in and announced the President was dead. I got a terrible sick feeling in my stomach. I remembered how I had seen him when he visited our fall training camp at Quonset Point, so happy and full of life. I just couldn't believe it had happened.

"The professor said we could stay or leave, and everyone started drifting outside. I went to the practice field. Everyone was standing there, dazed. Our team felt we were closer to President Kennedy than most people. He had visited us ... and also tossed the coin at the last Army-Navy game. Wayne Hardin, our coach, looked like he had been crying. He told us he didn't know what would happen to the Army game but that the afternoon practice was canceled. We knelt and said some prayers. Then we left."

All the banners and decorations on the Annapolis campus that were part of the traditional hoopla before the Army game were removed as the Middies joined the nation in mourning its fallen president. There was speculation that the Army game would be canceled, that Navy's season might be over. But the next Tuesday, the day after President Kennedy's burial in Arlington National Cemetery, two important messages arrived at Annapolis.

"The Pentagon said the Army game would be delayed one week, to December 6, and would be played in President Kennedy's memory at the request of his family," Staubach said. "And I got some other news. I had won the Heisman Trophy."

The team celebrated in the locker room with a big cake and threw Staubach in the shower, but he had mixed emotions.

"I was proud of the Heisman Trophy, but I felt no joy," he said. "There was so much riding on the Army game, but you had to wonder if we would be emotionally ready for it. As game time neared, I wasn't nervous, but I did realize the pressure was much greater than last year. Now I was the Heisman Trophy winner."

Staubach passed and ran brilliantly against Army, taking the Middies to a 21–7 lead in the fourth quarter before a crowd of 100,000 in Philadelphia Municipal Stadium (later renamed J.F.K. Stadium) and a national TV audience. Army rallied strongly, scoring once and driving to the Navy two-yard line as the game ended, giving Navy a 21–15 victory and an invitation to return to Dallas and play Texas in the Cotton Bowl on January 1.

"We couldn't have arranged a better game from Navy's standpoint, but there was a funny feeling about going to Dallas," Staubach said. "I felt very leery of the city. In fact, I didn't like Dallas. We had lost to SMU in a distasteful game and had received bad press coverage [reserve fullback Nick Markoff was charged with hitting some SMU players late, but the Middies felt the Mustangs threw more cheap shots at them]. Then there was President Kennedy's death. Stories in the national press made Dallas seem like a pretty bad place.

"Since I've made my home in Dallas, I've learned it was an altogether different atmosphere [then], but in December 1963 I was no lover of Dallas. We wanted to go back and knock the heck out of Texas. We were anxious to make amends."

It didn't quite work that way for Navy. Thirty years later, after four years of active duty as a Navy officer (including a year in Vietnam during the war), a star-spangled 12-year career with the Cowboys (including two Super Bowl titles), founding the Staubach Company, a national real estate and investment firm headquartered in Dallas, and raising four daughters and a son with wife Marianne, Staubach sat in his Dallas office and reflected back on the Cotton Bowl game.

Pat Donnelly, a tremendous fullback and linebacker for the Middies, pulled a hamstring four days earlier but started the game. Texas quarterback Duke Carlisle quickly capitalized on Donnelly's gimpiness, twice lofting touchdown passes over his outstretched hands to wingback Phil Harris. Texas won 28–6 after leading 21–0 at halftime.

Donnelly's injury and Texas's insurmountable early lead took away any Navy hopes of establishing a running game to open up passing and scrambling lanes for Staubach. He was dogged by the Longhorns' rush all afternoon but still completed 21 passes, a Navy and Cotton Bowl record.

"The game was a weird ending to a very exciting and emotional season, one in which we achieved a lot for Navy football," Staubach said. "After all, we were undefeated in 49 states. The Cotton Bowl game certainly didn't satisfy us, but we proved something there. We proved who was No. 1."

Staubach, named the NFL's player of the year in 1971, never left any doubt as to who was number one.

—*SAM BLAIR*

John Huarte

Surprise in South Bend

John Huarte (rhymes with Stewart) played for a grand total of one hour his first two years as a Notre Dame quarterback. He almost missed his final season in 1964 because of a serious shoulder injury he suffered in spring practice. Ara Parseghian, who took over the head coaching job at Notre Dame in 1964, had Huarte at the bottom of his depth chart in March of that year. As late as September, Huarte, a senior without one varsity letter, wasn't even mentioned as a contender for the Heisman Trophy.

The favorites that year included Joe Namath, Roger Staubach, Dick Butkus and Jerry Rhome. Even Huarte's teammate Jack Snow, a wide receiver, was mentioned as a possible Heisman candidate. As the 1964 season began, no one even gave Huarte a second thought.

In less than three months, however, Huarte became the sixth Notre Dame football player to win the Heisman Trophy in what Notre Dame publicists have referred to as "one of the biggest upsets in the history of the award."

Those less generously disposed toward Notre Dame have referred to the 1964 vote as just another of those Heisman victories achieved because the athlete played for Notre Dame, the nation's foremost college football power. "For any Heisman candidate, it helps to have Notre Dame as a mailing address," said Maury White, the highly respected sports editor of *The Des Moines Register*. Another controversial Notre Dame Heisman winner was Paul Hornung in 1956, the only man to claim the honor while playing on a losing team.

Both Staubach and Namath dropped out of contention for the award because of injuries. Rhome would finish second to Huarte in the voting, with Butkus third.

While a number of these 1964 college stars went on to become National Football League Hall of Fame heroes, Huarte rightfully says, "When people see the players who could have won the Heisman that year—Namath, Sayers, Frederickson, Butkus et cetera—they say who am I to slip in there. But just because you win the Heisman doesn't mean you're supposed to be a great pro. I won because I was able to put together 10 straight good games. I had to hustle, fight and scrap to do it, and I had to get lucky. I was unknown most of the year, and I just had a perfect season. All I ever wanted to do was win some games."

Notre Dame was 9–0 when the

Lucky seven produced a 9–1 record for a flagging Notre Dame program and a Heisman for its wearer.

Heisman ballots were counted and announced on Tuesday, November 24. Four days later the Irish were beaten in the final 95 seconds, 20–17, at Southern California, ending Parseghian's first year at the helm of the Irish with a 9–1 mark. Although Alan Page, Jim Lynch and Snow, a trio of future NFL stars, were on this Notre Dame team, Huarte's record-setting passes made him the single most important player in the big comeback. When it was all over, Notre Dame had its first winning season in six years.

Maybe there were some really good reasons why Huarte won the Heisman, after all.

"It was the dramatic aspect of Notre Dame having been down for a lot of years," Parseghian said. "And now with Notre Dame back, people wanted to know who was making it happen." Under coaches Knute Rockne, Elmer Layden and Frank Leahy, football had been virtually the driving force on the Notre Dame campus for 40 years. But in the past decade one mediocre season had followed another. The Irish of the early '60s were hoping for a return to those wonderful days of yore.

Huarte and Parseghian were the saviors.

It's doubtful that any of the "name" players of 1964 would have been better than Huarte at rehabilitating Notre Dame's football program. But given his minuscule contribution to the team in his first two years, it was somewhat nervy of Huarte to join with Snow and tell Parseghian before 1964 spring practice that "we are the best pass-catching team on campus." Snow later said, "It wasn't a braggart's statement; it was a last-gasp thing."

Parseghian told them they would have the chance to prove their worth. That satisfied them, and they seemed to make the grade until, in a late spring scrimmage, Huarte dislocated his right (passing) shoulder. Two doctors told him he needed immediate surgery. Two other doctors said rest would result in gradual healing. Parseghian and Huarte went for the rest and rehabilitation idea.

That summer, after weeks of coddling the shoulder, Huarte and Snow went to the California beaches where, day after day, they threw passes and caught passes for hours and hours. With their timing nearly flawless, and Huarte's arm strong again, Snow and Huarte, along with the other Irish players, were ready. They opened at Wisconsin, where the Badgers were highly favored. Huarte and Snow completed touchdown passes of 61 and 42 yards as Notre Dame won 31–7. The rest of the season went the same way, as Huarte–

to-Snow connections ignited scoring drives game after game. Huarte completed 114 passes that season. Snow caught 60 of them.

Huarte had an unusual style for a college passer. He tossed the ball sidearm, a method most coaches deplore because defenders can block that pass more easily than the pass thrown from an overhand motion. Yet Huarte, a superb medium distance thrower in that senior season, found targets regularly. The results included 2,062 yards passing in 1964 with 16 passing touchdowns, which were Notre Dame season marks at the time.

Notre Dame whipped Purdue in the second game, 34–15. Huarte and Snow had one touchdown together against the Boilermakers. A week later, on October 10, they made one more such connection, against Air Force, as the Irish won 34–7.

By this time both the nation and the Heisman voters were beginning to pay attention to the rebirth of Notre Dame football, driven by the passing and catching of Huarte and Snow.

Huarte was suddenly well known. And he was gaining momentum. Sometime in early November, while the Irish were still unbeaten, Huarte sped past the big names in the race for the Heisman. Just a few days after Lyndon B. Johnson won a totally predictable landslide election over Barry Goldwater for president of the United States, Huarte won a totally unpredicted Heisman race.

Huarte and Namath were both drafted by the New York Jets of the American Football League. Huarte was paid the huge sum of $200,000 for signing, but Namath set all kinds of records by signing for the unheard-of bonus of $400,000. The four-year-old upstart American Football League and the senior National Football League were at the height of a bidding war for senior college players. This war ended five years later with the merger of the leagues to form what is the modern NFL.

Huarte never really made it in the pros, playing for six teams before retiring after eight seasons. Upon retiring from football in 1973, he became the owner of an imported—ceramic tile company and now lives in Tempe with his wife and five children.

That 1964 season was a once-in-a-lifetime chance for Huarte. Along with the Heisman Trophy he won something else that season—his one and only Notre Dame varsity letter. No athlete before or since Huarte has won the Heisman as a returning nonletterman. Things aren't supposed to work that way. But in a season of surprises it made sense.   —GORDON S. WHITE JR.

Mike Garrett

First of a Great Tradition

When Mike Garrett was a small boy, his father died, and out of that tragedy he found a purpose that would shape his life.

"I wanted attention," Garrett said. "No one realized my father had died, and that made me very upset. Too many people pass from this earth unrecognized. There are a lot of great human beings who die and are never given any attention."

Garrett didn't have an easy time growing up in the Boyle Heights section of East Los Angeles. "My mother, along with my stepfather, raised my four sisters, brother, two nieces and me," Garrett said. "Mom did housework for people, worked in restaurants. I didn't know we were poor. I thought I was a middle-class kid. I didn't have the monetary things normal kids have."

But he quickly began to turn his childhood hunger for recognition into lasting achievement. He was an all-city baseball player at Roosevelt High School and a prep All-America as a football quarterback his senior season.

The odds were against him in college, however. He stood just 5'9" and weighed only 185 pounds. But what he lacked in size, he made up for in balance, body control, field vision and heart. Garrett had an odd, splay-footed stride that led his teammates to nickname him Duck and Ten to Two, because his left foot pointed to 10 o'clock and his right foot to two o'clock. But the unusual alignment of his feet led to a brilliant change-of-pace and breakaway ability. "Just a brush block will spring him into the secondary," USC tackle Chuck Arrobio said. "It takes the average college back about 2.5 seconds to get through the hole. Garrett gets through in 1.5. You can even feel him go by."

Garrett, who had a 45-inch chest and thighs the size of hams, was also not adverse to running over or through would-be tacklers when necessary. *Los Angeles Times* columnist Jim Murray said his nose looked like a baked potato because of all the hits he took.

Capable of a runover tactic when faced with would-be tacklers, Garrett usually opted for the simpler run-around.

No one knew how good or how tough Garrett would be in 1963, when Trojan coach John McKay gave him a try as starting tailback at what would come to be known as Tailback U. The first major clue came in fall practice before Garrett's sophomore season. McKay had Garrett carry the ball a dozen straight times in a scrimmage, and he not only held up, he also scored a touchdown. He then got the ball seven more times in a row and responded with another TD.

That, in effect, was the birth of McKay's vaunted tailback offense, with one workhorse runner carrying the ball 25 or 30 times a game.

By the time his three seasons at USC were complete, Garrett, who was also a fierce blocker, had accounted for 4,846 all-purpose yards. His 3,221 yards rushing (on 612 carries) broke Ollie Matson's 15-year-old NCAA career record. He also had 397 yards in pass receptions, 498 on punt returns, 700 on kickoff returns, and he scored 30 touchdowns.

"He's the best college ball-carrier I've ever seen," UCLA coach Tommy Prothro said after Garrett's final game as a Trojan. McKay, who later coached O.J. Simpson, said that while Simpson was bigger and faster, "nobody ever got more out of his ability than Mike Garrett."

In 1965 Garrett became the first player from a California school to win the Heisman. "After my dad died, I wanted to be immortal," Garrett said. "I figured I could do that by winning the Heisman, and I set out to do that in my freshman year at USC. When I got it, I was very proud."

Garrett didn't forget the contributions his mother, Ella Sigur, had made. Just after he got the word that he had been chosen for the Heisman, Garrett called her and said, "You won the Heisman." She replied, "You mean, you won." "No," Garrett said, "you did."

There were many doubts about his ability to play running back when he entered the pros. One pro scout said, "He's too small. The one place he can play is flanker, and he's almost too short and not fast enough for that. What are you going to do, roll the ball to him?"

The reservations notwithstanding, Garrett was drafted by both the Los Angeles Rams of the National Football League and the Kansas City Chiefs of the American Football League. He not only signed with the Chiefs, for much more money than the Rams had offered, but he also starred for them. As a rookie Garrett gained 801 yards rushing and 462 more on kick returns as the Chiefs won the AFL championship and the right to challenge the NFL's Green Bay Packers in the very first Super Bowl. In 1967 Garrett rolled up 1,087 yards rushing. And in 1969

1965 Mike Garrett

he led the Chiefs to another AFL title and into the 1970 Super Bowl. "The way he runs," one Chief said, "you feel you should get up and throw another block, because he might be back."

In early 1970 Garrett, who had starred as a baseball outfielder at USC and was offered a $65,000 bonus by the Pittsburgh Pirates after his junior year, announced that he was retiring from football to try professional baseball, keeping a promise to himself that he had made at a press conference when he signed with the Chiefs.

"I want to play football for just five years and then try to be a major league baseball player," he had said. "I think I can make it in baseball. At least I want to try."

But the attempt was not successful, and Garrett returned to pro football. He was traded to the San Diego Chargers during the 1970 season and in 1972 gained 1,031 yards rushing, becoming the first player to record more than 1,000 yards for two different teams.

The sensitive, introspective Garrett, who had majored in sociology at USC, retired in the summer of 1974, then spent several years in social work and community service. Later he started his own real estate company, went to law school and ran unsuccessfully for the Republican nomination for the California State Senate. Married, with two children, he is now the athletic director at his alma mater, USC.

He has taken considerable satisfaction over the years in having become the first great Trojan tailback. "I'm proud I set the mold for the other USC backs," Garrett said. "Not to sound conceited, but there's a tradition at USC that you never give up."

Garrett's pride in what he accomplished at USC definitely extends to winning the Heisman. "I first heard of the Heisman when I was 11 years old and growing up in a government project apartment," he said. "I used to watch football film clips on television and Howard 'Hopalong' Cassady of Ohio State became my boyhood idol. I loved the way he faked guys out and left them standing bewildered. That was the kind of runner I wanted to become."

When Cassady won the Heisman in 1955, Garrett had his introduction to the award. Ten years later he had the statue. The attention that came with winning it, he said, has never been a burden. "I can take whatever goes with it," he said. "I wouldn't have wanted to win it if I couldn't. I have to foot the bill for my fame. I accept that." —DWIGHT CHAPIN

1966

Steve Spurrier

Florida's Comeback Kid

Luck, they say, is where preparation meets opportunity. But by themselves those two will not make a hero. On a Saturday afternoon in late October 1966, Steve Spurrier added one more component to the equation. Guts.

Spurrier, the quarterback at the University of Florida, played the position with absolute confidence. Eight times in his career Spurrier had brought the Gators back in the fourth quarter to win—often drawing up plays in the dirt in the huddle. When those all around him, including coach Ray Graves, were losing their heads, Spurrier was the picture of calm.

"Steve had a way of making the rest of us believe in whatever he believed," said Alan Trammell, Spurrier's college roommate. "Steve was so nonchalant, and he always believed we would find a way to win."

By October 29, 1966, the Spurrier legend had spread beyond the South and into the consciousness of the nation's sportswriters. That was due in part to Spurrier himself, who had carried the Gators to a 6–0 record and a No. 7 national ranking, and in part to the tireless work of Norm Carlson, the Florida sports information director, who would spend eight hours on the phone every Sunday telling the sportswriters around the country about the latest exploits of Florida's swashbuckling star.

One must remember that this was in the days before the big-money media blitzes of the 1980s and '90s. Carlson, in addition to the phone calls, sent out 11,000 photographs, put 1,300 people on Florida's mailing list and produced 425 highlight tapes—before videotape had been invented. Even the governor of Florida got into the act. When Haydon Burns found out that his beloved Gators would not be on TV in 1966, he ordered the State Tourism Department to create and mail 5,000 film clips of Spurrier highlights to TV stations nationwide. At taxpayer expense.

So on this October Saturday the Florida press box was full of sportswriters from all over the country who had come to see what all the fuss was about. *Sports Illustrated* had sent John Underwood, its top college football writer, to Gainesville earlier in the week to put together a profile for the next issue.

There was one other piece of helpful timing for Spurrier that day. When the writers arrived in Gainesville, they

Spurrier's skills were honed by a boyhood spent throwing pass after pass to his older brother.

had just received their Heisman Trophy ballots. Those ballots were due back in New York a week later.

Against this backdrop, Florida took on Auburn before 60,511 just slightly crazy people at Florida Field.

With 2:12 left in the game, Spurrier had already done enough to leave an indelible impression on the minds of the Heisman voters on hand. He had completed 27 of 40 passes for 259 yards and a touchdown. He had also punted seven times for a 46.9-yard average. But the score was tied at 27–27, and Florida faced a fourth-and-long at the Auburn 25-yard line. Coach Graves called timeout. There was a big decision to make.

Florida placekicker Wayne Barfield was deadly accurate, having kicked an NCAA-record 51 straight extra points, but the 42-yarder was beyond his range. Spurrier had a hot hand, but going for a long fourth down against a stacked defense would be tough. A bad snap, a dropped pass, a missed block, and the drive would be over. Graves knew it would probably be Florida's last possession.

Graves was still pondering his options during the timeout when Spurrier trotted over to the sidelines. "Coach, let me give it a shot," he said.

At first the request did not register with the Florida coach, who was deep in thought. Spurrier was the team's long-range field goal kicker, but he had only attempted three all season and had only made one, that coming in the first game. Spurrier asked Graves again, shaking the coach. "Go kick it, Orr," Graves said to him, calling Spurrier by his middle name. Spurrier, meanwhile, had already put on a kicking shoe.

The field goal, of course, was good. Florida won 30–27, and Spurrier had the Heisman firmly in his grasp.

The Heisman balloting wasn't even close. He led the balloting in every section of the country except the Midwest, which went for Purdue's Bob Griese. Spurrier's total of 1,679 points was twice that of Griese's 816.

Spurrier had begun his football life as a fullback. Too slow, they said, to ever be a quarterback. But a quarterback is what this Presbyterian minister's son wanted to be. Every day after football practice was over at Science Hill High School in Johnson City, Tennessee, Spurrier would drag his older brother out to a nearby park so that he could throw passes to him.

As a sophomore Spurrier finally made the varsity, as a placekicker. Still too slow to play quarterback, they said.

Finally, as a junior at Science Hill, Spurrier got his chance. And he never gave the position back to anybody.

"He was too slow," said Kermit Tipton, Spurrier's high school coach. "But he made up for it with quickness and smart football."

Alabama offered a scholarship, but Spurrier wanted to play right away. The Crimson Tide already had two guys on scholarship, named Namath and Sloan. Spurrier decided to visit Florida. He fell ill while in Gainesville and wound up in the Florida infirmary. Coach Graves rarely left his side, knowing an opportunity when he saw one.

The rest is delicious football history.

Freshmen did not play varsity football in those days but in three years as a starter Spurrier gave Florida fans one memorable moment after another. The win over Auburn in 1966 is his most famous game, but just as impressive was the Sugar Bowl of January 1, 1966, when the Gators trailed Missouri 20–0, with less than 11 minutes left in the game. Spurrier led Florida to three touchdowns in the closing minutes, passing for two and running for one. But the coaching staff decided to go for two points after each score, and Florida lost the game 20–18. Still, Spurrier is the only MVP in the Sugar Bowl to have played for the losing side.

Spurrier did not find the same glory as a professional player as he did in college, mostly serving as a backup to John Brodie for eight years with the San Francisco 49ers. He did, however, start 10 games in 1972 after Brodie broke an ankle and led San Francisco to a division championship. He later finished his career with the Tampa Bay Buccaneers.

It took a year away from football for Spurrier to realize that coaching was what he wanted to do. After several stops as an assistant, where he was successful with a wide-open brand of football he called the Fun 'n Gun offense, Spurrier was named head coach of the Tampa Bay Bandits of the now defunct USFL. Spurrier later became the head coach at Duke, where he was the ACC Coach of the Year twice.

On December 31, 1989, Spurrier came back to Florida as its head coach and was hailed as a conquering hero. He has not let those people down. In his first four years as coach Spurrier has won two SEC championships and would have won another in his first year but for the Gators' being on NCAA probation for violations committed by the previous coaching staff.

So for Steve Spurrier, the Heisman Trophy winner of 1966, his life continues to read like a storybook. And each year he just keeps adding a new and exciting chapter.

—*Tony Barnhart*

Gary Beban

Master of the When

Gary Beban is best judged not on his stature or his statistics, but on his successes. At six feet and 195 pounds, the UCLA quarterback was physically unimposing, lacked blazing speed and was not a pure passer. But when he put everything together as the leader of Tommy Prothro's Bruins in the mid-1960s, he was a marvel.

"He has no weaknesses," Prothro said when Beban was a senior. "Maybe some quarterbacks can run or throw better. But I don't know anyone else who can do it all like he can. He makes big yardage and comes up with the big play in close games. The more pressure, the better he is."

A scout for a rival team agreed, saying, "You don't judge Beban on how *much* he does. He beats you with the *when* he does something. Invariably it's at the perfect time." And teammate Rick Purdy said, "There's something about the way he manages things out there that gives everyone confidence. You just know whatever he calls is right."

In three seasons the poised Beban quarterbacked the Bruins to 24 wins against just five losses and two ties. So many of the victories were so spectacular that Beban was given the nickname the Great One.

Greatness, however, had an unlikely beginning.

As a youngster growing up in the San Francisco suburb of Redwood City, Beban loved baseball and basketball. The only son of a an Italian mother and a Slavic father who worked on the Bay Area docks, Beban played Pop Warner football as a 120-pound lineman but only reluctantly went out for football at Sequoia High School. Coach Joe Marvin was struck by Beban's big hands and coordination and made him a single wing tailback. By his senior year he was all–Northern California.

But the bowlegged Beban was overlooked by the two major colleges close to home, Stanford and Berkeley, and was recruited instead by UCLA's Bill Barnes, who was fired before he could coach his "find" in a varsity game. Beban then came under the tutelage of the chain-smoking Prothro, who had turned another quarterback

Blessed with a cool head, Beban led the Bruins to a three-year record of 24-5-2.

1967 Gary Beban

blessed mainly with intangibles, Terry Baker of Oregon State, into a Heisman Trophy winner in 1962.

The union between Beban and the brainy Prothro, one of the most underrated coaches in college football history, became one for the ages. Prothro could direct Beban to do almost anything in the Bruins' quick-hitting option offense, which often resembled the chess games Prothro pursued when he wasn't coaching. "Tommy's intelligence, strategy and preparation made us better than we were. We had trick plays, sleeper plays," said Beban.

The Bruins lived on improvisation. "You have to think about what you're going to do, yes," Beban said. "But you try to make it all a natural reaction. I tried to make taking the ball from center as natural as breathing. When I run to the corner on the option, what I do there has to be an instant, natural reaction. I can't pause and think about it. The pause can mean the loss of a second, which can be the loss of a step, which is the loss of a play."

Time and again, Beban would make a big play at the best possible time.

In the 1965 game against crosstown rival USC, the Bruins trailed by 10 points with just four minutes to play. But the then sophomore Beban threw 34- and 52-yard touchdown passes, and UCLA won 20–16.

In the 1966 Rose Bowl game against heavily favored Michigan State, the nation's No. 1–ranked team, Beban scored two TDs (after setting up one with a 27-yard pass) as the Bruins upset the Spartans 14–12.

In UCLA's season opener in 1967, against Tennessee, Beban twice rallied his team from deficits, but the Bruins trailed the Volunteers 16–13 with four minutes remaining. UCLA had the ball on Tennessee's 27-yard line with fourth and two, and Prothro called the weary Beban to the sideline. "I want you to run one more great play," Prothro said. Beban nodded, and on the next play he wriggled to his right, cut back, outran five Tennessee linemen and broke two tackles in the secondary to score and give UCLA a 20–16 win.

"I've gotten to the point where I expect so much from Gary that he doesn't impress me anymore," Prothro said.

In 1967 Beban was the early Heisman favorite, but another leading contender quickly emerged a few miles from Westwood—USC's great tailback, O.J. Simpson.

Their personal duel came down to a showdown between their teams that November in Los Angeles. UCLA was ranked No. 1 nationally at the time; USC was No. 3. So this was a matchup for city, state and potential national supremacy.

140

The game was a classic. Beban, despite playing with bruised ribs and getting a heavy rush from the Trojans, was brilliant, completing 16 of 24 passes for 301 yards and two touchdowns. But Simpson may have been even better, scoring twice, including a 64-yard run that led to a 21–20 Trojan victory and a berth in the Rose Bowl.

There was a lot of controversy before the Heisman Trophy balloting. A number of people thought Simpson, the junior, should win over Beban, the senior. By a narrow margin Beban was the choice, but some years later Beban himself said, "I'm still not so sure O.J. shouldn't have won it. He had a phenomenal season."

Looking back, however, Beban seems a perfectly logical choice. In three seasons he passed for 4,087 yards, rushed for 1,271 and scored 35 times. And few have fit or continued to fit the Heisman image any better.

With antiwar and antiestablishment protests beginning to proliferate on college campuses, Beban was a straight arrow, a handsome, clean-cut guy (some said he resembled a young Marlon Brando without the black motorcycle jacket) who was as comfortable in a business suit and tie as he was in a football uniform.

Beban would go on to marry, father two children and prosper in industrial real estate sales. He's now president of CB Commercial Brokerage and Management Services, with offices in Chicago and Los Angeles.

His good fortune did not extend to professional football. Beban was drafted in the second round by the Los Angeles Rams but was immediately dealt to the Washington Redskins, where he struggled for three seasons. He failed in one last attempt, with the Denver Broncos in 1971.

But he has always been philosophical about his lack of success in the pros. "There is no such thing as a Heisman jinx," he said. "As a Heisman winner, I didn't feel any extra pressure to make it, but I was aware of the pressure exerted by the press and the fans. They seem to know more about a Heisman winner than the winner himself."

Over the years, his pride in winning the Heisman has deepened, as have his associations with the other winners. "The people whom I have come to know who won the trophy are active, principled men," he said. "Many have had very successful businesses and lives outside football. Some of my most vivid memories are talks with the former winners."

Beban, an unlikely hero, has been the only player from mighty UCLA to win the Heisman Trophy.

It's almost as if Beban feels a touch of awe at being included in this select company. Of all the star quarterbacks at UCLA—from Bob Waterfield to Billy Kilmer, Troy Aikman and Tommy Maddox—and the other great Bruin players, only Beban's name is on the Heisman.

So maybe it's just that he has been able to keep the honor in clear perspective. —*Dwight Chapin*

It is a deeply ironic note that the times have found Simpson's face blanketing newspapers and magazines and his story captivating the TV networks. For since his earliest days, O.J. Simpson has had a commanding presence and a special touch with the media. Even before he was old enough to vote, Simpson was almost as good at working a crowd as he was at carrying a football. A few days before his USC team was to play Ohio State in the 1969 Rose Bowl, O.J. stood in a garden at the Tournament of Roses house in Pasadena, holding court. Remarkably, this kid from a San Francisco ghetto was so polished, so poised, so comfortable that he had veteran reporters from all over the country squarely in the palm of his hand.

It was little wonder to those who knew him then that he went on to careers in acting and sports broadcasting when his football days were over, becoming the most recognized Heisman winner. Simpson's broad smile became familiar to TV watchers and moviegoers worldwide as he raced through airports in advertisements for Hertz, served as color commentator on ABC's "Monday Night Football" in the 1980s, and analyzed football for NBC in the early '90s.

Simpson grew up in a housing project in San Francisco's Potrero Hill district, not the world's most placid environment, and as a teen-ager he was the leader of a street gang named the Superiors. His parents, Jim, a bank janitor, and Eunice, a hospital orderly, separated when he was 3, and O.J.—short for Orenthal James, a name given to him by his aunt, and one he never really liked—was reared by his mom. It was not an easy childhood.

"His legs were badly bowed [because of a calcium deficiency and rickets] since birth and unable to support his upper body," Eunice Simpson said. "Doctors kept telling me that they should operate to straighten his legs, but I didn't like that idea, and said so. We finally agreed to put metal braces on his legs, and he wore braces and then special shoes until he was more than two years old."

The legs that once caused SImpson such problems catapulted him to astonishing heights in football.

Maybe because of those early problems, Eunice Simpson always worried about her son playing football. She would have preferred that he pursue a professional baseball career, like his cousin, Hall of Fame shortstop Ernie Banks of the Chicago Cubs.

1968

O.J. Simpson

A Life in the Spotlight

directly to college.

He landed, instead, at a community college close to home. In his two seasons as a running back and wide receiver for City College of San Francisco, he was spectacular, scoring 54 touchdowns and leading his team to a 17-2-1 record.

That caught the attention of recruiters nationwide. UCLA, Arizona State and California all made strong pitches for Simpson. "Everywhere I went on a recruiting trip," Simpson said, "everyone tried to impress me with how big they were. At USC, it was different. Everyone was so regular. Mike Garrett, who had just won the Heisman Trophy, was driving a Chevrolet and wearing jeans and tennis shoes."

When Simpson finally committed to USC, canny Trojan coach John McKay was thrilled, but hastened to add that O.J. still had to be taught a few things about running with a football. To which Simpson's junior college coach, Dutch Elston, responded, "Teaching Simpson how to run is the same as teaching Bing Crosby how to sing."

But McKay knew exactly what he had in mind for his prize recruit. Simpson would be a Mike Garrett-type runner, only more so. He would carry the ball again and again, as much as his once-weak legs could stand.

McKay had a ready response for those who asked whether he wasn't overusing Simpson, who was 6'1" and weighed a sturdy 205 pounds in college, by having him run 35 times a game. "The ball isn't very heavy," McKay would say. Then he'd add, "Besides, O.J. doesn't belong to any union, so we can work him as much as we want to."

McKay ran Simpson as a tailback out of the I-formation, on plays he half-jokingly called "Student Body Left" and "Student Body Right." When Simpson came at you, it often seemed as if it was the whole Trojan Student Body.

"I enjoyed running [with the ball] that much," Simpson said. "It made me feel like I was in the game. It helped my concentration. Also, I think it helped my running. The more you run, the more you learn."

Simpson always seemed to gain strength in the second

His legs still weak, Simpson was cut by a Pop Warner team when he was 12. But the legs eventually strengthened to the point that at San Francisco's Galileo High School, Simpson starred in football (he was briefly a tackle before being shifted to running back), baseball and track. But he didn't star in the classroom, so he didn't have the grades to move half, as he wore opponents down.

"He gets faster in the fourth quarter," McKay said, "and I get smarter."

In two seasons the Trojan Horse gained 3,295 yards, scored 34 touchdowns and led USC to a 19-2-1 record, two Rose Bowls and a national championship in 1967. Simpson scored three touchdowns against Notre Dame that season, and, in a battle for No. 1 in the nation against UCLA, he scored on two scintillating runs, one a 64-yarder, as USC won 21–20.

Many people thought that Simpson should have won the Heisman Trophy in 1967, but it went to UCLA's Gary Beban.

The diplomatic Simpson said he wasn't disappointed, but the night after the Rose Bowl, while visiting Garrett's home, he saw the trophy. "For the first time," he said, "I was aware how close I had come to winning it—and how badly I really wanted it. I wanted to be considered by everyone the best college player in America. It wasn't just the award. You don't want the trophy just to look at it. It's what it stands for. If you believe in your heart that you are the best college football player in the country, it's nice to have that substantiated by a vote."

In 1968 Simpson set NCAA single-season records with 334 carries for 1,654 yards. And he got his trophy. His 1,750-point margin over Purdue's Leroy Keyes was the largest ever in Heisman balloting.

"They all say O.J. is the greatest," said Minnesota coach Murray Warmath, whose team was victimized by Simpson, "but he's been misrepresented. He's greater than that."

As a collegian, Simpson was a rare combination of speed, elusiveness and power. A 9.4 sprinter, he had been part of USC's world-record-setting 440-yard relay team. He had the ability to run through tacklers, but, more often, he would choose to employ his quickness, switch gears and go around them rather than give them a clear shot at him.

USC linebacker Jim Snow, who played against Simpson frequently in practice, said, "When most backs come through the line of scrimmage, you can miss them once and still have a second chance at tackling them. That's not true with O.J. If you miss him, that's it. He's gone."

The pros, in time, learned the same thing. All he did in the National Football League was to establish himself as perhaps the greatest runner of all time, the likes of Red Grange, Jim Brown, Gale Sayers and Walter Payton notwithstanding.

It has been a precipitous fall from grace for a man who once seemed to rise so effortlessly above the crowd.

O.J. (he was nicknamed Orange Juice, which was later shortened to just Juice) was drafted No. 1 by the talent-poor Buffalo Bills, who agreed to pay him $150,000 a year, which in 1969 was a record for a rookie.

Simpson was already a very wealthy young man even before he turned pro. After his college playing career ended, he went on a postseason tour, exuding warmth and charm all along the way as he signed contracts with Chevrolet, Royal Crown Cola and ABC-TV that made him a millionaire.

Simpson was worth the money the Bills paid him, too, although it took awhile for that to become apparent. In his first three NFL seasons, when the Bills went just 9–33, he was frequently used as a blocking back, and even a

more than 2,000 in one season. On his final rush of the day, on a snowy, frozen field, Simpson gained six yards to give him a total of 2,003.

Three seasons later, he gained a then-NFL record 273 yards in a game against the Detroit Lions. Spectacular games were almost commonplace. After a 227-yard performance by Simpson against Pittsburgh, Steeler defensive end Dwight White said, "O.J. leaps, he soars, he twists and turns and flies through the air. He's the greatest I ever saw."

Clearly, Simpson loved what he did, too. "Nothing," he said, "can compare to the feeling of being in a stadium of 80,000 people and they're all yelling, 'Juice, Juice, Juice!' My God, it's such a high."

In 1985, Simpson became the first Heisman Trophy winner to be enshrined in the Pro Football Hall of Fame, effectively ending the argument that Heisman winners never did well in the NFL.

But the charmed life abruptly ended in June 1994 when, as an astonished and riveted country looked on, Simpson was arrested for the brutal murder of his wife, Nicole Brown Simpson, and her friend Ronald Goldman.

Although acquitted, O.J.'s future still remains unknown. Perhaps that is only in keeping with the drama of a life whose reality has far outpaced the dreams - and now the nightmares - of most.

—*Dwight Chapin*

wide receiver.

But when Lou Saban took over as head coach in Buffalo, he put together a strong offensive line—the "Electric Company"—and gave Simpson the ball the same way McKay had. O.J. blossomed overnight.

In 11 seasons as a pro with the Bills and the San Francisco 49ers, Simpson led the league in rushing four times, finishing with 11,236 yards total and 61 rushing touchdowns. He had 1,000-yard seasons five straight years and gained 200 yards in a game six times.

Perhaps his most memorable achievement as a professional came in 1973. That December 16, he went into a game against the Jets at New York's Shea Stadium needing 197 yards rushing to become the first man ever to gain

In 1969 college football and the U.S. were in transition. These changes were best reflected by the December 5, 1969, issue of *Time* magazine. Its cover story about the My Lai massacre in Vietnam would fuel a tremendous amount of turmoil on college campuses across the country. The magazine also carried its annual upbeat story on that season's new Heisman Trophy winner, this one entitled "Boomer Sooner" in recognition of the powerful Oklahoma back who had been chosen to carry on the great Heisman tradition.

My Lai proved to be a turning point in the public's perception of the war. In a different arena, Steve Owens also represented change, a bridge between the old and new in the world of football.

At 6'2", 215-pounds, Owens was bigger than most running backs of his day but not as fast as the future big backs would get. He played most of his games on grass but would end his Sooner career on artificial turf in the first bowl game played indoors—the Bluebonnet Bowl in the Houston Astrodome.

There are more pictures of Owens in black and white than there are in color. That seems fitting. Owens wore black shoes, played on muddy fields and was one of the last backs to wear the T-bone face mask, with a vertical bar splitting his face and adding to the impression he gave of a charging rhino.

He had a gift for playing football, but it was his grit that made him such an unusual success. Owens was as consistent as a player could be, averaging 4.3 yards per carry every season in his three years at Oklahoma.

Owens received the Heisman as much for a sterling three-year career as for a dominating senior season. He ended with more carries (905) for more yards (3,867), more touchdowns (56) and more points (336) than any NCAA player before him. He was a two-time All-American and twice Big Eight player of the year. He still holds the NCAA record for touchdowns (56) and points (336) for a three-year career.

A homegrown Sooner star, Owens was raised in Miami, a small town in northeast Oklahoma with an often harsh climate. He was one of nine children. His father was a trucker who drove 18-wheelers and taught a strong work ethic, which Owens adopted.

Steve Owens

Mr. Consistency

"I'm a firm believer that if you work hard, you'll have rewards," Owens said. "I didn't have great speed.... So I worked harder to develop my strength and quickness and my blocking. I refined the talents I had."

He was one of many who grew up following Oklahoma under its legendary coach Bud Wilkinson. Six years old when the Sooners started their 47-game winning streak in 1953, Owens was 10 when it finally ended.

"I can't think of anything that brought as much glory to the state as those teams did," Owens once said. "Everybody followed them. When I was working at Hub's Bootery on Main Street, we didn't sell many shoes between noon and four on Saturdays."

Owens always wanted to play for the Sooners. But even though he had gained 4,000 yards rushing in a standout high school career, the Sooners still weren't sure where to play him. Barry Switzer, an Oklahoma backfield coach when Owens arrived as a freshman in 1966, wasn't all that impressed at first sight. "He looked slow and clumsy.... We had about decided to use him as a tight end," Switzer said.

Yet with time the verdict on Owens was to change.

It was production—not grace—that proved to be Owens's forte on the field. He specialized in running between tackles, not around end. Owens lined up in the traditional deep set as the tailback in the Oklahoma I formation, and he hit the line going full speed.

"He can fake people," one Oklahoma coach said. "But more often he just splatters 'em."

As both a junior and a senior, Owens distinguished himself by breaking records. He set seven NCAA marks, including one for going 17 consecutive regular-season games with 100 or more yards rushing and a single-game record of 55 carries against Oklahoma State in 1969. In the Big Eight he broke the career rushing record of Gale Sayers of Kansas and set the single-game record for touchdowns (five, against Nebraska, in 1968).

While Oklahoma struggled with injuries and compiled a 14–8 record under coach Chuck Fairbanks in 1968 and 1969, Owens remained a constant source of success, averaging 35 carries per game. He once had 150 carries in an Oklahoma practice. And despite his bruising style, he never missed a game.

The race for the Heisman that year was nationwide. Owens was the top running back, leading the nation in

Natural ability, hard work and true grit contributed to Steve Owens' great success.

rushing (1,523 yards) and edging out Cornell's Ed Marinaro. Ohio State had a trio of stars in quarterback Rex Kern, fullback Jim Otis and defensive back Jack Tatum. The top quarterbacks were Mike Phipps of Purdue, Mississippi's Archie Manning, Stanford's Jim Plunkett and Kansas State's Lynn Dickey.

The race came down to Owens and Phipps. Owens was sitting by the Oklahoma president's office and Phipps by Purdue's on November 25, 1969, when Owens was announced the winner by a vote of 1,488 to 1,334.

For Owens it solidified his place in college football history. "It's hard for me to realize I'm in this position," he said. "It's the greatest, greatest moment of my life." The day after the Heisman ceremony in New York, Owens flew with President Nixon on Air Force One to Fayetteville, Arkansas, to watch Texas beat Arkansas. Along the way Owens swapped memorabilia with Nixon, trading his Heisman cuff links for Nixon's, which were embossed with the presidential seal.

Following his college career, Owens was drafted in the first round by the Detroit Lions. His lack of speed had handicapped him among pro coaches. "The best compliment I received as an athlete was from a Cincinnati Bengals scout who said, 'Owens may run a 4.8-second, 40-yard dash, but he runs a 4.5 in his mind,'" Owens said. "He was right. I had to think faster, not make mental errors, be able to read defenses. I also had a high pain threshold, which allowed me to carry the ball a lot game after game."

Plagued by injuries his rookie season, Owens finally proved himself in the NFL by becoming the first Lion to rush for 1,000 yards in 1971 and earning All-Pro honors in 1971 and 1972. He played for six seasons before retiring in 1976 because of a severe knee injury.

Owens, whose son Mike became a freshman Sooner receiver in 1993, has remained close to the Oklahoma program and plays every year in the Sooners' alumni game. In the 1994 alumni game Owens broke free for a touchdown and was eventually brought down by Switzer in the end zone after Switzer had playfully jumped on Owens's back.

Off the field Owens has been as successful as he was in his playing days. As a Norman, Oklahoma, businessman, with interests in insurance and banking, he was a founding member of the Norman Public School Foundation and the Miami (Oklahoma) Public School Foundation. He has also been a spokesman for the Ronald McDonald House, which helps families with children who must endure long hospital stays, and is active with the Heisman Foundation. —DAVID MCNABB

Jim Plunkett

Against All Odds

One of the greatest quarterbacks in the history of college football almost didn't get to play the position.

Jim Plunkett got off to a late start his freshman season at Stanford because of neck surgery to remove a benign thyroid tumor. The operation left him weak, and his showing in the three games he played at quarterback did not impress coach John Ralston, who had serious thoughts of shifting him to defensive end.

Plunkett, even though his primary characteristic was shyness in those days, quickly balked at that idea.

"I am a quarterback," he informed Ralston.

And so he was, eventually. Big (6' 3", 204 pounds), strong (he could throw a football almost the length of a field) and accurate, Plunkett turned into a classic dropback quarterback, in three seasons passing for an NCAA-record 7,544 yards and rolling up 7,887 yards in total offense. And in 1970 he became Stanford's only Heisman Trophy winner.

Plunkett's story would have been a perfect plot for a Horatio Alger novel. A Mexican-American, he grew up poor, the son of William and Carmen Plunkett, both of whom are blind. Aided by welfare, William Plunkett supported his wife, son and two daughters by selling newspapers at the San Jose post office.

"My folks were poor and uneducated," Plunkett said, "but they didn't complain. They accepted what was good in life and what was bad. For me and my sisters, our lives were pretty much the same as our friends'. No one in our neighborhood had much money. The only difference was that because our parents were blind, we had to stay around the house a lot to make sure they were all right." Plunkett added to the family income by delivering newspapers and working as a gas station attendant and as a grocery clerk.

He first caught the notice of football scouts at the age of 14, when he threw a ball 63 yards in a schoolboy contest. And as a high school senior, he led James Lick High School of San

Plunkett, who threw so hard he left receivers' hands tingling, set NCAA marks for passing.

Jose to an undefeated season.

Plunkett wanted to stay close to his parents when it came time for college, so he only considered three schools—Stanford, Berkeley and Santa Clara. He chose Stanford but then had to overcome Ralston's doubts. Plunkett spent the entire summer after his freshman year throwing between 500 and 1,000 passes a day to convince himself that he had the strength and accuracy to make it

as a quarterback.

With three other quarterbacks on the Stanford roster, Ralston decided to redshirt Plunkett in his sophomore season. But once in the lineup, Plunkett quickly became a budding record breaker, and Ralston wisely changed his offense to take advantage of Plunkett's passing skills.

Ralston later said, "The difference between a great college quarterback and a great pro quarterback is often the ability to throw the ball hard. Jim has that talent. He can wear the skin off your hand if he can talk you into playing catch with him. After four passes you say, 'Forget it, Jim.' "

Because of his redshirt year, Plunkett had a chance to turn professional after his junior season, but he decided not to do so for two reasons. First, he said, he and his teammates still had something to accomplish: beating USC, then the West Coast's dominant team, and advancing to the Rose Bowl.

The second reason he opted to stay in school was more personal. "We are always telling kids not to drop out, to finish school, to set targets and work toward them," Plunkett said. "What would those kids think if I were to drop out now for professional football? I want to show them, by example, that dropping out of school is not the right move, especially for minority students."

In 1970, his last season, Plunkett was the cream of a terrific class of college senior quarterbacks that also included Archie Manning, Joe Theismann, Dan Pastorini, Ken Anderson and Lynn Dickey. UCLA coach Tommy Prothro called him "the best drop-back passer I've ever seen in college football." Plunkett not only led his team to a win over the Trojans, but he also helped Stanford upset Woody Hayes and Ohio State 27–17, in the Rose Bowl, shortly after he won the Heisman.

Receiving the award left him limp. "I'm in an emotional knot," he said in barely audible tones after the voting was announced. "I'm extremely honored. I feel this is a reflection on my coaches, and I would like to share the honor with them."

As expected, Plunkett, who graduated from Stanford with a degree in international relations, was the No. 1 pick in the 1971 NFL draft. He became an immediate starter for the New England Patriots, passing for 2,158 yards and winning rookie of the year honors. But over the next few seasons Plunkett had to scramble for his life behind a porous Patriot line. The battering he took led to two knee surgeries and three operations on his left shoulder during the next three years.

Plunkett chose Stanford in order to remain close to his parents, both of whom are blind.

Plunkett came home to the Bay Area in 1976, when the Patriots traded him to San Francisco, but he couldn't recapture his early pro magic and was released before the 1978 season began. Signs were that his professional career was over, but Al Davis, who had watched Plunkett go 0 for 11 in a 49er exhibition-game loss to the Oakland Raiders just before he was discarded, was there to pick up Plunkett on the rebound.

Plunkett didn't really get a chance to show what he could do until 1980, when he became the starter after Oakland quarterback Pastorini broke his leg. Plunkett went on to lead the Raiders to a victory in the 1981 Super Bowl where he was named the most valuable player.

"It was fun again to step on the football field," Plunkett said after that triumph. "I had almost begun to dread it, but all the good feelings returned, the things that make football so exciting for me—leading a team downfield, calling the play that works, throwing the long, beautiful spiral for a touchdown."

Plunkett remained the Raiders' No. 1 quarterback into the 1983 season, when Marc Wilson replaced him. Then when Wilson broke his shoulder, Plunkett was back in charge again and once more guided the Raiders to a win in the Super Bowl.

Plunkett, the man who more than once had been relegated to pro football's scrap heap, was 40 when he finally retired from the NFL. He had played 17 seasons. Pro Football Hall of Famer Ted Hendricks, a teammate on the Raiders, once said, "The offensive linemen love Jim so much they won't let anyone touch him."

Billy Sullivan, owner of the Patriots when Plunkett turned pro, paid him an even higher compliment. "Of all the people I've dealt with in sports—players, coaches, owners, fans, family—I've never met a finer person than Jim Plunkett.... When he started having success with the Raiders and finally won a championship, I don't think there was anyone happier for him than I was. I just can't say enough about Jim Plunkett."

Over the years Plunkett became a master at surviving adversity, including 11 operations, and finding a way to win. "I've had a lot of setbacks," he said, "but I'm the kind of guy who doesn't let them upset me. The setbacks have taught me not to get discouraged, even thought it's hard not to at times. I keep plugging away."

In 1988 Plunkett was named winner of the first Ernie Davis Award, which honors the All-America running back from Syracuse who died 17 months after winning the Heisman Trophy. The award salutes football players who display Davis's dedication to mankind, love of humanity and athletic prowess.

Plunkett now lives in the Bay Area with his wife, Jerry, and two children. An avid tennis player, he has a beer distributorship in San Jose and has worked as a radio and television sports commentator, which represents another huge step for a man who used to be so uncomfortable in the spotlight. —*DWIGHT CHAPIN*

Pat Sullivan

Rising to the Occasion

From 1969 to 1971, a lot of adjectives were used to describe the play of Auburn quarterback Pat Sullivan. But the one that seemed to stick was simple. Sullivan was inspiring.

How else to explain the burst of feeling from Auburn coach Shug Jordan, who was not known to be a man of great emotion, after watching Sullivan's memorable performance at Georgia on November 13, 1971? Jordan and about 60,000 others at Sanford Stadium in Athens had been mesmerized that day by Sullivan, who completed 14 of 24 passes for 248 yards and four touchdowns as the Tigers beat the previously undefeated and favored Bulldogs 35–20.

Sullivan had made successful throws from every spot on the field and from every position imaginable. One 27-yard completion to Dick Schmalz came while Sullivan was falling. He was literally sideways but used his powerful right arm to muscle the ball down the field.

The ultimate impact of Sullivan's memorable performance went far beyond keeping the Tigers undefeated. For it was common knowledge, or at least the common perception, that Sullivan was entering the game trailing in the race for the Heisman Trophy to Cornell running back Ed Marinaro.

Marinaro was a handsome, all-purpose back who would later go on to become a successful actor. Aside from his talent on the field, he was accessible, intelligent and had more national appeal than Sullivan, the sedate Southerner whose school had mounted only a low-key campaign. No Ivy League player had won the Heisman since Dick Kazmaier of Princeton in 1951, so Marinaro had another point in his favor.

But after watching Sullivan perform miracle after miracle against Georgia on that cool autumn afternoon, Jordan, the staid Auburn coach, became downright indignant when someone suggested that his quarterback might not win college football's highest honor. "Maybe not," said Jordan, "but if someone else does get it, I'll bet he's Christ reincarnated!"

Jordan then collected himself. "Hold it. I'm a religious man, and now I'll be up all night saying Hail Marys. Maybe I had better say that if someone else gets it, he'll have to be, uh ... magnificent."

Yes, Ed Marinaro was a very good football player, and he went on to have more success as a pro than Sullivan did. But when the votes were counted, Sullivan had edged Marinaro by 152 points in one of the closest Heisman races ever. Marinaro, in fact, had finished first in three of the five geographical voting areas—the East, the Midwest and the Far West—with Sullivan taking the South and the Southwest. Sullivan, however, received 60 more first-place votes.

The word came at halftime of the nationally televised game between Georgia and Georgia Tech in Atlanta. Unlike today, when the nominees are flown to New York for the ceremonies, Sullivan and his wife and daughter watched the game on TV with his parents. They had planned to watch the announcement at Auburn. But the television malfunctioned, and everyone raced over to a local hotel. Officials from the Downtown Athletic Club had to be called so that they could reach Sullivan by phone to officially give him the word.

The tiny little village of Auburn was overcome with emotion when the news came that one of its own had been named college football's best player. Immediately after the announcement, over 2,000 students converged on Toomers Corner, a downtown meeting area used to celebrate big football victories. Another huge crowd turned out at the school's basketball arena, where a press conference was hurriedly arranged.

Sullivan's road to the Heisman began when he went out for football in the sixth grade in his hometown of Birmingham, Alabama. It was an inauspicious start. His first coach put him at center, which Sullivan hated enough to quit. He came back a year later, and by then the parochial school coach, Brother Christopher, had noted young Sullivan's speed and throwing ability during baseball season. He moved him to quarterback—a position Sullivan would never relinquish.

Sullivan became a football legend at John Carroll High in Birmingham and was heavily recruited. But Auburn had an advantage. Assistant coach Gene Lorendo had begun recruiting Sullivan when he was a junior. After watching Sullivan perform in his first game that year, Lorendo hurried back to Jordan. "I don't care if I never recruit another soul for Auburn," he told the head coach. "Pat Sullivan is the boy to lead us out of the woods, and I want him."

Sullivan made his debut at Auburn in 1969 in spectacular fashion. The Tigers scored touchdowns on six of their

On that magical Saturday, Sullivan beat both Georgia and Marinaro.

first seven possessions and destroyed Wake Forest 57–0. The Auburn faithful could not believe their eyes. A new era was dawning for Tiger football and Mr. Sullivan was about to take them all on a wonderful three-year ride.

As a junior Sullivan set an NCAA record for yards gained per play (8.58), while leading the nation in total offense (259.6 yards per game), completion percentage (59.4 percent) and touchdown responsibility (26 running and throwing).

So Sullivan was certainly not unknown when the 1971 season began. He was the leading Heisman vote-getter returning from 1970 and had almost the same team around him for what would hopefully be a great season.

But Sullivan believed, as did his coach, that the award had to be won on the field. There would be no massive media campaign on his behalf. "Coach Jordan and I sat down that summer and discussed it," Sullivan recalled. "Basically he told me if I win an award, it will be because of the team's success. He told me just to play the season and let everything take care of itself."

Jordan remained true to his convictions. Sullivan's statistics for 1971 could have been even more impressive, but Jordan pulled his quarterback shortly after halftime in four of Auburn's first eight games. Jordan knew that if Sullivan was destined to win the Heisman, his moment to shine would come.

That brilliant Saturday afternoon in Athens, Georgia, was Sullivan's moment. It was a ticket scalper's dream come true. The demand to see the game was so great that men dressed in suits were climbing over fences to get into Sanford Stadium. There was an overwhelming sense that day that something special was going to take place. Sullivan did not disappoint.

"There can be no doubt that Pat Sullivan won the Heisman Trophy that day," said Georgia's Vince Dooley, who retired as coach of the Bulldogs after the 1988 season. Dooley's team was denied at least a share of the SEC title by Sullivan's heroics. It turned out to be the only loss in Georgia's 11–1 season.

Though Sullivan was named head coach at Texas Christian in 1992, a year after he was inducted into the College Football Hall of Fame, he is still remembered best for that one brilliant afternoon many years ago. "That day Sullivan did what many players only dream about," Dooley added. "He was a super player having a super day. I coached for 25 years, and I only saw it a handful of times. But that day we were beaten by the best quarterback I've ever seen." —TONY BARNHART

1972
Johnny Rodgers

From the Ghetto to Greatness

It was the game that football fans everywhere had talked about for weeks: defending national champion Nebraska, with a string of 20 consecutive victories, against Oklahoma, ranked No. 2, with a 9–0 record. From coast to coast, the late-season grudge match was billed as the Game of the Century. And when it was finally played, on Thanksgiving Day, November 25, 1971, the game actually lived up to the hype.

In front of 63,385 fans in Oklahoma's Owen Stadium and millions more watching on ABC-TV, Nebraska and Oklahoma swapped touchdowns evenly, four for four, and Oklahoma added a field goal. But there was one play that astonished the crowd: a sudden, shocking, dazzling punt return by Nebraska's Johnny Rodgers.

"It was one of those insanely thrilling things in which a single player, seized by the moment, twists, whirls, slips, holds his balance, and sprinting makes it all the way to the goal line," Dan Jenkins wrote in *Sports Illustrated*. "Rodgers went 72 yards for the touchdown, one which keeps growing larger in the minds of all."

When Rodgers raced over the line for the touchdown, the packed house erupted in pandemonium. Up in the press box, Lyle Bremser, the veteran voice of Nebraska football, shouted, "Take me now, Lord. I've seen it all." At the end of the game the scoreboard read 35–31, Nebraska. It was a sight Cornhusker fans would cherish for years.

On the field Rodgers was one of a kind. He overcame his size (5'9" and 173 pounds) with a jittery, swirling running style, piling up yards every way he could—catching passes, running kicks, sneaking the occasional carry out of the backfield. In three years he gained 5,586 all-purpose yards and scored 45 touchdowns. Indeed, it was Rodgers who made "all-purpose yards" a meaningful category (though the NCAA would not make it an official statistic until six years after he had graduated).

Off the field Rodgers's life has also been singular. A product of Omaha's northside ghetto, he has lived a life of

Rogers's twisting, twirling runs produced 17 touchdowns during his Heisman-winning senior season

controversy and contrasts.

Rodgers ran away from home at 14, rebelling against his mother and stepfather, who wanted him out earning money, not dreaming of athletic glory. He did not meet his father until he was 17. At 13, while horsing around with a pistol, Rodgers accidentally shot a friend in the stomach. Two years later he was stabbed in the back at a party. As his four-sport stardom made him a target of envy, Rodgers had to fight his way through high school. His coaches repeatedly took knives away from Rodgers, whose response was, "How am I going to get home?"

At Nebraska, Rodgers made himself famous with his on-field acrobatics and infamous by getting drunk on the last day of his freshman year and robbing a local grocery store. He and his pals got away with $91. Got away, that is, until Rodgers became a football hero as a sophomore, and one of his buddies began to brag about the robbery he had pulled with the great Johnny R. Soon everyone—including the police—knew the story. Rodgers was convicted but given a suspended sentence.

Heisman voters in 1972 had an unusual decision to make: Should college football's highest honor be given to a convicted felon? When they voted "yes," Rodgers became only the third receiver to win the Heisman Trophy. The others were ends Larry Kelley in 1936 and Leon Hart in 1949, athletes who, in a one-platoon era dominated by the single wing and other dense formations, were primarily blockers and defensive players.

Rodgers was something else entirely, a speedy dancer who specialized in the spectacular. His stunning cuts and 360-degree twists came not only from his brilliant athletic ability, but also from the fact that tacklers were continually surprising him. "He is half-blind," his high school coach and longtime friend, Dick Christie, once explained. "He has terrible vision. I asked him once how he caught the ball, and he told me, 'I just look for something fuzzy and brown and grab it.'"

In 1972 Nebraska coach Bob Devaney fielded a group that some consider the best college team of all time: Jerry Tagge at quarterback, Jeff Kinney at halfback and a defensive line that featured three All-Americas—end Willie Harper, tackle Larry Jacobson and noseguard Rich Glover.

Rodgers was the first of the great all-purpose runners, capable of rushing, receiving and returning kicks.

Most of all, though, Devaney had Rodgers. With no previous model for a multifaceted runner, Devaney had to concoct new ways to get Rodgers the ball in the open field. "I owe a lot to Coach Devaney," Rodgers has said. "It was an experimental type of thing. If I had to depend on just getting the ball as a running back or wingback or just catching passes, I wouldn't have had it often enough to make a difference." But make a difference he did. Rodgers possessed a gift for making big plays in big games. In the 1972 Orange Bowl he contributed another punt return masterpiece, a 77-yard run through mystified Alabama tacklers as Nebraska won 38–6 to lock up a second national championship.

During Rodgers's senior year Nebraska's record was "only" 9-2-1. But, if anything, Rodgers raised his game. He scored 17 touchdowns and set Cornhusker single-season marks for catches (55) and yards receiving (942). He also pioneered a theatrical tradition now widespread, finishing a 64-yard punt return against Minnesota by high-stepping into the end zone … *backwards*.

In his last game, against Notre Dame in the 1973 Orange Bowl, Rodgers put on one of the greatest displays of multitalented excellence in college football history. Moved to deep back in the I formation for the only full game of his career, he skittered for 81 yards and three rushing touchdowns. He also caught three passes, sprinting 50 yards with one for a touchdown. Finally, in his first passing attempt of the season, he lofted a perfect spiral to Nebraska end Frosty Anderson for 52 yards and six points. Those five touchdowns made it easy for the Cornhuskers, 40–6.

Rodgers's pro career proved anticlimactic. He spent four years with the Montreal Alouettes, even though the San Diego Chargers had drafted him in the first round. In his first two years in Montreal, where he was brilliant when used, his personal style—featuring a Rolls-Royce and a different fur coat for every day of the week—earned him the cheers of Canadian fans and the nickname Johnny R. Superstar. But in his final two Canadian seasons, Rodgers skipped meetings and missed games with injuries. He later signed with the Chargers, but saw his career fizzle out with a succession of leg injuries. After retiring from football Rodgers founded a successful magazine publishing firm. In 1993 he returned to the University of Nebraska to finish his degree.

Looking back at it, the 1972 college football season was memorable for many reasons. As the Heisman race between Rodgers and Oklahoma's Greg Pruitt began to heat up, a number of sportswriters took shots at Rodgers because of the $91 robbery. To their credit, though, most saw Rodgers for what he was: a spectacular talent outgrowing a horrific childhood. In 1972 he was the best player in the country. No one else was close.
—BOB OATES AND BOB OATES JR.

1973

John Cappelletti

Something for Joey

When John Cappelletti accepted the Heisman Memorial Trophy, he dedicated the award to his 11-year-old brother, Joey, who was already battling the leukemia that would take his life in April 1976. It was an act that touched the hardened hearts of Wall Street merchants and had cynical journalists and professional athletes wiping their misty eyes.

Speaking to a gathering that included Vice President Gerald R. Ford and other luminaries, the big Penn State tailback offered a gift to Joey from deep in his heart.

"The youngest member of my family, Joseph, is very ill. He has leukemia. If I can dedicate this trophy to him tonight and give him a couple days of happiness, this is worth everything."

With Joey and his parents in the audience, John Cappelletti continued, "A lot of people think that I go through a lot on Saturdays and during the week as most athletes do. You get your bumps and bruises, and it is a terrific battle out there on the field. Only for me it is on Saturdays, and it's only in the fall. For Joseph, it is all year round, and it is a battle that is unending with him. He puts up with much more than I'll ever put up with, and I think that this trophy is more his than mine because he has been a great inspiration to me."

Asked to give the traditional blessing at the conclusion of the Heisman Trophy dinner, Archbishop Fulton J. Sheen said, "Maybe for the first time you have heard a speech from the heart and not from the lips. Part of John's triumph was made by Joseph's sorrow. You don't need a blessing. God has already blessed you in John Cappelletti."

The first Heisman Trophy winner at Penn State, Cappelletti himself was not unfamiliar with adversity. He had coordination problems as a child, constantly tripping when he walked or ran. As a senior at Penn State he suffered a painful deep thigh muscle bruise in preseason practice in the summer of 1973. But with his leg taped tightly every Saturday afternoon, Cappelletti went on to become only the third man in Penn State's glorious football history to gain over 1,000 yards in a season and the first to rush for more than 1,000 yards in two seasons.

Cappelletti's large frame carried him over and around tacklers for a total of 1,522 yards in 1973.

Cappelletti spent his sophomore season at Penn State as a defensive back. He did this as coach Joe Paterno directed two of the nation's best running backs of 1971, Franco Harris and Lydell Mitchell. The following year, with Harris and Mitchell off to the pros, Paterno switched the powerful 6' 1", 205-pound Cappelletti to tailback, where over the next two seasons he would lead Penn State to a 22–2 record.

Paterno and his Penn State publicists didn't have to raise a finger on Cappelletti's behalf. He won the Heisman Trophy in a cakewalk after a season of 1,522 yards rushing and 19 touchdowns, including more than 200 yards rushing in each of Penn State's last three regular-season games. Those 200-plus efforts in three straight games established a major college record at the time and included 220 yards in a 35–29 victory over Lou Holtz's North Carolina State team.

These numbers assured the Nittany Lions of a spot in the 1974 Orange Bowl against Louisiana State. Penn State won the New Year's game 16–9, despite the fact that Cappelletti played with a sprained ankle on a surface still slick from a heavy downpour that preceded the kickoff. He gained 50 yards and scored one touchdown, just a so-so outing for his final game as Penn State's tailback. But bowl games had always been sort of a jinx for Cappelletti. A year earlier he missed the Sugar Bowl game against Oklahoma because he was sick with the flu and had a 102° temperature at game time. Penn State lost that game 14–0, one of only two losses for the Nittany Lions in Cappelletti's two seasons on offense. The other loss was at Tennessee in Penn State's 1972 opener.

After rather easy triumphs on the road against Stanford and Navy to open the 1973 season, Penn State played the first of its six home games that year against Iowa on Homecoming Day, September 29. By this time Cappelletti was the talk of the East, if not the nation. National recognition would come as the victories mounted along with Cappelletti's yardage.

Cappelletti was also the talk of the Beaver Stadium press box at Penn State. Each Saturday bets were made among the reporters just before Penn State, with Cappelletti at tailback, staged its first play of the predictable Paterno attack. The wagering was made over the earth-shaking issue—Would Cappelletti go off right tackle or would he go off left tackle on the first offensive play of the game?

Cappelletti always tested the defenders right up the gut on opening plays. But the Penn State sweep was also a show as Cappelletti went fast and powerfully around the wide corners behind the blocking of Mark Markovich, the guard who was one of his best friends. Cappelletti once quipped during the 1973 season that "I've followed Markovich around so much on the field that I'm starting to follow him around on campus."

Paterno had a fine bunch of blockers in addition to Markovich, making it imperative that he stick with his sometimes monotonous offense of Cappelletti right, Cappelletti left. One Air Force defender expressed total surprise when told that Cappelletti did not actually carry on every single play as Penn State whipped the Falcons 19–9 on October 6, 1973. "You can't prove it by me," he said. "I thought he was in there every play. Felt like it."

Cappelletti was a fullback at a tailback's position at Penn State. His was a one-man attack of rushing power and speed. The plunge, the sweep and the strength needed for each made up Cappelletti's artistry. Like all successful coaches, Paterno knew how to highlight his players' skills to best advantage. So if his tailback was a powerful full-back type, naturally Paterno developed a program empha-sizing power running.

The result in 1973 was that by pounding team after team with Cappelletti's running, the Nittany Lions had a perfect season. The big tailback won the Heisman Trophy by a two-to-one margin over his nearest rival, John Hicks of Ohio State.

Cappelletti went on to a good professional football career as a fullback, starting out with the Los Angeles Rams in 1974 behind the well-established National Football League running star Lawrence McCutcheon. Then at San Diego he was a running back in a pass-ori-ented attack. Injuries and illness interfered with his pro career, but he completed a decade in the NFL before retiring to go into the real estate business in California.

Cappelletti married his high school sweetheart, the for-mer Betty Berry, and has four sons. He was inducted into the College Football Hall of Fame in 1993.

Through all his success, the big, gentle man remained rather humble. That was spelled out clearly in his famous Heisman Trophy acceptance speech which remains his primary legacy. His speech was so touching that CBS-TV aired a two-hour movie in 1977 about the football play-er and his family from Upper Darby, Pennsylvania. It was entitled, *Something for Joey*.

After all, the 1973 Heisman Trophy was and will always remain just that: "Something for Joey."

—*GORDON S. WHITE, JR*

1974·75
Archie Griffin

In a Class of His Own

There were players who ran for more yards. There were players who instilled deeper memories of their spectacular dashes to glory. There definitely were players who went on to have better pro careers and some whose national fame endured long after their last run.

Yet of all the great college football players, only one has two Heisman Trophies. For that achievement Archie Griffin will always hold a unique and treasured place in college football history.

Griffin was an unlikely Heisman candidate. The press guides claimed that he stood between 5'9" and 5'11", but in reality Griffin was just under 5'8" and weighed only 182 pounds. His first coach in the NFL, Cincinnati's Bill Johnson, said of him, "When you first look at him, you say, 'My god, look how little he is.'"

Griffin clearly was a fighter. He always talked of "the three D's: determination, dedication and desire." This wasn't a corny slogan for Griffin, it was a way of life—and what set him apart on the football field.

Woody Hayes called Griffin the greatest runner he ever saw, which takes in more than a few outstanding players. What impressed the hard-nosed Hayes most was Griffin's ability to block. "Archie Griffin is the greatest back I've ever seen or coached," Hayes said. "He's also the most popular player we've ever had, by far. In fact, we value Archie's attitude more than his football ability. Which is saying something, because he can do everything. He's a great blocker, a great faker and a great broken-field runner, one of those rare backs who can run over you or around you. It's like Rommel's wide-front attack or Sherman maneuvering through Georgia. No one ever knew which way they were going either, and from there on it was strictly option football."

Though Hayes praised him for his blocking, Griffin ran for 100 yards in 31 games, an NCAA record.

Indiana's Lee Corso said of Griffin: "He has unbelievable peripheral vision. I saw him go through a hole in our line that wasn't there. It was off-tackle to the left. You could see the hole develop, but then three of

our men played it perfectly and closed it up. Griffin suddenly got through for 12 yards. It was one of the greatest runs I've ever seen."

Griffin's roots with Ohio State went extremely deep. He was born in the campus hospital in 1954, the fourth of James and Margaret Griffin's eight children. His father used to work several jobs to support the family. Archie called him "the hardest-working man there ever was." His father's goal was to send all of his children to college. He met that goal. In addition, two of Archie's brothers, Ray and Keith, also went on to have careers in the National Football League.

When it came time to pick a college, Griffin almost chose Northwestern. He liked its academic reputation, and he thought he was too small to play at Ohio State. Hayes, though, had different thoughts. He put a full-court press on both Griffin and his family. Hayes's wife, Anne, even took Mrs. Griffin to lunch. Hayes always said after-

ward that that had sealed the deal.

Griffin's college career had an unimpressive start. In his first game he bobbled a pitchout for a five-yard loss. Officially, in 1.5 minutes of action he did not carry the ball. The next game, though, was a different story. Griffin didn't expect to play, but Rudy Hubbard, one of Hayes's assistants, implored the coach to put in Griffin. Hayes would never again think twice about using Griffin, who had runs of 32, 22 and 55 yards. When it was over he had rushed for 239 yards in a 29–14 win over North Carolina. A stunned Tar Heel coach Bill Dooley said, "We came here not even knowing Archie Griffin existed, and now you tell me he's a freshman!"

Griffin finished his freshman year rushing for 772 yards and three touchdowns. As a sophomore he emerged as a bona fide star, rushing for 1,428 yards, averaging 6.3 yards per carry and finishing fifth in the Heisman balloting. In that year's Rose Bowl, Griffin ran for 149 yards in the

Buckeyes' 42–21 win over USC.

There was no stopping Griffin during his junior year. He gained 1,620 yards rushing and ripped through the Big Ten, with hated rival Michigan looming in the season finale. Griffin's presence only fueled the already intense rivalry between Hayes and his protégé, Bo Schembechler. Before the game a Wolverine player said, "If Archie Griffin gains 100 yards, it will be over my dead body." Griffin wasn't bothered by the remark, but it fired up the Buckeyes' offensive line. Griffin rushed for 111 yards in Ohio State's 12–10 win, which sent them to another Rose Bowl.

A few weeks later Griffin won his first Heisman, easily outdistancing Southern Cal's Anthony Davis and prompting a popular bumper sticker in Columbus: THANK YOU, MRS. GRIFFIN. During his emotional acceptance speech, Griffin said, "To me, football represents the good things in life. I'll do everything in my power to set the greatest example. If today's young people look up to the Heisman winners and other stars the way I did, they'll do as I did."

The only dark spot for Griffin came in the ensuing Rose Bowl. The Buckeyes blew a shot at the national championship, suffering a heartbreaking 18–17 loss to the Trojans.

Of all the legendary players who have won the Heisman, only Griffin has done so twice.

All eyes were focused on Griffin the next year. Could he win a second Heisman? His mother had a premonition. "When he was in high school, I saw it all in a dream," Margaret Griffin said. "I saw Archie standing with the Heisman Trophy. I saw us standing beside him and all the people gathered around. Well, I had that dream more than once."

Griffin, though, knew it would be tough. It's one thing for a defensive player to apply a solid hit on an ordinary running back. It's quite another to cream a Heisman Trophy winner. "Arch gets hit almost every play, and when he has the ball, he gets hit about four times," Hayes said. He had Griffin use linemen's thigh pads to soften the blows, but they did little good. The bruised and battered Griffin was rarely able to practice before Wednesday after Saturday's game.

"Being tagged the Heisman winner, naturally guys on other teams were after me more," Griffin said. "They all tackled me clean but hard. They might say a few things like, 'Get up, Heisman winner.'" But Griffin prevailed. He was the dominant force on a Buckeye team that went through the regular season undefeated.

When it came time for the 1975 Heisman vote, there was some sentiment for California's Chuck Muncie, who had outrushed Griffin by 103 yards that season and had a 6.4-yards-per-carry average, compared to Griffin's 5.5. Nevertheless, over a remarkable three-year stretch Griffin had an NCAA-record 31 games where he rushed for more than 100 yards. The award went to Griffin.

Practice obviously makes perfect. After being overcome by emotion in his first Heisman ceremony, Griffin was much more composed the second time around. "Winning the Heisman is a dream I first had when I was nine," Griffin said. "To have it happen once was great. Then to go back again … it's a great feeling."

His career ended on a sour note when UCLA upset the No. 1 Buckeyes in the Rose Bowl, 23–10. Griffin called it "the biggest disappointment" in his career. He quickly got over it, graduating ahead of his class. Griffin then went out and gave motivational talks to youngsters, spreading his motto of "Determination, dedication and desire."

Griffin's pro career was average. The Bengals picked him in the first round of the 1976 draft. He finished his rookie year rushing for 625 yards, and in 1979 he ran for 688 yards (a 4.9 average) and had 43 pass receptions. Unfortunately, Griffin never got to carry the full load for the Bengals. When Cincinnati earned a trip to Super Bowl XVI in January 1982, Griffin had only one rush for four yards. The Bengals didn't offer him a contract after the 1983 season, thus ending his NFL career. The next year he had a brief fling with Jacksonville in the USFL.

Bengal owner Paul Brown called Griffin "a class person," stating that Griffin should be proud of his years in Cincinnati. Griffin agreed. "People don't think I'm happy with my NFL career. But I averaged four yards per carry, and I caught a lot of passes. I had a good Super Bowl year. I really do feel satisfied."

After football there was only one logical place for Griffin to land: Ohio State. Hayes suggested that Griffin go back to work for his alma mater. Griffin now serves as an assistant athletic director and one of the school's top ambassadors.

"College, in general, was the greatest time of my life—the people I know, the people who have helped me, the education I received. Those things will be with me forever. The Heisman is a part of all this."

Actually, two parts of it. For two glorious autumns in Columbus, Griffin stood on top of the college football world. And when it comes to future Heisman winners, Griffin will continue to be the measuring stick.

—*ED SHERMAN*

It was a moment that changed Tony Dorsett's life.

When he was a junior in high school, Dorsett saw his steel-worker father walk out of the mill in Aliquippa, Pennsylvania, for the first time. He was so covered in dirt and grime that his son barely recognized him.

"My dad always told me not to get stuck in a steel mill, and that day convinced me," Dorsett said. "I made up my mind right there, I'd be a great football player."

That determination helped make him one of the greatest college and pro players of all time. During four All-American years at the University of Pittsburgh, he gained an NCAA-record 6,082 yards, broke Glenn Davis's collegiate scoring mark, with 356 points, won the Heisman Trophy and led a school that was 1–10 the year before he arrived to three bowl games and a national championship.

"He's the most exciting running back I've ever seen," said Pitt coach Johnny Majors during Dorsett's freshman season. "He has the most running ability I've ever seen. He's the best young running back I've ever seen—period!"

"I hate to practice against him," said Pitt teammate Al Romano. "Trying to tackle him is like trying to catch a fly." Dorsett developed his moves on a rock-covered playground in Aliquippa, a rough neighborhood where gangs battled with bats and bottles. "I was too scared to fight those big guys," Dorsett said. "That's how I think I got so fast—running away from those bloody fights."

Though he weighed only 155 pounds, Dorsett's running ability made him one of the top high school players in the nation. Majors got his first glimpse of Dorsett at a high school all-star game, where he dazzled everyone with his clever cutbacks, blazing speed and surprising power. "I had to control my enthusiasm in the press box," Majors said. "I was very enthusiastic, but I walked out of there very quietly ... went back to the motel and shouted 'Hallelujah!' when I closed the door to my room."

Dorsett, nicknamed Hawk because of his wide-set eyes, could have gone to a perennial power such as Penn State or Southern Cal. But he chose to stay close to home and help Majors revive the lowly Panthers, who hadn't had a winning season since 1963. It didn't take long for them to turn the program around.

Dorsett rushed for 101 yards in his first game and went on to gain 1,586 yards in 1973, at the time the most ever by a college freshman. He led the Panthers to a 6-5-1

1976

Tony Dorsett

"Like Trying to Catch a Fly"

record and a berth in the Fiesta Bowl, their first postseason appearance in 17 years. "We knew he was good," Majors said, "but we had no idea he'd do so well so soon."

As a sophomore Dorsett gained 1,004 yards and set the school's career rushing record in only his 15th game. The following year he rushed for 1,544 yards, including an amazing 303-yard performance against Notre Dame. He closed his junior season with 142 yards and two touchdowns in a Sun Bowl victory over Kansas, the Panthers' first bowl triumph since 1937.

But Dorsett, now a chiseled 5'11", 192-pounder, saved his best for last. As a senior he led the country in rushing, scoring and all-purpose yards as Pitt went 12–0 and won the national championship. The Panthers opened the season at Notre Dame, which had devised new defensive schemes to stop Dorsett. They didn't work. Dorsett rushed for 181 yards, including 61 on his first carry, as Pitt prevailed 31–10. "We called a direct dive up the middle, and Tony became like a man possessed," Majors said of Dorsett's long run. "He squirmed through a hole, broke three tackles, slipped and slid and damn near took my breath away. He ran for 61 yards, and it broke Notre Dame's heart."

Opponents occasionally contained Dorsett for a quarter or a half but not for an entire game. After Penn State held him to 51 yards in the first half, Majors switched him from tailback to fullback. Dorsett responded with 173 yards and a touchdown in the second half as Pitt broke open a close game for a 24–7 victory. Asked to describe Dorsett, Penn State coach Joe Paterno said, "How many ways can you say *great*?"

Heisman Trophy voters were equally impressed. Dorsett won the award by a huge margin, beating runner-up Ricky Bell of Southern Cal by 1,011 points. "Ever since I made All-America as a freshman, this trophy has been what I wanted most," Dorsett said. "It recognizes me as the best."

Dorsett was at his best in the Sugar Bowl, rushing for 202 yards and a touchdown as Pitt defeated Georgia 27–3 to capture the national title. "T.D. is quicker than a hiccup and tougher than week-old bread," bragged a Pitt assistant coach. As Majors said: "He has the heart to back up his feet. He won't shrink from

Dorsett evaded tacklers and outdistanced the Heisman field en route to an equally brilliant career in the pros.

a challenge. When one presents itself, he gets tougher."

Drafted in the first round by the Dallas Cowboys, Dorsett gained more than 1,000 yards in eight of his first nine NFL seasons; the exception was the strike-shortened 1982 season. He was named NFC Rookie of the Year in 1977 and helped the Cowboys beat the Denver Broncos in the Super Bowl. Dallas returned to the Super Bowl the following year, losing to Pittsburgh despite a 96-yard rushing effort by Dorsett.

On January 3, 1983, he set an unbeatable record with a 99-yard touchdown dash—the longest from scrimmage in NFL history—against the Minnesota Vikings in a televised Monday-night game. Remarkably, the Cowboys only had 10 men on the field, and Dorsett wasn't even supposed to run the ball. The intended ballcarrier, fullback Ron Springs, got his signals crossed and mistakenly left the field. So Dorsett took the handoff from quarterback Danny White, cut right, eluded a tackler, sprinted down the sideline and straight-armed the last defender in his way. "Ron Springs has some pretty good moves himself," said Cowboy assistant coach Al Lavan, "but there were a couple of things on that play that only Tony could do."

Injuries slowed Dorsett in 1986, but he still led the Cowboys in rushing for the 10th consecutive season. He was traded to Denver in 1988 and gained a team-high 703 yards in his first season with the Broncos. But a knee injury forced him to miss the entire 1989 season, and he never played again.

"When you think about great players, maybe Tony Dorsett would be considered because I gave people their money's worth," he said after announcing his retirement in 1990. At the time Dorsett owned a Super Bowl ring and, with 12,739 yards, a spot just behind Walter Payton on the NFL career-rushing list. As a pro, Dorsett played in two Super Bowls, four Pro Bowls and five NFC Championship Games. But his fondest football memories were of those glory days at Pitt. "I think back to those college days often, and I can't help but smile," said Dorsett, now a businessman in Dallas. "I've never had more fun in my life. We were a part of history. We helped save Pitt football."

Dorsett's son, Anthony Jr., is now following in his father's footsteps by playing for Majors at Pitt. He avoids comparisons, though, by playing defense. It is a wise decision. As Majors once said, "I could coach another hundred years and never get the opportunity to coach another back like Dorsett." —RICK WARNER

Earl Campbell

The Pride of Tyler, Texas

Earl Campbell had some ambitious goals when he entered the University of Texas in the fall of 1974.

"Before I leave, I want to gain 2,000 yards in one season, win the Heisman Trophy, be on a national championship team and help us win the Southwest Conference the next three years. Then I want to turn pro and sign for enough money to buy Mama a new house," he wrote in a freshman paper.

Had Texas coach Darrell Royal seen that paper, he probably would have whistled softly and exclaimed, "Way to go, Earl!" But Royal was already certain that his prized recruit, a soft-spoken farm boy from the Tyler rose fields, could become one of football's alltime great running backs. "Earl was good enough as a freshman to go into pro football," Royal said a few years later, after Campbell had won the Heisman Memorial Trophy, signed with the Houston Oilers as their No. 1 choice and built Ann Campbell a lovely brick home about 50 yards down Texas Farm Road 492 from the faded three-bedroom frame house where she and her late husband, B.C., had raised 11 children. "I'm not saying he would have been a star immediately. He wasn't ready to play, but no one would have had the guts to cut him and let him go somewhere else for seasoning, because you could see the raw talent there."

Earl brought that raw talent with him to Austin after leading John Tyler High School to the Texas Class 4A championship and earning schoolboy All-America honors in 1973. But getting there hadn't been easy. His father, an expert rose budder—one who takes a limb from a bush and ties it into a seedling, which a year later produces roses—died when Earl was 11. Before B.C. died he taught his children this skill. "When I was five he took me to the fields," said Earl, the sixth child in the family. "That was very important later."

After her husband's funeral Ann Campbell was determined that she and her children stay together. "I told them I was by myself now, and I had to have

Inspired by the changes made in the Longhorn offense, Campbell averaged 6.5 yards per carry in 1977.

their help. I told them I would put clothes on their backs and food in their mouths, but that I couldn't afford to pay their fines if they got in jail. If they got in trouble with the police, they'd just have to take care of it themselves."

But Earl soon fell to drinking and carousing with a group of older guys. In later years he called this his "Bad Earl" period. He never got into drugs, but he was heading for trouble. "Earl was going over Fool's Hill," Ann Campbell said. "I finally sat him down and gave him a talking to. I told him to get hold of himself. If he did, he could go places in life."

Earl didn't shape up until ninth grade, when the school district started busing students to achieve racial integration. Earl was transferred across town to Moore Junior High, a previously all-white school that also had a new head football coach, a black man named Lawrence

LaCroix. "Coach LaCroix always would sit me down and tell me about things outside of football," Campbell said. "I guess it was like a father seeing potential in his kid when the kid can't see it himself. Lots of afternoons he'd give me a ride part of the way home, and he'd talk about how there could be so many good things ahead. 'Now, Earl, you can do it,' he'd say, 'but you've got to do it this way, because this is right.'"

Campbell ultimately found the way. In the years ahead he would move to a different type of fast lane. This one took him all the way to the Heisman Trophy and the Pro Football Hall of Fame.

College football's most famous schools pursued Earl after his smashing senior season at Tyler High, but some tried to land him by offering him more than the NCAA allowed, promising cars, clothes, cash and help for his mother. On a cold January evening in 1974, Royal visited Earl and his mother at their home. Royal made it clear that Earl would be welcome at Texas on a scholarship, but that he would not be offered anything illegal. "Earl, if this is a factor, and that is what you want, please don't string me along," Royal said. "Some way or another, let me know you're not interested in us if you're going to go for that kind of a deal."

Earl looked Royal straight in the eye. "Coach, my people were bought and sold when they didn't have a choice," he said. "Nobody is going to buy Earl."

"That impressed me," Royal said. "I knew he had tremendous pride." A few weeks later Earl signed with the Longhorns and became the cornerstone of a strong recruiting class, one that Royal, college football's Coach of the Decade in the 1960s, hoped would take the University of Texas to the top again.

Campbell, 6' 1" and 220 pounds, with powerful legs and a sprinter's speed, had played half-back in high school but quickly adjusted to the demands of playing fullback in Royal's wishbone offense. He lined up two yards behind the quarterback and one step up from the halfbacks and was the key to the offense, with its premium on strong running. As a freshly minted fullback, Campbell rushed for 928 yards and a 5.7 average during Texas's 8–4 season in 1974, then gained 1,118 yards (a 5.6 average) in 1975 when Texas went 10–2. That year Campbell made the Coaches' All-America team, but on the first day of spring practice in 1976 he pulled a hamstring. He missed the rest of the spring workouts and ballooned to 240 pounds.

Hampered by the bad leg and the extra weight,

Few Heisman winners were more deserving than NCAA rushing and scoring champion Earl Campbell.

Campbell played erratically most of his junior year and so did the Longhorns. He missed three games as Texas went 5-5-1—Royal's only nonwinning record in 20 UT seasons—and rushed for a mere 653 yards (a 4.7 average).

Royal retired after the 1976 season, leaving with a .778 winning percentage, the highest in SWC history. He also endowed his successor, Fred Akers, with an athlete who would become an incredible force in 1977.

Once spring practice arrived Campbell was healthy again, but Akers was unhappy with his weight of 242. He told him to lose 23 pounds. "Where am I going to find 23 pounds to lose?" Campbell asked veteran UT trainer Frank Medina. "I don't know," Medina replied. "It might be in your butt, but we are going to lose it."

Thus began Campbell's pursuit of the Heisman Trophy.

While Campbell reported to Medina at 7 a.m. daily, spending 25 minutes in the steam room wearing a sweat suit and a rubber suit, then doing 300 sit-ups, Akers revamped the Texas offense. He junked the wishbone and put Campbell at left halfback in the veer formation and at tailback in the I. That fall, playing at his old freshman weight of 220 pounds and running with a fury sparked by this exciting new offense, Campbell blew out of the gate and brought the Longhorns with him. They outscored Boston College, Virginia and Rice by a total of 184–15 and climbed to a No. 5 national ranking. After Campbell delivered a virtuoso performance in a 13–6 win over No. 2 Oklahoma, Sooner coach Barry Switzer sought him out to shake hands. "I hope you win the Heisman Trophy," Switzer said, "and I think you should."

At the end of an 11–0 regular season Texas was ranked No. 1, Campbell was the national rushing champion, with 1,744 yards (a 6.5 average), and Heisman voters across America had come to agree with Switzer.

The UT delegation that came to the Downtown Athletic Club that December night filled 10 tables, with a chair of honor reserved for Ann Campbell. Earl, who was wearing a yellow rose in the lapel of his tuxedo, accepted his trophy from Jay Berwanger, the original Heisman winner, and 1968 recipient O.J. Simpson. As Campbell and his mother stood amid the flash of photographers' lights in the big ballroom, the bad times and the hard times seemed far away. "Mama, this is your award," Earl told her. "You've worked so hard. If it hadn't been for you, I wouldn't have gone as far as I did in life."

Campbell knew that countless people in Texas were rejoicing with him that night, so he took the trophy back to Austin where thousands could see it. Then he took it home to Tyler, to his mama's house.   —*Sam Blair*

1978
Billy Sims

He Sparked a Border War

When Oklahoma touts its successful tradition, some Texans scoff. At the top of their list of complaints is Billy Sims.

Depending on which side of the Red River the view is from, the Sooners either stole or recruited Sims from Hooks, Texas in a near legendary recruiting battle. Sooner coach Barry Switzer put a premium on luring talented players out of Texas. And Switzer wanted Sims so much that he had an Oklahoma assistant spend 77 nights in a motel near Hooks so that they could land the gifted athlete. Switzer once even called Sims at halftime of a Sooners' rout over Colorado.

The NCAA would later institute reforms limiting such contacts in an effort to end the overwhelming intensity in the recruiting of players like Sims.

But it was unanimously agreed on both sides of the border that Sims was worth the effort. The heralded running back would win the Heisman Trophy as a junior, in 1978, and finish second in the balloting the following year. In 1980 Sims would become the NFL's Rookie of the Year.

Sims moved from St. Louis to tiny Hooks (population 2,500) in East Texas when he was 13 years old. Along with Earl Campbell of Tyler and Eric Dickerson of Sealy, Sims quickly became one of the reasons for the legendary quality of East Texas high school football.

There's no doubt where Sims considers home. When his 4.5 year NFL career with the Detroit Lions was ended by a severe knee injury, Sims returned to his farm near Hooks.

In high school Sims gained more than 100 yards in each of his 38 games and scored a total of 78 touchdowns. In half of his games he had more than 250 yards. "He had it all when he came here," Switzer once said. "He was a great back in high school. He was a superstar. You looked at him and it made you laugh and giggle to know he was coming here. You took great pride in the fact he was coming to Oklahoma."

Sims was a star among stars at Oklahoma in 1978 and 1979—when the Sooners' only two losses likely cost them back-to-back national championships. As a freshman, however, Sims played only sparingly on the Sooners' 1975 national championship team. His rise to the top would take some time. A cracked shoulder and a severe ankle injury held him to 545 yards on 83

Sims often took to the air while picking up 1,762 yards in his Heisman-winning junior year.

carries in his first three years. Sims was granted a medical hardship after playing only one game in 1976, giving him an extra year of eligibility.

Switzer's support for Sims helped him through those first trying years. "I felt like going home, because it wasn't working out at all," Sims said. "But I was never a quitter. I never shied away from hard work. I knew that sooner or later, I'd stay healthy and have a good season. There was another reason I stayed—Barry Switzer. He never gave up on me. He told me I could be a great player."

That greatness would come in 1978.

Sims exploded in his junior season. He moved into the national spotlight in the fourth game of the season, when he rushed for 131 yards as Oklahoma beat Texas 31–10. A powerfully built six-foot, 205-pound halfback in Oklahoma's wishbone attack, Sims became the first Big Eight player with three consecutive 200-yard rushing games (against Iowa State, Kansas State and Colorado). He ended up as the nation's leading rusher, with 1,762 yards, and the No. 1 scorer, with 20 touchdowns.

His biggest tests came against the Sooners' Big Eight rival, Nebraska. On November 11, 1978, Nebraska knocked Oklahoma off its No. 1 perch with a 17–14 victory. A key play in the game occurred when Sims lost a fumble at Nebraska's three-yard line with 3:27 remaining. Even though Sims had scored the Sooners' sole touchdown and rushed for 153 yards, many thought he would only be remembered for the crucial fumble.

"I got hate mail after that game saying, 'You fumbled the Heisman away,' " Sims said upon receiving the 1978 Heisman award. In the tightest Heisman race since 1956, Sims held off Penn State quarterback Chuck Fusina. Sims actually had fewer first-place votes (163–151) than Fusina but won with 77 more total points.

The memories of the ill-fated Oklahoma-Nebraska game stayed with Sims. He would not let a repeat occur. In a dramatic rematch of their regular-season game, Sims was named the offensive MVP in a 31–24 victory over the Cornhuskers in the 1979 Orange Bowl. He led his team on a 17-point, third-quarter burst which gave Oklahoma a 31–17 lead. Sims ended the contest with 134 yards rushing on 25 carries and two touchdowns.

Of all the tremendous running backs Oklahoma fielded over the years—Steve Owens, Greg Pruitt, Joe Washington—Sims is considered by many to have been the best. "He's stronger than any running back we've ever had," Switzer said. "He can bench-press 350 pounds. That's fullback strength. He's got great strength in his legs, and he's like all our backs, who run 4.5 or 4.4 in the 40. He's elusive. He's what I call a snake runner. He's got great balance, and he runs low. He just kind of slithers down the field."

Another Sims trademark was to leap over would-be tacklers. It was characteristic of his all-out effort to gain yards, but the reckless style also led to his one weakness—fumbles. "I wish he'd stay on the ground a little more," Switzer said. "But that's Billy."

Ironically Sims's most memorable outing for the Sooners came the year after his Heisman season. Oklahoma's national championship hopes had been dashed early in a 16–7 loss to Texas. When the Sooners met Nebraska for the Big Eight title, the Cornhuskers were ranked No. 3 and vying for a national championship. The Sooners, with Sims's production lower than in 1978, were clearly the underdogs. Some thought Sims had been gliding through the season in order to remain healthy and protect his status as the projected No. 1 pick in the upcoming NFL draft.

It took a matchup with the Cornhuskers to get his adrenaline flowing. "Billy and I are sitting on the sideline the Thursday before the Nebraska game," Switzer said. "It's going to be his last home game. I asked him, 'You got one more in you?' He grinned, laughing, and said, 'I got one more, Coach. I got one more.' "

Before a sellout home crowd of more than 72,000, Sims broke free on a 71-yard run that set up the winning touchdown in the Sooners' 17–14 victory over the stunned Nebraskans. Sims blasted over right guard from the Sooners' 21-yard line. In typical style he broke two tackles and veered down the sideline, where he was finally hauled down at the Cornhuskers' eight-yard line.

Sims ended the game with 247 yards—not counting a 68-yard touchdown run that had been wiped out by a clipping penalty behind the play. Of Sims's 1,506 yards in 1979, 529 came in the final two games. "I asked myself how Sims could not get the Heisman again," Switzer said after the victory over Nebraska in 1979. "And I know the answer. It's because people have made him out to be more than he is. They expect him to rush for 211 yards every game, forgetting that 100 yards is a great, great day for anyone.

"Also, he makes it look so easy. A great play for him is just another ho-hum. There will never be another player like him at Oklahoma." —*DAVID MCNABB*

Charles White

The Vanishing Man

As a freshman at USC in 1976, Charles White found himself staring wistfully at the two Heisman Trophies displayed in the school's Heritage Hall.

One belonged to Mike Garrett, the first Trojan to win the award, in 1965, and by so doing, defining USC as Tailback U. The other Heisman belonged to O.J. Simpson, who nearly won the trophy twice, finishing second in 1967 before registering his lopsided Heisman victory the following season.

White, born January 22, 1958, and raised in the Los Angeles area, knew about the legacy. The Southern California High School Athlete of the Year in both track and football, White had just one name on his wish-list of colleges: USC. It was the reason Trojan coach John Robinson barely had to lift a finger during recruitment of the San Fernando High School star, other than to hand White a pen to sign the scholarship papers. "You don't have to say a thing," White told Robinson during a visit. "I'm coming."

Once there, White casually said while eyeing the USC Heisman collection that he would like to win a pair for himself. As it turned out, one would have to do. And it did. Quite nicely, too.

"I don't know why I said that," White would say later. "It was just stupid." Or wishful thinking.

White's 1979 Heisman victory came with surprising ease. The senior running back more than doubled the point total of Oklahoma halfback Billy Sims, who had entered the season with a chance to become only the second player to win consecutive Heisman awards. A year earlier Sims had led the nation in rushing and scoring, but White wasn't far behind—either in yards gained or Heisman votes earned. Sims won the trophy, but lurking in fourth place was White.

Roles were all but reversed in 1979, as White received 453 of the

White proved that he belonged in the trophy case with the likes of Simpson and Garrett.

available 698 first-place votes on his way to a dominating 1,695-point total. Sims was next with 82 first-place ballots and 773 points.

White's quest for a place in Heisman history began as a second-stringer on the Trojan depth chart. Stuck behind Ricky Bell, White seemed destined to serve at least a season as an apprentice to the talented upperclassman. But then Bell suffered an injury, forcing—if you can call it that—Robinson to insert the six-foot, 185-pound White into the lineup. White gained 858 yards and established himself as a potential star. The following season, with Bell graduated, White rushed for 1,478 yards.

As a junior White became part of Rose Bowl lore with his infamous phantom touchdown against Michigan, a score that ultimately guaranteed USC a 12–1 season and a share of a national championship. Faced with a second-and-goal from the Wolverine three-yard line, Robinson called for a simple dive play up the middle. White, of course, would get the ball.

But keeping it was something else entirely. As White leaped toward the end zone, the ball fell from his arms just before he cleared the goal line. Despite the apparent fumble, the officials ruled the run a touchdown and USC won 17–10.

At season's end White and Sims were invited to a banquet, where the Sooner star offered a confession of sorts. As the dinner audience looked on, Sims said that while he now owned a Heisman, he had yet to duplicate a certain football achievement of White's.

"I wish I could score like he did," said Sims, glancing at White, "without the football."

White would later admit that, yes, he fumbled the ball before he reached the goal line. But what was he going to do after the officials' call—give the touchdown back?

Mystery score or not, White had become one of college football's elite players. As a junior he gained 1,859 yards and led the country in all-purpose yardage, averaging 174.7 per game. The following year White improved upon this performance, gaining 2,050 yards in total offense and averaging more than 186 yards per game. And for the second straight season White led the nation in all-purpose running.

As with almost any Heisman season, there is a game that separates the leader from the candidates. For White it came on October 20 at Notre Dame.

White carried the ball 44 times for 261 yards and four touchdowns in the Trojans' 42–33 victory. It might well have been the day White convinced the voters and a national television audience that he deserved the Heisman.

The following Saturday against Stanford, White again rushed 44 times and led USC to a 24–14 win. Afterward Robinson was informed of his star running back's work load.

"Eighty-eight times in two weeks," Robinson responded. "Wow. Charles is going to want an extra scholarship."

White didn't want another scholarship; he wanted the ball. Robinson, who loved the idea of punishing opponents with a power rushing attack, was happy to oblige. "He's the best football player in America," Robinson once said, "a fierce competitor who is both elusive and powerful. He is the most durable football player I have ever coached. Other players occasionally get tired, but I think White could play a doubleheader.

"I've seen opposing players stand over him after a tackle and try to intimidate him by yelling at him or shaking their fists at him," said Robinson. "But his only reaction is to get up and walk away, and that's smart in my book. People who criticize me for running him 44 times evidently don't know that a football isn't heavy."

Nor, apparently, was the weight of carrying the USC backfield legacy, a decision which had its beginnings with Frank Gifford and Jon Arnett. "I don't know what people expect from me, for me to be like Garrett or O.J.," White told reporters during the 1979 season. "But I'm not like their image. I'm Charles White. This is my time right now."

The Heisman voters thought likewise, which was amply justified in the 1980 Rose Bowl, where USC again turned to White for the decisive scoring run. With only 5:21 remaining in the game, and the Trojans trailing 16–10, USC began its drive on its own 17-yard line. As expected White got the ball early and often. Robinson called for eight consecutive running plays, six of them going to White. White thanked him by gaining 71 of the Trojans' 83 yards (60 on his first two carries) during the drive, including a game-winning one-yard scoring plunge with 1:32 left to play. Not surprisingly White, who finished with 39 carries and a Rose Bowl-record 247 yards, was named the player of the game.

Asked once about his occasional appearances as an extra in television shows and movies, White revealed more about his inner self than about show business. "In Hollywood everything is fake," he

White was No. 1 indeed after gaining 2,050 all-purpose yards in his sterling '79 season for USC.

said. "Everyone is really someone else playing a role. So when I'm running the ball, I'm someone else. I feel like I'm in a fantasy world. I think I'm a bowling ball running through pins, only this bowling ball is able to change course as it goes along.

"Or I think of the football as a piece of important mail, and it's got to be at a certain place at a certain time. Or I tell myself that I can vanish into thin air. You'd be surprised how that one works. You run right at a guy, and he's breathing hard and foaming and thinking, 'Oh, I got him now. I got the best running back in the country coming at me, and I've been telling all the fellas back home that when I get the chance I'm really going to get him.' And here you come and ... *shoom!* ... he's grabbing air and saying, 'Now where'd he go?' And after the game they ask him, 'What did you think of Charles White?' and he says, 'Well, one time I thought I had a real good shot at him, and, I don't know, somehow I missed him.'

"That's what I like to hear most."

White, who heard his share of applause, also fought the demons. A first round NFL draft pick by the Cleveland Browns in 1980, White suffered a series of injuries that forced him to miss the better part of two seasons. He had troubles of another sort as well. In the summer of 1982 he admitted himself to a drug rehabilitation program for treatment of a cocaine problem. He spent his off-seasons speaking to youth groups about the problems of addiction.

Cut by the Browns in 1985, White was quickly picked up by the Los Angeles Rams and reunited with Robinson, who was the head coach. In 1987 White led the NFL in rushing, with 1,374 yards, and earned a place in the Pro Bowl.

After retiring from the league in 1988, White returned to USC in 1990 as a special assistant to the athletic director and later became an assistant coach to—guess who?—Robinson.

"Somehow," said Robinson, "I always feel better with Charles White standing next to me. He was the toughest, most intense running back I've ever coached."
—GENE WOJCIECHOWSKI

The Georgia—South Carolina game on November 1, 1980, was one of those classic individual battles that is usually more hype than substance and rarely lives up to its advanced billing. But as it turned out, this game fulfilled everyone's expectations.

The two best college running backs in America were on the field that day: Georgia's magnificent freshman, Herschel Walker, and South Carolina's senior, George Rogers, who was from nearby Duluth, Georgia, less than an hour away from Sanford Stadium in Athens. Georgia was undefeated, ranked No. 4, and, thanks to Walker's brilliance, on the way to winning the national championship. South Carolina had lost only once, on the road at Southern Cal, and, in Rogers, had a back many said could win the Heisman with just a little exposure.

Rogers, near the end of his third straight 1,000-yard season, had never played on national television or gotten much attention. Despite his 1,681 yards as a junior, bested only by Heisman-winner Charles White, Rogers had finished just seventh in that year's Heisman voting.

If the truth be known, ABC really never intended to show the Rogers-Walker battle, thinking it would appeal only to Southern viewers. But in the days leading up to the game, the network's offices in New York were inundated with requests. On one day alone ABC received 136 letters, including one written in crayon that simply said: PUT GEORGE ON!!!!!!!

So ABC did just that. And they were never sorry.

What ABC and the rest of the nation got was a titanic confrontation between two talents destined to make their marks on college football history. Walker's performance was stunning as he rushed for 219 yards, including a 76-yard touchdown run that still ranks as one of his greatest ever. Rogers's numbers weren't as high, but his effort was equally heroic. He pounded a Georgia line determined to stop him for 35 carries and 168 very impressive yards. But he also suffered a running back's worst nightmare by fumbling inside the Georgia 20-yard line in the final minutes, ending South Carolina's chances of winning.

George Rogers overcame tremendous personal hardship and a paucity of media coverage to win the Heisman.

So Georgia and Walker won the war, 13–10, but Rogers won respect and the recognition of being the best college football player in America. Even Walker, who would win the

1980
George Rogers

A Soft-Spoken Miracle Worker

Heisman in 1982, said after the game, "I'd vote for George Rogers. I don't think I'm as good as he is right now."

As it turned out, the Heisman voters agreed. For after Rogers ended the regular season by leading the nation in rushing, with 1,781 yards, those voters made him the 46th winner of the Heisman Memorial Trophy.

"The first day, the first practice, the first time he tucked the ball under his arm, I knew we had something special," said Jim Carlen, South Carolina's head coach at the time. "Because what you had in George was the total package. He could run over people or around them. And he had the heart of a lion. When you think about where he came from, his success is phenomenal."

"If you only knew what it took for me to get there," said Rogers.

No college football player has come from more dire circumstances to win the Heisman Trophy. Rogers was born into poverty in rural Duluth. His parents were divorced when he was six years old, and his father eventually went to prison for eight years for fatally shooting a woman with whom he was involved. Rogers, with his mother and two brothers and two sisters, moved eight times while he was a boy, "to stay ahead of the bills," he said.

In junior high Rogers skipped school and lied about his age in order to work in a labor pool for $1.80 an hour. He wanted to play football in junior high but could not come up with the $2 necessary to pay for the athletic insurance. His clothes were ragged hand-me-downs. The neighborhood children would taunt him and call him Dirty Boy. Often at night he would cry himself to sleep out of hunger or frustration.

"You can't forget stuff like that," said Rogers, the memories still strong. "It really hurt."

When Rogers was a teenager, the family lived in a cramped Atlanta housing project. Both of Rogers's teenaged sisters already had babies. Most of his friends in the project had gotten into drugs. Rogers had one dream left—to emulate his cousin who was a football star back in tiny Duluth. He decided to leave the housing project and move in with his Aunt Otella and go out for football. Otella welcomed her nephew under the following conditions: She would not wait on him, meaning he had to learn to cook and clean and do his part around the house. And, most important of all, he *would* go to school.

As a sophomore at Duluth High School, Rogers came

under the wing of coach Cecil Morris. What Morris saw was a physically gifted youngster who, despite the hard hits life had given him, was afraid of contact on the football field. "I was chickening through the hole," Rogers recalled of his early practices. "My coach reached down and picked me up from the bottom of the pile. He started shaking me and said, 'You're gonna run the ball, or I'm gonna kick your rear end.'"

The admonition brought tears to the young man's eyes, but later Morris took Rogers off to the side. "Keep trying, son," he said. "You can be anything you want."

Rogers's turn came in the third game of his first season. When the starting tailback left with an injury, Rogers replaced him and ran for four touchdowns. He went on to become the Georgia Class AA Player of the Year in each of his final two seasons.

Before Rogers arrived at South Carolina the school had not won eight games in a season since 1903. And in that season South Carolina played two high school teams and the local YMCA. With Rogers, South Carolina went 8–3 in both 1979 and 1980, and twice played in bowl games. He had three consecutive years of over 1,000 yards and a career average of 5.5 yards per carry. Rogers finished his career with 21 consecutive games with 100 yards rushing or more.

And the man who shied away from contact in high school became as a collegian the most bruising tailback in America. At 6'2", 224 pounds, he had 19-inch biceps, 28-inch thighs and could bench-press over 380 pounds, a weight normally lifted by only the big linemen. Because South Carolina relied on him so heavily, Rogers would often take a tremendous pounding in games. But time after time Rogers proved he could dish it out as well as take it.

In Rogers's senior year Carlen was convinced that the only way to beat NC State was to give Rogers the ball again and again. The Wolfpack was just as convinced that it could pound on Rogers enough to limit his effectiveness. By the end of that day Rogers had hit two NC State players so hard that they had to be removed from the game. In another collision, with a linebacker, Rogers split the opponent's helmet down the middle. He finished that day with 193 yards and three touchdowns. South Carolina won 30–10.

But Rogers is best remembered in Columbia, South Carolina, as a man who cared not only for himself but also for his teammates. During his freshman season Rogers was playing so well that he beat out the starting fullback. Upon being informed by Carlen that he had won a starting job, Rogers asked to remain No. 2 because he didn't

If one word could describe George Rogers, it would be caring.

want to hurt the other guy's feelings. As a junior, on the day he learned that he had been named All-American, Rogers cried when he heard that no teammates had been so honored.

The New Orleans Saints made Rogers the first pick in the 1981 draft, and his first act upon signing a five-year contract was to buy a new house for his mother. In his first season he was the NFL's rushing leader, was named Rookie of the Year and was selected to play in the Pro Bowl.

Rogers's life, however, did not become all bliss once he turned pro. In the summer of 1982 he told federal investigators that he had spent more than $10,000 on

cocaine during his first year in the league. He under-went testing and treatment for drug abuse at a Florida clinic in July 1982 before returning to football.

In 1985 Rogers was traded to the Washington Redskins, where he played until his retirement in 1988. Rogers eventually returned to the University of South Carolina, where he works for the school's athletic depart-ment in several different capacities. He spends his free time working with young people and counseling them on the pitfalls and the temptations of life. "You know," he said, "for a kid brought up like me, football makes you or breaks you."

Football made George Rogers: from a socially awkward teenager to a confident adult who became an in-demand public speaker; from a high school player scared of phys-ical contact, to a bruising collegian willing to take on any man in cleats; from a kid with no future and no hope to a Heisman Trophy winner.

It was a tough journey but worth it—every bit of it.

—TONY BARNHART

Marcus Allen

First Over 2,000 Yards

In the summer before his senior season in 1981, Marcus Allen, the University of Southern California's starting tailback, had a little chat with the Trojans' offensive coordinator, John Jackson.

A talk seemed to be in order. Allen's career at USC had been spotty. As a freshman he had been used lightly, backing up the great tailback Charles White. As a sophomore he had been switched to fullback to block for White during White's Heisman season.

As a junior the tailback position had finally been his, and by most measures his season was spectacular. Carrying the ball 354 times, he scored 14 touchdowns and gained 1,563 yards, second in the nation behind Heisman-winner George Rogers of South Carolina. But at USC tailbacks were measured by different standards. Their names were Mike Garrett, O.J. Simpson, Anthony Davis, Ricky Bell and Charles White, and all but Davis and Bell had been Heisman winners at the end of their senior seasons.

As he looked ahead to his own senior season, Allen had reason to be a little discouraged. His career at USC had not quite lived up to the promise he had shown in high school. While growing up in San Diego, Allen's dream was to win the Heisman as a USC tailback because his boyhood idol was O.J. Simpson, the runaway winner of the 1968 Heisman when Allen was eight. However, playing tailback at USC or anywhere else seemed unlikely, partly because Allen was a particularly good defensive back at Lincoln High School, one who once made 30 unassisted tackles in one game. But his high school coach, Vic Player, saw something special in the mature youngster, something he called charisma. "I never considered Marcus a kid," Player once said. "He was like a grown-up playing with school kids."

To take full advantage of Allen's potential for leadership, Player switched him to quarterback his senior season, over Allen's objections. "Marcus just wanted to be one of the boys," the coach said. "He didn't want to be the honcho." In his first practice at quarterback Allen fumbled on almost every play. Player, seeing through the ploy, kicked him off the team. The next day Allen apologized and was welcomed back—at quarterback.

Before the season was over he had learned to like the role of honcho. Allen led Lincoln to a 12-0-1 record and emerged a superstar after scoring all five Lincoln touchdowns in the San Diego city championship game.

The performance earned Allen the designation as the California high school player of the year and a trip to a national awards banquet in New York. At the banquet Allen met Simpson and promptly won over his idol, even dragging him to a phone to call Allen's mother—who wasn't home.

Recruited by USC as a defensive back, Allen played the position for just three practice days before coach John Robinson switched him to tailback. But it wasn't until his junior year that Allen finally got his chance to shine. Yet for all his impressive rushing and touchdown totals, something seemed a bit off. As the starting tailback Allen was inevitably (and usually unfavorably) compared to previous USC greats. He was not as fast as Simpson or as powerful as Bell. In addition, Allen was forever slipping and falling on cuts, and even when he stayed on his feet he seemed, as one coach put it, half a step behind.

All through the season Jackson worked closely with Allen, teaching him, as he later put it, "to run with his eyes," paying close attention to his blockers and potential tacklers and not simply trying to run over them.

Allen must have thought he had learned his lessons well. For when it came time for his preseason chat with Jackson in 1981, he blurted out, "Hey, I want to get 2,000 yards this year." Jackson must have thought Allen was crazy. For 2,000 yards was not only more than 25% over what Allen had gained the year before, it was more than any college running back had ever gained in a single season, half a football field longer than the record 1,948 yards set by Pitt's Tony Dorsett in 1976.

Under Jackson's skeptical look, Allen came to his senses. As he later recalled it, "Then we settled down and set some realistic goals." Allen never said what those "realistic goals" were, but from the very first game, the man Simpson called E.T. was off on an extraterrestrial tear.

Now half a step ahead, sure of his footing and using his speed, his power, his finesse and his blockers to perfection, Allen became the first runner in college history to gain 200 or more yards a game in the first four games of a season, then the first to reach 200 yards in five consecutive games and eventually the first to rush for 200 yards in eight games in a season.

When he topped the 2,000-yard mark in the next-to-the-last game of the season, at Washington State, the rival crowd gave him a thunderous ovation, but for Allen the milestone

Allen, so expert at eluding would-be tacklers, finished his senior season as the possessor of 15 NCAA records.

Legendary columnist Jim Murray talked with Marcus Allen in 1993, at a moment in Allen's pro career when he might have been forgiven for some heavy-duty gloating. What Murray discovered was a lesson in class.

Listen. Have you ever been fired from a job and, in your dreams, fantasized about coming back for another company and conspiring to put your former company and boss out of business?

Have you ever been rejected socially or fraternally as not equal to, even inferior to, your former associates and plotted to come back and make them pay for their rejection?

Heady stuff, right?

They tell us revenge is an unworthy motive. A sick response. Vengeance is mine, saith the Lord. Vengeance is desolation, said William Tecumseh Sherman.

Hah. It's sweet getting even. You sleep better knowing you have settled a score, right? Let the philosophers warn that vengeance is an empty emotion. What do they know?

So, I go down to the locker room at the Coliseum on Sunday to see an old colleague who had cashed in on the most basic of emotions, the get-even, the mood of well-how-do-you-like-it?

I found Marcus Allen toweling his neck. He had crushed a team that let him go with a shrug last year after 11 years of star performance for them. [Allen is pictured at right during his Raider days.]

Marcus had run for an average of five yards against his former mates, the Raiders. He had scored, almost by himself, the most important touchdown, the one that broke the Raiders' back.

Here was the situation: The Raiders were in command, 17–7, in the middle of the third quarter. Kansas City had the ball on L.A.'s 44-yard line. The ball was given to Marcus. He darted, twisted, faked and juked his way through the entire defense, burst open and dashed down to the Raider five. Two plays later, he took the ball again and negotiated the toughest four yards in the game, the last four into the end zone. He carried a Raider safety on his back the last two.

It was the backbreaker. It put the Chiefs back in the game, it buoyed them, it shook the Raiders. It was the difference, really.

"Aren't you going to gloat?" I asked Allen at his locker. I was ready for the wicked gleam in his eye, the I've-got-a-secret look. I was waiting for him to beat his chest and crow. After all, this is a sport now where they dance in the end zone after touchdowns, jump in the air with fists raised after sacks, taunt pursuers when they get open, wave the ball in their faces and otherwise humiliate them past the line of scrimmage. I was ready for some major trash-talking.

"Hey!" I said to Allen. "Aren't you going to say, 'I wonder how they like that!' Aren't you going to say, 'This was a team I won a Super Bowl for with a 74-yard run from scrimmage for a touchdown and 191 yards total that day. This was a team I rushed for 8,500 yards in the regular season, scored 98 touchdowns, caught more than 400 passes. This was a team that brought in Bo Jackson, Eric Dickerson and a half-dozen other all-timers, but every time they wanted to score, they gave the ball to Marcus.'

"Aren't you going to add, 'This was a town where I was the biggest hero since O.J. Simpson, where I went to the Rose Bowl twice, won the Heisman, had 11 200-yard rushing games. I sold tickets, baby! And they put me on a bus. And then they told me to clean out my locker and that they would see me around.' "

Well, that's what we were hoping for. Gloat sells. Gloat makes headlines.

But Allen simply stood there with this typical small smile on his face. He is leaving vengeance to the Lord.

"I know it makes wonderful copy," he began, "but really, I didn't feel any special enjoyment out of this. It's just one game. The good news is, we won.

"I'd rather let sleeping dogs lie. I was here a long time and the fans welcomed me today as if I were still one of their own, and that warmed my heart. I know NBC and ESPN and all made a big thing of it. But I'd like to say right now, there were never any hard feelings between me and [Raider coach] Art [Shell]. We spoke before the game, and I have great respect for him."

How about [owner] Al Davis? Allen is asked. He smiled. "No. We didn't speak," he answers.

"I was just glad to put some points on the board. But it was just a road game. It was a very big win for us, not for Marcus Allen. After all, what we're about is, we're trying to win a division, not get even with anybody." Well, it was hardly King Lear. More like that other Marcus—Marcus Antonius who said he had come to praise Caesar, not to bury him. This Marcus came to bury the Raiders, not to censure them. For they, too, are all honorable men. Marcus's mission is not revenge, it's the Super Bowl, he told reporters.

A Super Bowl, for his new team? Now, that would be revenge. Worthy of Marcus Antonius to say nothing of Marcus Allen.

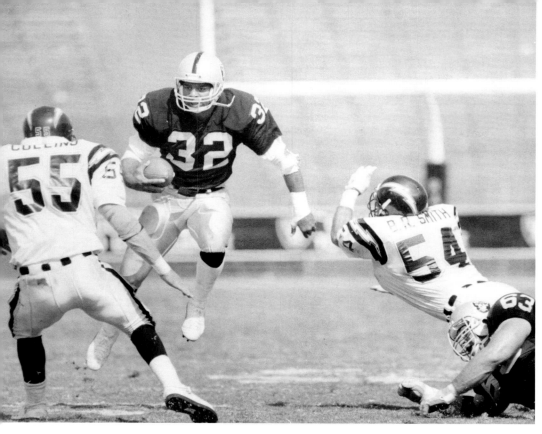

league in '85 with 1,759 yards while setting a league combined rushing/receiving record of 2,314 yards and winning recognition as the league's most valuable player.

Although occasionally hampered by injuries, Allen continued to lead the Raiders in rushing and added important help as a receiver and blocker through the 1988 season. But after a contract dispute in 1989, his playing time abruptly dropped. Allen blamed Al Davis, the Raiders' owner. Davis denied it, but Allen was used less and less, despite being at the top of his form. The nadir came in 1992 when the man who had carried the ball more than 200 times in six straight seasons was used only as a third-down back, running the ball only 67 times the entire season although his 4.5-yard average was powerful evidence that he was still one of the best in the game.

With the advent of free agency in 1993, Allen, who for years had all but begged the Raiders to trade him, began his career anew. At the age of 33 he signed with the Kansas City Chiefs. A starter from Game 9, Allen displayed his blazing skills of yore, leading the team with 764 rushing yards and leading the American Conference with 15 touchdowns, just one behind Jerry Rice's league-leading 16. The '94 season brought more success as Allen led the Chiefs with 709 rushing yards and seven TDs, bringing his career totals to 10,018 yards, ninth on the alltime list, and 120 touchdowns, fourth best ever.

As the 1995 season loomed nobody who saw Allen playing at 34 was prepared to write him off at 35. Whatever his future brings, Allen, who lives with his wife, Kathryn, in Brentwood, California, knows that his past is secure. Some things don't change.

USC tailbacks are still measured by different standards. Their names are Garrett, Simpson, Davis, Bell, White—and Allen. —*ROBERT McG. THOMAS JR.*

was marred. USC lost the game 13–3, costing it a trip to the Rose Bowl.

"What I did doesn't mean all that much right now," Allen said after the game. "All I'm thinking about is that we didn't win."

After a final 200-yard game, against UCLA, Allen, who led the nation with 23 touchdowns, finished the season with 15 NCAA records, among them the single-season rushing total of 2,342 yards on a record 403 carries. When he won the Heisman it was noted that half of the 30 running backs who had won the award up to that time had not carried the ball 403 times during their entire careers.

In the 1982 National Football League draft, Allen was selected by the Oakland Raiders on the tenth pick of the first round, the third running back taken. It didn't take Allen long to establish that the tenth shall be first. In the strike-shortened 1982 season he started nine games, gained 697 yards on 160 carries, led the league in scoring, with 84 points (11 touchdowns rushing and three receiving), and was the unanimous choice as Rookie of the Year.

Over the next six seasons Allen did nothing less than establish himself as one of the league's dominant running backs. In 1983, repeatedly demonstrating a breathtaking ability to stun a crowd with a single breakaway cut, he gained 1,014 yards and led the Raiders to a 38–9 rout of the Washington Redskins in Super Bowl XVIII. His two touchdowns and 191 rushing yards, including a Super Bowl-record 74-yard run, earned him the game's most valuable player award.

He had an 1,168-yard season in 1984, then led the

1982

Herschel Walker

Adonis in Pads

Most Georgia football fans can tell you where they were that hot, humid Saturday evening in September 1980 when the legend of Herschel Walker was born. A packed house of 96,000 was on hand for the contest at the University of Tennessee. And 86,000 of these folks were Big Orange fans.

It is extremely unusual in college football for someone to make such an impact in his first varsity competition, but Walker did, and what followed was remarkable. Nothing limited Walker's fame, not even the size of his hometown in central Georgia, Wrightsville, population about 2,000, capital of Johnson County.

From the first time he faced the press at Georgia, he had his interviewers hanging on every word. It was fascinating to watch him drop a phrase or observation to test their reactions. To this day he still speaks his mind, witnessed by his occasional proclamation that it is his "dream" to be an FBI agent. "The subject of crime and why people are criminals has always interested me," he explains. On occasion he would become the poet and recite some of his verse. Most of his poems were written when he had trouble on his mind.

Trouble didn't strike him much after his first days in playground football games. When one of the older boys told him he was too slow and fat to play, Herschel went to Tom Jordan, who would in time become his confidant, and asked the coach's advice on how to build up his body. "Push-ups," Jordan said. "Start doing push-ups."

Herschel started and never quit, doing push-ups by the hundreds, claiming at one time that he did 3,000 a day. He also did morning runs—his "joggers," he called them. All of this until the fat began to turn to muscle, the body began to develop an athletic trim, and by the time he reached junior high school, he was bigger than most linemen who had to tackle him. Perhaps the most amazing thing about Herschel was that he never lifted weights or subscribed to any bodybuilding regimen. But muscles bulged, neck and shoulders came together in one sinewy mass. He walked like a Greek god and ran with the harsh grace of a rhino.

Walker paid immediate dividends for the Philadelphia Eagles, rushing for 1,070 yards in 1992.

As a halfback at Johnson County High School, he was the most sought-after recruit the South has ever known. In three varsity seasons he gained 6,317 yards rushing and scored 86 touchdowns. He was such a wrecking force that his coach rarely played him more than half a game. "I thought that was a good thing, that everybody should have a chance to get into the game," Walker would say. In his senior year alone, he rushed for 3,167 yards and scored 45 touchdowns to lead Johnson County to the Class A state championship. Walker was named *Parade* magazine's National Back of the Year, a sign of the national spotlight that would come to shine on him at Georgia.

Vince Dooley, the historically conservative Bulldog coach, was reluctant to start freshman players, and despite all of Walker's potential and aplomb, and the fact that he far overshadowed an upper-class running back, Dooley stuck to his beliefs when the Bulldogs opened the season against Tennessee in Knoxville on that Saturday night in 1980.

After the first two halfbacks failed to get anything done, Dooley went to his third-stringer, the freshman from Wrightsville. The Bulldogs were losing 9–0 the first time Walker came in. The second time he appeared the margin had become 15–2. Then from the Volunteers' 16-yard line, Walker took the ball over tackle, and when a Tennessee defensive back tried to tackle him at the five, Walker dragged the Vols' safety man into the end zone. A few minutes later Walker scored again, and with the conversion of the extra point Georgia beat Tennessee 16–15, and the third-stringer had become first-string.

That game was as close as Georgia came to losing that season. Walker made every All-America team in the book. He set a record for yardage gained by a freshman, with 1,616 yards. He was third in the Heisman voting. One wire service named him College Back of the Year. But he wasn't through yet and wouldn't be until he had carried the Georgia team one step closer to perfection.

In the 1981 Sugar Bowl game he suffered a separated left shoulder in the first quarter but remained in the contest. Playing on guts and sheer determination he gained 150 yards, scored two touchdowns and was the outstanding player as Georgia beat Notre Dame 17–10 for undisputed possession of the national championship.

Georgia would win two more Southeastern Conference championships while Walker was there, but following his freshman season the pro leagues began rearing their heads. In the spring of 1982 *Sports Illustrated* ran a cover story on Walker and his flirtation with the pros. He said in that

Just days before Herschel Walker became the 1982 Heisman winner, Dave Anderson examined Walker's remarkable college career and the many reasons for his much anticipated winning of the trophy.

For three seasons now, the Heisman Trophy has been a silent inspiration for Herschel Walker, a silent ambition. Not simply the idea of winning the Heisman Trophy, but the actual bronze Heisman Trophy itself, the one that Frank Sinkwich of Georgia was awarded in 1942, the one that he donated to the university about a decade ago, the one that is inside a glass case perched on a pedestal near the student mail boxes in the lobby of McWhorter Hall, the athletic dorm where Herschel Walker lives.

"Herschel has to see it every time he goes through the lobby," says Claude Felton of the Georgia athletic office, "but I've never heard him talk about it."

Be assured, however, that Herschel Walker is thinking about it now. Tomorrow the voting for this year's Heisman Trophy will close. Saturday evening the winner will be announced, the winner of what is really an election to determine the nation's outstanding college football player. And judging by conversations with the campaign managers for the three leading candidates, running back Herschel Walker will be the winner, ahead of John Elway, the Stanford quarterback, and Eric Dickerson, the Southern Methodist running back.

The players haven't been saying much. But their campaign managers, alias the sports information directors at each college, have been trying to gauge how approximately 1,000 sportswriters and sports broadcasters will vote.

"I feel pretty confident," says Claude Felton of Georgia.

"Elway will probably carry the Far West and Dickerson the Southwest, but I think Herschel will carry the South, the Midwest, the Northeast and the Mid-Atlantic."

Spoken like a national campaign manager for a presidential candidate. For a campaign manager, being "pretty confident" is virtually a victory speech. Especially when the campaign managers for John Elway and Eric Dickerson sound as if they're about to compose a concession speech.

"I feel John still has a shot," says Steve Raczynski of Stanford, "but not as good as he once had."

"The Heisman isn't won in one year," says Bob Condron of SMU. "It's usually a cumulative award."

Over three seasons, no college football player has ever accumulated the credentials Herschel Walker has—5,259 rushing yards, third on the career list behind two other Heisman Trophy winners, Tony Dorsett, who had 6,082 at Pitt, and Charles White, who had 5,598 at Southern Cal.

In leading the Bulldogs to their second 11–0 regular-season record in his three seasons there, Herschel Walker ran for 1,752 yards this year.

"Except for the opener against Clemson this year, when he had a broken thumb and got only 20 yards, Herschel has had 22 straight games with 100 or more rushing yards," Claude Felton says. "Even so, I thought he got off to a slow start this year while Elway was getting off to a fast start, but Herschel got stronger and stronger, Stanford lost a few games, then Herschel ran for 219 yards and three touchdowns against Florida on national television."

Frank Sinkwich, now a Miller beer distributor in Athens, Georgia, remembered Herschel Walker as a high school junior.

"He was so big, I thought he was a tackle," Sinkwich

story, "Everybody tries to hold you back from making your own decisions. I want to be successful and want to be happy, and it's my life." In the end, he wouldn't go—until a year later, after his junior season, and after he had finally won the Heisman Trophy. That was exceedingly important to him, to have his own Heisman, just like the one he had seen in the trophy case at Georgia, donated by Frank Sinkwich.

At the end of the 1982 football season the New Jersey Generals of the now extinct USFL offered the Heisman winner $5 million for three seasons. He signed, then changed his mind—almost tearing up the just-signed contract, then changed his mind again and made it stick. "No one realizes more than I that I am a human being,"

he said. "I apologize to Coach Dooley. I ask for your forgiveness, and I ask God for His forgiveness."

Walker's career in the upstart USFL proved to be a statistical and box-office success. In three seasons he rushed for more than 5,500 yards, had 61 touchdowns and nearly 1,500 yards in pass receptions. As the league's most valuable player in 1985, Walker set an alltime pro football rushing record of 2,411 yards. But it was not enough to save the fledgling league. When the USFL collapsed he signed with the Dallas Cowboys of the NFL, which held his rights. He had several bright moments with the Cowboys, including one season where he rushed for over 1,500 yards and was named to the Pro Bowl. Still, Dallas coach Tom Landry never found a way to utilize both

said. "His speed for his size is amazing."

Once upon a time, the Heisman Trophy understandably was criticized as a phony award. In the years before so many games were on television, none of the voters were able to see enough of the best players to evaluate the one best player. Now television enables the conscientious voter to see most of the best players at least once, if not several times.

But just as the benefit of being on television often during their college careers has helped the Heisman campaigns for Herschel Walker and John Elway, the relative lack of television exposure because of SMU's probation until this season has hurt Eric Dickerson's appeal. With 1,617 yards in only 232 carries, he had a seven-yard average this season.

"Walker and Elway had a running start going into the season," says Bob Condron of SMU, "and then Eric wasn't on national TV until the seventh game."

Herschel Walker, of course, has been a Heisman candidate almost from his opening game as a freshman. He finished third in the voting that year, behind George Rogers, now of the New Orleans Saints but then a running back at South Carolina, and Hugh Green, now a linebacker for the Tampa Bay Bucs but then a defensive end at Pitt; last year Walker finished second to Marcus Allen, now of the Los Angeles Raiders but then a running back at Southern Cal.

"I think Herschel probably played well enough to deserve it as a freshman, but human nature hurt him," Claude Felton says. "I think the voters considered that Rogers and Green were seniors, and that Herschel was only a freshman who had three more years. Then last year, Herschel again played well enough to deserve to win it but Marcus Allen was the first back to go over 2,000 yards. It's hard to say Allen didn't deserve it."

Each year Herschel Walker reacted calmly, as if he knew his Heisman eventually would come.

"When he finished third two years ago," Claude Felton recalls, "I went over to the dorm and told him. All he said was, 'Well, those guys are both great athletes.' Last year, we had a game the day of the announcement. I knew the Heisman people were going to call me if they needed him to be in New York that evening. After the game I told him, 'I haven't gotten a call.' All he said was, 'That's fine.' Then he got on a plane to go to Phoenix for the Kodak All-America banquet instead of going to New York for the Heisman."

But this Saturday, look for Herschel Walker to be on display at the Downtown Athletic Club when the Heisman Trophy winner is announced over the ABC network. Then there will be two Heisman Trophies in McWhorter Hall on the Georgia campus: the one belonging to Frank Sinkwich in the lobby, the other in Herschel Walker's room.

Walker and fellow Heisman winner Tony Dorsett in the backfield. In 1989 Walker became the centerpiece in a major trade with Minnesota. But in three seasons with the Vikings, Walker didn't fit their plans.

In 1992 he was signed by the Philadelphia Eagles. There he quickly found new life and rushed for 1,070 yards, had 278 yards in pass receptions and a total of 10 touchdowns. On the heels of Walker's rebirth, the Eagles made it to the second round of the playoffs that season. In 1993 Walker settled into the role of team leader and accumulated over 1,350 yards in rushing and pass receptions. He was named the team's most valuable player while leading the Eagles into the playoffs once again. The 1994 season was a disappointing one for the Eagles, but Walker continued to play well, again gaining a combined total of more than 1,000 rushing and receiving yards.

So after 12 seasons in professional football, the Herschel Walker legend continues. His numbers to date—more than 13,000 rushing and 5,000 yards in pass receptions for a total of 140 touchdowns in both the USFL and the NFL—have ensured him a spot in the pro football history books.

Yet for those who saw him in those early days at Georgia, charging like a rhino around end or hurdling high over a defensive goal line stand for a touchdown, the awesome ability of this great athlete was a sight that will be long remembered.   —FURMAN BISHER

Mike Rozier

Iron Mike

In the autumn of 1983 Nebraska running back Mike Rozier accomplished a rare feat: he lived up to his Heisman hype.

At the beginning of an era when publicity seemed as important as actual achievement, Rozier proved himself as good as his pre-season billing. He set what was then an NCAA single-season record, with 29 rushing touchdowns. He also led the country with an average of 7.81 yards per carry for a total of 2,148 yards. By the time he was finally announced the winner in December it seemed like old news.

"I'm starting to learn more about the trophy and its history," Rozier said upon receiving the Heisman Trophy. "I probably won't realize how much it means until I'm old and gray."

Rozier was honored as much for his performance as for his part on what many consider to be one of the greatest collegiate teams. He was one third of a backfield that included quarterback Turner Gill and wingback Irving Fryar. Together they helped Nebraska compile a 33–5 mark in three years. In 1983 Nebraska would set the NCAA record for points (624) in a single season.

Yet a disappointing one-point loss in the 1984 Orange Bowl to Miami foreshadowed a turbulent future for Rozier. After gaining 147 yards on New Year's Day against the Hurricanes, Rozier was forced to the sidelines with an ankle injury. On Nebraska's two-point conversion attempt in the final seconds for a national title, Gill's pass was knocked away at the last second from the intended receiver—Rozier's backup. Miami thus ended Nebraska's 22-game winning streak with a 31–30 defeat.

Following the Orange Bowl, Rozier signed a $3.1 million, three-year deal with the Pittsburgh Maulers of the upstart USFL. The next season his contract was purchased by the USFL's Jacksonville franchise. In all, he played for three professional teams in his first three years and had to weather a controversy after he indicated he had broken NCAA rules by signing with an agent before finishing at Nebraska. Rozier's playing career ended in 1991 after eight solid, if not spectacular years in the USFL and the NFL (with the Houston Oilers and the Atlanta Falcons).

But Rozier's imprint at Nebraska is clear.

At 5'11" and 210 pounds, he was a combination of power and strength. Rozier's lack of blazing speed limited his pro career, but his quick bursts and toughness were his trademarks at Nebraska. Defenders were kept off balance because they didn't know whether Rozier would try to run over them or around them.

"If there is a hole, he hits it," said Nebraska guard Dean Steinkuhler. "If there's not a hole, he makes it."

Nebraska assistant Frank Solich found his place in Cornhusker lore on a 1980 recruiting trip to New Jersey. Solich was looking for a tight end whose name he no longer remembers. He returned with a running back who would become the school's alltime leading rusher (4,780 yards) and scorer (312 points).

Rozier was a fullback in a wishbone offense at Woodrow Wilson High School in Camden, New Jersey. He spent a year at Coffeyville (Kansas) Junior College to gain his academic eligibility before arriving at Nebraska. As a junior he would break a 32-year-old Nebraska single-season record by rushing for 1,689 yards.

"The game I most remember about him was our junior year," said Gill, now a Nebraska assistant. "We were playing Missouri. He had cracked ribs.... I went out with a concussion. Mike got 200 yards or more while playing with a flak jacket [for protection]. He showed a lot of heart."

Rozier was named Big Eight player of the week after Nebraska's 23–19 victory over Missouri. He had not been expected to play because of severe hip and rib injuries but came off the bench to rush for 139 yards on 17 carries.

Despite his gregariousness Rozier did not receive all the accolades his play merited. Rather than face the constant glare of the media himself, Rozier would sometimes send out his brother, Guy, to do interviews and never tell the interviewer he had been tricked. Rozier was criticized by some for his flamboyant playing style, but Gill said he wasn't seen that way by the Cornhuskers.

"On the bench he'd get water and give it to the [offensive] linemen," Gill said. "He'd do it for the defense. He was a team player, but maybe some people didn't see him that way."

In 1982 the Heisman went to a heralded junior, but it wasn't Rozier. Georgia running back Herschel Walker won the award while Rozier finished 10th in the balloting.

High stepping hig way to the Heisman, Mike Rozier actually proved himself as good as his pre-season billing.

The following year when Walker signed a professional contract and Oklahoma's star running back, Marcus Dupree, surprised everyone by dropping out of school, Rozier became a clear favorite for the Heisman. The prestige of the award was undisputed, as were its benefits to the winner's school. Intensive media campaigns were conducted by colleges, which sent posters and weekly updates of potential candidates to voters across the country.

Even though Cornhusker coach Tom Osborne has always stressed a team-oriented philosophy, Rozier became the focal point of a Heisman campaign when he was featured in the 1983 Nebraska media guide. Nebraska had four players who could have vied for the award that season, but they had no problems with putting a stronger effort behind Rozier rather than splitting potential votes.

Rozier met the expectations. By October 10, *Sports Illustrated* had already conceded the Heisman race to the Nebraska back.

"Rozier will win the Heisman because of the kind of effort and talent he displayed on three third-quarter runs against [Syracuse]," wrote SI's Douglas Looney. "Syracuse stopped him at the line, whereupon he bulled, dove, fought, scratched and clawed for six yards—six Heisman yards.... Rozier took a pitch and battered his way for eight Heisman yards on a play that should have produced no gain.... On a fourth-and-one, he again was hit immediately but lowered his head and picked up four more Heisman yards and a first down."

Nebraska needed another standout performance to complete its regular-season with a 12–0 record. Rozier rushed for 205 yards and a touchdown in a 28–21 victory over archrival Oklahoma.

The national championship eluded the Cornhuskers because of the loss to Miami in the Orange Bowl. But Rozier was one of many Heisman winners to suffer the same fate. From 1976 to 1993 only two Heisman winners were able to guide their teams to national titles.

In the Heisman voting, Rozier won by a landslide, with 482 first-place votes. Brigham Young quarterback Steve Young finished second with 153 first-place votes. Gill was the No. 4 finisher with 11 first-place votes.

"The best man won this trophy," said Young.

—*David McNabb*

1984
Doug Flutie

Little Big Man

The Pass.

Whatever else Doug Flutie does in his life, he will forever be known as the little man who threw one of the biggest passes in college football history.

On November 23, 1984, Flutie's Boston College Eagles trailed defending national champion Miami 45–41 with six seconds left on a rainy, windy day at the Orange Bowl. Boston College had the ball near midfield, with time for one more play. In the huddle Flutie called for a Flood Tipa play—three receivers would line up on the right side and sprint toward the end zone, where one of them hoped to catch a Hail Mary pass or tip it to a teammate.

Flutie dropped back, scrambled away from the Miami rush and launched the ball more than 60 yards in the air. Though surrounded by three Miami defenders, Gerard Phelan made a diving catch in the end zone for the winning touchdown.

"I didn't see anything much until the referee raised his arms," Flutie said after the game. "Then, I admit, I couldn't believe it, even when everybody started yelling and picking me up."

Boston College fans had come to expect miracles from their charismatic 5'9", 175-pound leader, who was once considered too small to make it as a college quarterback. Flutie led B.C., a school that had not made a post season appearance in 4 decades, to three bowl games. He became the first major-college player to pass for 10,000 yards, and he gave New England its first Heisman Trophy winner since Yale's Clint Frank in 1937.

But Flutie will be remembered more for style than statistics. He was one of the most exciting and entertaining players of his era, a diminutive David who frustrated the giant Goliaths with his acrobatic scrambling, daring improvisation and surprisingly strong arm.

"The first time I saw him play, I knew he was special," said his college coach, Jack Bicknell. "You can't teach what Doug has, and we wouldn't try

Though famed for one spectacular pass, Flutie made a lot of things happen for Boston College.

to take credit for it."

Flutie's athletic flair was apparent at an early age. In a Little League game he once fielded a grounder at shortstop and faked a throw to first in order to confuse the runner at second. The strategy worked. The runner tried to go to third and was tagged out by Flutie.

During a high school football game, Flutie's Natick (Massachusetts) High team was losing by one point with three seconds remaining. They had the ball on the opponent's 21-yard line. Although he had never kicked a field goal, Flutie begged his coach to let him try one. The coach agreed, and Flutie booted the game-winner.

Despite such heroics, few colleges recruited Flutie because of his size. Bicknell gave him a scholarship, but Flutie was a bench warmer as a freshman in 1981 until late in the fourth game when he was sent in for mop-up duty with Boston College trailing Penn State 38–0. He passed for 135 yards and a touchdown and earned the starting job. "He went into that game, and it was like someone threw a switch," Bicknell said.

With Flutie at the controls, Boston College won four of its last seven games. The following year he passed for a school-record 2,749 yards and led the Eagles to an 8-3-1 record and a berth in the Tangerine Bowl, their first postseason appearance since the 1943 Orange Bowl. They lost to Auburn 33–26, but Flutie was sensational, passing for 299 yards and having a hand in all but four of the Eagles' points.

As a junior Flutie guided the Eagles to a 9–3 mark, including a 19–18 loss to Notre Dame in the Liberty Bowl. He threw three touchdown passes on a bitterly cold day in Memphis and was named the game's most valuable player. In the final Associated Press poll that year, Boston College was ranked 19th, its best finish since 1942. And Flutie finished third in the Heisman Trophy voting, behind runner-up Steve Young of Brigham Young and winner Mike Rozier of Nebraska.

Although Flutie was now a full-fledged star, he didn't consider himself a celebrity. "It's not an ego trip for me, being an All-America and a Heisman candidate," he said. "I play because I love the game. I don't want to be a big shot."

Flutie's reputation continued to grow during his senior season, when he led the nation in passing, completing 60% of his throws for 3,454 yards and 27 touchdowns. He made headlines early in the year by rallying Boston College from a second-half, 17-point deficit to a 38–31 victory over Alabama, running

Flutie's famed fling gave the Eagles a shocking 47–45 win over defending national champion Miami.

for one touchdown and passing for another.

Flutie was just warming up for his miracle in Miami, where he and Hurricane quarterback Bernie Kosar put on a record-setting passing display. Kosar passed for 447 yards and two touchdowns, but ended up playing second fiddle to Flutie, who threw for 472 yards and three TDs. The game was like a toe-to-toe slugfest between hard-hitting heavyweights. Flutie directed an 82-yard drive to put the Eagles ahead 41–38 with less than four minutes left, but Kosar countered with his own long scoring drive to give Miami a 45–41 edge with 28 seconds remaining.

Then came the Pass. "I think they lost track of Flutie's arm and how far he can throw it," Bicknell said.

A week later Flutie won the Heisman Trophy in a landslide. "It's like putting your mark in the history book," he said. "It's what I've been striving for."

Flutie capped his college career by leading Boston College to a 45–28 win over Houston in the Cotton Bowl. He tied a Cotton Bowl record with three touchdown passes as the Eagles completed a 10–2 season, their most victories since 1940. "I'll never see anything like him again," Bicknell said. "He always made things happen."

A month later Flutie signed a reported five-year, $7 million contract with the New Jersey Generals of the United States Football League. The new league suspended operations after Flutie's first season, and he bounced around the NFL for four years without much success. He spent three years with his homestate New England Patriots, but started only 11 games. "Once you get labeled as a backup, you're a backup, and there's nothing that's going to change their mind," he said.

Flutie's career was revived in the Canadian Football League, where the larger field and more wide-open style were better suited to his skills. He was named the CFL's outstanding player three straight years, set league passing records for most yards and touchdowns in a season and led Calgary to the Grey Cup championship in 1992. Calgary was almost eliminated from the playoffs that year in the Western final, but with 19 seconds left Flutie scored the game-winning touchdown after one of his shoes fell off during the run.

"Things happen in our games that you can never imagine happening," he said. "If you leave your seat for a hot dog, you might miss two scores before you get back."

Doug Flutie always did things that were hard to imagine—from a decoy play in the Little League to an improbable pass in the Orange Bowl. —RICK WARNER

1985

Bo Jackson

A Life on the Edge

A decade ago, when the legend of Bo Jackson had yet to achieve full critical mass, someone asked the then Auburn University running back about his choice of funeral arrangements. It was an unusual question posed to an unusual person.

Jackson considered the inquiry and decided he would prefer cremation and a sprinkling at sea. If circumstances required a more traditional burial, Jackson said his tombstone should read:

VINCENT JACKSON

?

This, of course, was vintage Jackson. Simple. Directly vague. Strangely eloquent and altogether appropriate.

From the moment he came into the world on November 30, 1962, the eighth of 10 children, Jackson has been as unpredictable as the flight of a humming-bird. Even his selection as the 51st winner of the Heisman Memorial Trophy was steeped in intrigue and guesswork. Until he was summoned to the podium to accept the award, Jackson was unsure about the voting outcome. Iowa quarterback Chuck Long was considered a serious challenger, so much so that the usually unflappable Jackson could barely sit still during the announcement ceremony.

"It's been on my mind all day," said Jackson that afternoon. "I thought my heart was going to jump out of my shirt. There was doubt in my mind when I heard the vote was close. I even prepared myself to lose."

As it turned out, Jackson's margin of victory was the narrowest in Heisman history—a scant 45 points out of a possible 4,456. But to anyone who saw him play in 1985, when he gained 1,786 yards and scored 17 touchdowns despite an assortment of injuries, there was little question

With weightlifter strength and sprinter speed, Jackson may have been the most multi-talented Heisman winner of all.

about the award's proper owner.

Of course, the storied surroundings of the Downtown Athletic Club were a long way from Bessemer, Alabama, where Florence Jackson Bond had struggled to raise her 10 children. It was there that the evolution of a nickname began. It was there that a mother warned her son that he would be wearing prison stripes by his 21st birthday if he didn't change his ways.

A juvenile delinquent, really, Jackson used to shoplift, extort lunch money, pelt pigs with rocks, smoke dope and treat school with indifference. His family compared his personality with that of a wild boar—thus, his first nickname, "Boar," which was later shortened simply to "Bo."

But his prodigious athletic talents couldn't be hidden. At McAdory High School in McCalla, Alabama, Jackson was a three-sport star. He was the two-time state champ in the decathlon, hit a national high school record 20 home runs in one season and gained 1,173 yards on 108 carries and scored 17 TDs in his senior year. Although drafted by the New York Yankees in the second round of the 1982 baseball draft, Jackson rejected a multiyear contract in order to attend Auburn.

It was at Auburn that Jackson established himself as a person who no longer defied authority but defied description. His freshman season he led the Tigers with 829 rushing yards, played on the baseball team and listed liver as his favorite food. As a sophomore Jackson led the Southeastern Conference in rushing (with 1,213 yards) and decided to run track during the spring. Not surprisingly Jackson's name was beginning to gain strength as a Heisman candidate.

In his first game of the 1984 season Jackson gained 96 yards against Miami but injured his ankle doing it. The next game, this time against Texas, a limping Jackson was caught from behind after a 53-yard gain. He separated his shoulder on the play and later tried to pop it back into place. The team trainer informed Auburn coach Pat Dye that Jackson's shoulder was hurt but that no more damage could be done to it.

"I send him back in the game, and he plays a half-quarter or so, and he scores a touchdown with a separated shoulder," recalled Dye. "I just thought he had a bruised shoulder. I found out later in the locker room that he had a separated shoulder. I felt like an idiot."

Doctors examined the shoulder and decided that Jackson's season—and Heisman hopes—were all but finished. In a rare display of emotion Jackson broke down and cried.

Then came 1985, the season to cherish, to mystify.

Healthy for almost the entire schedule, Jackson ran as if he were making up for lost time. He rushed for 200 yards or more in four games and carried the ball 30 or more times in six games.

But it wasn't simply the yards that created his legacy, it was his flair and mystery and arrogance. He could move his 222 pounds across 40 yards of grass field in 4.22 seconds, about the time it takes to scratch a good itch. He could walk into the Auburn weight room, bench-press 365 pounds, then 380, then 400 and then ask the stunned Tiger strength coach, "Is that enough?" He could run over or around would-be tacklers. Jackson could prompt Dye, the famed disciplinarian, into allowing him to get ready for a game at his own pace. He could keep a hunting rifle in his dorm room. He could keep a nation in suspense.

"I don't like people knowing my every move," he said once. "I like to keep people guessing, no matter what the situation is. I've always done that."

By the time he left Auburn in the spring of 1986, Jackson had become the first three-sport SEC letterman in 30 years. He hinted that he might pursue a track career "and give Carl Lewis a run for his money." He talked lovingly of baseball and football but never committed himself.

NFL scouts considered him a sure thing, and his ratings, among the highest ever, reflected it. Confident they could sign him, the Tampa Bay Buccaneers made him the first selection in the league draft and offered him a reported five-year, $7.6 million contract.

Meanwhile, major league baseball scouts generally ranked Jackson among the country's best prospects, if not No. 1 outright. That explains why the Kansas City Royals decided to take a chance and chose Jackson in the fourth round of the June draft.

In the end Jackson did what he does best. He confounded those who thought they knew him.

"I went with what is in my heart," he said at a June 21, 1986, press conference. "My first love is baseball, and it has always been a dream of mine to be a major league player." In a hastily planned batting practice that day at Royals Stadium, Jackson, using a borrowed Steve Balboni bat, swung and missed the first pitch. But by the end of the brief session he had sent six balls over the fence, including one that landed near the base of the stadium scoreboard.

"That's damn near 500 feet," said Royal second baseman Frank White.

Jackson continued to amaze. After calling football "my hobby," Jackson signed a contract with the Los Angeles Raiders, with the provision that he would join the NFL team only after the baseball season was completed. That done, Jackson eventually became an All-Star in baseball, an All-Pro in football and an all-global in endorsement ventures.

In a January 13, 1991, game against the Cincinnati Bengals, Jackson injured his left hip, producing a condition which was later diagnosed as a vascular necrosis, a degenerative condition that severs the blood flow to the hip area. Doctors advised him to retire from sports. Jackson, released by the Royals about two months later, instead signed a one-year deal with the Chicago White Sox.

In the spring of 1992 Jackson underwent hip replacement surgery and missed the entire season. But much to the astonishment of his physicians, teammates and fans, he returned to the plate as a pinch hitter in the White Sox's home opener on April 9, 1993. On an 0–1 pitch from New York Yankee Neal Heaton, Jackson drilled the ball over the rightfield fence, his first home run since September 1991. Jackson went on to belt 16 homers in less than 300 at bats, proving that the potentially career-ending surgery hadn't affected his powerful stroke.

Financial considerations and continuing doubts about his hip eventually led the White Sox to release Jackson before the start of the 1994 season. Not to worry. The California Angels, whose Anaheim Stadium was the site of a Jackson All-Star Game homer, happily signed the unemployed designated hitter/part-time outfielder to a contract.

Several years ago, after thousands of well-wishers had written to him and claimed him as postoperative inspiration, Jackson offered a piece of advice. "I tell them, 'Don't expect to come back from surgery like Bo Jackson,'" he said. "After all, I'm a little crazy, I'm young, and I'm as strong as a horse. And I like to live on the edge. That helps."

Life on the edge has its dangers. But as Jackson has proved again and again, you can't beat the view.

—*GENE WOJCIECHOWSKI*

An All-Pro in football, an All-Star in baseball— Jackson could do it all, including hitting home runs like this in the 1989 All-Star game.

Vinny Testaverde's quest for the Heisman Trophy began with a dream. But it wasn't his dream. It was his father's. Alonso Testaverde, or Big Al, as his friends know the 260-pound construction worker from Elmont, New York, had a dream that his son would win the Heisman Memorial Trophy, and he had it well before his wife bore him his first and only boy.

When Josephine finally did get around to giving birth to their son, on November 13, 1963, after having two daughters (two more girls would follow), she couldn't blame her husband for wanting to get a football into young Vincent Frank's hands as soon as possible. She just thought he might have waited a little longer than the baby's first day home from the hospital.

That day, when Big Al put a real leather football into the bassinet next to his son, the dream was still fresh. The football was his way of passing it on.

The gesture worked, but it takes more than a dream to become a star quarterback for the University of Miami Hurricanes, shattering school passing records, winning the 52nd Heisman Trophy and becoming the first pick in the National Football League draft. It takes an early start and hard work.

To his father's delight, Vinny fell in love with football right away. Shortly after his stint in the bassinet league, Vinny played catch with Big Al every chance he got. By the time Vinny was old enough to play peewee football, he had grown so tall, his father made a point of bringing his son's birth certificate to games. The strong-armed boy liked and excelled at playing quarterback. This was fine with his father, who was already concocting a new fantasy: his son becoming the next Johnny Unitas. Vinny, however, wanted nothing to do with this dream—his idols were Joe Namath and Terry Bradshaw.

By his junior year at Elmont's Sewanhaka High, Vinny seemed ready to take over as starting quarterback. But his coach, apparently unaware that Vinny was fulfilling an important dream, had other ideas. He relegated Vinny to the second team, a decision that seemed to bother Big Al more than it did his son. Vinny was surprisingly patient for someone so young and talented. He knew he would get his chance.

That chance came in his final game as a junior. Vinny went in at wide receiver, where he took a step back from the line of scrimmage, caught a long lateral from the quar-

Vinny Testaverde

A Father's Dream Fulfilled

terback and rifled a 60-yard touchdown pass, giving his team the Nassau County championship.

Vinny became the starter his senior year, and although his coach used a run-oriented veer offense, he got to pass just enough to provide convincing evidence that he had a future as a college quarterback. There was a slight problem, however.

Vinny was so consumed by sports (he lettered in baseball and track as well as football) that his grades slipped enough that he needed an extra year of school to qualify for a scholarship at a top football college. Vinny was disappointed, but he cheered up when he got a call from New York Jet quarterback and receivers coach Pete McCulley, who had seen him play. McCulley liked Testaverde's size (he was already 6'4") and was impressed with the way he set up and delivered the ball. All he needed, McCulley said, was a little seasoning and more discipline, both of which, he suggested, Vinny could get at the Fork Union Military Prep School in Virginia.

Vinny was elated. "After that phone call," he said, "all my doubts disappeared." Following McCulley's advice he headed for Fork Union, and the extra year paid off. He made the grades he needed. His football skills improved. And college football recruiters came knocking. Testaverde fell in love with Miami, its warm weather and its pro-style offense, even though Miami coach Howard Schnellenberger told him that the Hurricanes were recruiting another top quarterback—Bernie Kosar.

Both Testaverde and the redshirted Kosar watched from the sidelines as Jim Kelly finished out his stint as Miami's starting quarterback in 1982. To Testaverde's dismay, the following year he was redshirted, and Kosar was named the team's starter. Kosar led Miami to the 1983 national championships, a bittersweet victory to Testaverde. It meant he had to spend another season backing up the "star."

If Testaverde couldn't take the snaps, he prepared himself to take the hits. He spent hours in the weight room, diligently working out until he was squatting 500 pounds and bench-pressing 325—numbers that put him in a class with many of Miami's linemen. Testaverde, now 6'5" and 220 pounds, knew that his strength, size and mobility set him apart from most

Testaverde almost transferred from Quarterback U, but hung on to become Miami's first Heisman winner.

quarterbacks, and he wasn't about to let go of that advantage. But he was beginning to lose a valuable asset—his patience.

Jimmy Johnson became Miami's head coach in 1984 and, as expected, stayed with Kosar. Testaverde, realizing that Kosar still had two years of eligibility left, started to think seriously about transferring. Kosar apparently hadn't heard of Big Al's dream. Or maybe he had. As the deadline neared for Testaverde to transfer, Kosar told him that he was leaving Miami to enter the NFL and play for his homestate Cleveland Browns.

At long last the door to Big Al's dream was finally open. Yet when Vinny walked through it, he promptly stumbled. In his first start, against Florida, Testaverde made a 13-yard touchdown run, but Florida won the game, hardly a credit to a Heisman dreamer. The game was noteworthy, however. It would be Testaverde's only regular-season loss in two seasons as a starter.

Despite going on to win its next four games, Miami received no support in the polls, and no one paid much attention as Testaverde threw eight touchdown passes and ran for another in those games. Then in Game 6, against Oklahoma—ranked No. 2 and No. 3 in the major polls—Testaverde threw for two touchdowns and ran for a third in a 27–14 upset. Suddenly Miami was on the map, and Testaverde was on the Heisman frontier.

Although Testaverde finished the 10–1 regular season with 3,238 passing yards and 26 touchdowns, including a 339-yard, four-touchdown outing in a come-from-behind victory over Florida State, he finished only fifth in the Heisman voting.

The road to the 1986 Heisman wasn't so much a race as a triumphant procession. Big Al's dream was played out in technicolor on the national screen. From his first tentative game of the year, 231 yards and one touchdown in a 34–14 victory over South Carolina, to his last regular-season appearance, when he eclipsed Kosar's career passing record of 5,971 yards, in a 23–10 victory over Tulsa, Testaverde was the wire-to-wire Heisman leader.

Although impressive in every game, Testaverde nailed down his claim on the trophy with two true Heisman performances. Against top-ranked Oklahoma he completed 21 of 28 passes, including 14 in a row and four touchdowns, in a 28–16 victory, prompting Oklahoma coach Barry Switzer to call him the best quarterback he had seen in his 21 years in coaching.

Then, when Testaverde connected on 10 of 11 fourth-quarter passes against

> **Testaverde, to his dad: "We dreamed it together, we did it together, and tonight I'm proud to say we won it together.**

Florida State, scoring three touchdowns to turn a close game into a 41–23 rout, Seminole coach Bobby Bowden was beside himself. "Testaverde's the cold flat difference, the stinking difference," he said. "He is flat-cold-out the most dominating individual I've ever seen on a football team. That includes O.J. Simpson and anyone else you want to name."

Throughout a season in which some of his teammates were getting into a number of well-publicized scrapes, Testaverde was a model of decorum. But for all his reticent off-field ways, he was the accepted leader of a team of self-styled renegades, in part because when the game began there was no fiercer competitor on the field. Still, it seemed to humanize him a bit when he banged himself up in a motor scooter accident and had to miss the last game, against East Carolina.

Even so, in only two full seasons as the Hurricanes' starting quarterback, Testaverde set team records in career passing yards (6,058), career touchdown passes (48) and career passing efficiency. When it came time to award the Heisman, there were no surprises.

Testaverde beat out running back Paul Palmer of Temple by 1,541 points, at the time the second-greatest margin of victory in the Heisman's history. As Testaverde accepted the award on December 6, 1986, Big Al looked on in what must have been a classic case of déjà vu. First he had dreamed it. Now he was living it. Or, as his son put it, "Dad, we dreamed it together, we did it together, and tonight I'm proud to say we won it together."

After winning the Davey O'Brien Award, the Maxwell Award and the Walter Camp Award in addition to the Heisman, Testaverde was selected No. 1 by the Tampa Bay Buccaneers in the 1987 NFL draft. He played six seasons with the Buccaneers and established many Tampa Bay records, including career passing yards (14,820) and touchdown passes (77), before signing as a free agent with the Cleveland Browns in 1993 as a backup to his old friend Kosar.

As the 1994 season approached, Cleveland's coach, Bill Belichick, released Kosar and named Testaverde his quarterback of the future. The move was puzzling to some but not to anyone who had heard about Big Al's other dream, the one about his son becoming the next Johnny Unitas.

—*Andrew L. Thomas and Robert McG. Thomas Jr.*

Of the first 52 Heisman Trophy winners, exactly three were players who didn't line up behind center. Ends Larry Kelley and Leon Hart won the Heisman, as did flanker Johnny Rodgers. After Rodgers's victory running backs won the next 11 Heismans. The streak reflected the dominance of the running game in the 1970s, when the wishbone left America's dinner table and became a part of the football lexicon.

To restore some balance to offensive football, the NCAA rules poo-bahs began loosening the restrictions on pass blocking in 1980. Linemen could extend their arms. That fall, passing yardage increased nearly 10% and four years later quarterback Doug Flutie threw enough miracles to win the Heisman. In 1986 Vinny Testaverde strode through the door opened by Flutie. Cross off one taboo. The next year Tim Brown of Notre Dame, a flanker and kick returner, crossed off another.

Brown's victory served as a symbol of more than the revitalization of the passing game. His performance became proof that Notre Dame, the school America loved to love/hate (choose one), had returned to the top. Twenty-three years had elapsed since a Fighting Irish player had won the Heisman. Though Brown was the seventh Notre Dame player to win the award, there had never been a longer hiatus between Irish appearances at the D.A.C. And the Irish hadn't been ranked nationally since Dan Devine's final season in 1980.

But in the second season under head coach Lou Holtz, Notre Dame roared back, thanks in large part to the threat presented by Brown. "Tim Brown is the best football player I've ever seen in my life," Holtz said at the end of the 8–3 regular season. He added, "No matter what you say, Tim Brown is the reason we are going to the Cotton Bowl."

Although not a big man (he began his senior year at six feet, 195 pounds and by season's end had dropped down to 182), Brown seemed larger than life. He caught the ball. He ran it. He returned kickoffs. He returned punts. In each of his two seasons under Holtz, Brown averaged more than 20 yards per reception, returned three kicks for touchdowns and scored at least once on the ground.

None of this was anything Brown hadn't done before. At Woodrow Wilson High in Dallas, he played nine different positions, from quarterback to cornerback to kick returner. "Put it this way," his high school coach, Richard Mason, told *Sports Illustrated*. "If Tim Brown didn't get on

Tim Brown

Heir to a Great Tradition

the bus, I didn't get on the bus."

Woodrow, as the high school is known in Dallas, won four games during Brown's career. That didn't scare away the recruiters. Brown narrowed it down to Notre Dame and the local school, SMU. But he didn't like the way SMU recruited him—something about promising him more than the NCAA allowed. Brown went north, and let the record show that the year he won the Heisman, SMU didn't field a team. The NCAA had given the Mustangs the "death penalty."

At Notre Dame, head coach Gerry Faust installed the fleet freshman as his kickoff returner. In his very first game Brown fumbled a kickoff that Purdue converted into a field goal. The Boilermakers went on to upset the eighth-ranked Irish 23–21. Notre Dame didn't reappear in the Top 10 until Brown's senior year.

Brown caught one touchdown pass as a freshman reserve. As a sophomore starter he caught three scoring passes and returned a kickoff for a touchdown. Then Holtz took over for the beleaguered Faust in 1986 and quickly discovered the identity of his best weapon. Holtz made sure that the ball got into Brown's hands whenever possible.

The Irish lost four of their first five games under Holtz. Five minutes before the season ended, the Irish had a 4–6 record and a 37–27 deficit at USC. But with an incredible performance by Brown, Notre Dame gave a preview of things to come. "By himself in the fourth quarter," said former Trojan quarterback Pat Haden, who covered the game for CBS, "Brown brought them back. It's a 60-minute game, but for the past 56 they had gotten beat. Notre Dame had to score. It drives down a couple times just by the sheer athletic ability of one guy. That doesn't happen often in team sports."

Quarterback Steve Beuerlein threw a 49-yard pass to Brown, the key to an 80-yard scoring drive that pulled the Irish to within 37–35. The defense then forced the Trojans to punt. Brown returned it 56 yards to the USC 16. With no time remaining Notre Dame kicked a field goal to make it 38–37. That punt return, by the way, was only the second of Brown's college career.

Brown finished his junior year with 1,937 all-purpose yards, highlighted by two kickoff returns for touchdowns and 45 catches for 910 yards and five scores. But forget the stats. **Brown's explosive speed was what enabled him to end Notre Dame's Heisman drought.**

As the Heisman vote approached in 1987, Dave Anderson offered his readers this rationale for the coronation of Notre Dame's Tim Brown.

As part of its 100th anniversary celebration early next year, Notre Dame intends to display each of the Heisman Trophies that its football players have won. Asked to return his trophy for the exhibit, Paul Hornung preferred to bring it to the campus himself rather than risk shipping it. So not long ago the 1956 winner was walking through the South Bend, Indiana, airport, carrying the bronzed statue of a running back as if it were a football. Suddenly a stranger stared at him.

"Show-off," the man said.

Must've been a South Bend old-timer who remembers when the Heisman Trophy was considered a campus fixture. Angelo Bertelli, John Lujack and Leon Hart have also returned their trophies. Johnny Lattner and John Huarte have yet to comply. But before the exhibit opens, Notre Dame is expected to be applauding its seventh Heisman winner, its first in 23 years: Tim Brown, the wide receiver and kick-returner on the 8–1 team apparently on its way to the Cotton Bowl in only Lou Holtz's second season as coach.

Over the years the Heisman Memorial Trophy, awarded annually to the nation's "most outstanding college football player," has created one of America's most controversial elections. For many of the more than 1,000 sportswriters and sports broadcasters who vote, publicity is often more important than performance, psychology often more important than skill.

Of this year's other candidates, a strong case can be argued for Don McPherson, the Syracuse quarterback, and Lorenzo White, the Michigan State running back. Gordon Lockbaum, the Holy Cross two-way throwback, had 32 first-place votes last year, more than anybody except the winner, Vinny Testaverde, now the Tampa Bay Buccaneers' rookie quarterback. And if Gaston Green, the UCLA tailback, had not missed almost all of three games because of a pinched nerve in his neck, his yardage would be even more impressive.

Most candidates shrug modestly that their team's record is more important than the Heisman Trophy, but Don McPherson says quietly and refreshingly, "I think I've done the type of job that's worthy of the Heisman Trophy." And he has. But even the campus campaign managers for the Syracuse quarterback and this year's other leading candidates sound willing to concede that Tim Brown will be the winner when the announcement is made December 5 at the Downtown Athletic Club.

With two more nationally televised games remaining, against Penn State and Miami (Florida), the Notre Dame All-America appears to have everything going for him: the publicity, the performance, the psychology and the skill.

"I think Tim came into the season as the favorite to win the Heisman," said Roger Valdiserri, his campaign manager as Notre Dame's associate athletic director. "And I can't think of a week when he's lost it."

Brown has caught 32 passes for 729 yards, averaged 21 yards on kickoff returns and 12.3 yards on punt returns. As an occasional running back, he has rushed for 133 yards in 29 carries. He has scored seven touchdowns.

"I've never seen a flanker put so much pressure on the

The USC game set up Brown as the leading Heisman contender for 1987.

Though the D.A.C. didn't award Brown the trophy until December 5, he won it on September 19, when the Irish played Michigan State at Notre Dame Stadium. The game had been moved to an evening kickoff by ESPN, which televised it opposite the Miss America pageant on NBC. In other words, two winners were crowned on that Saturday night.

It didn't even take Brown the whole game. He needed only two punts, four downs apart, late in the first quarter. Brown took the punts 71 and 66 yards, respectively, for touchdowns. When he scored the second touchdown a Notre Dame band member leaped into his arms, the only

person in uniform to lay a hand on Brown. And as Brown made his way toward the tunnel to leave the field, the students serenaded him with chants of "Heisman! Heisman!"

Roger Valdiserri, who had been Notre Dame's sports information director since 1965, called Brown's performance the most exciting moment he had witnessed at Notre Dame Stadium.

The only things missing were a crown, roses and a runway.

His senior year statistics matched his spectacular numbers of the year before despite a late-season injury to his shoulder. Brown caught 39 passes for 846 yards and three touchdowns. He averaged 19.7 yards on his kickoff returns and 11.8 yards returning punts, three for touch-

defense as this kid does, and he's the best kick-returner since Johnny Rodgers won the Heisman at Nebraska," said Hornung, hardly an unbiased observer but certainly a respected one. "I've only known one other football player who brings the crowd to its feet every time he touches the ball—Gale Sayers when he was with the Bears. This kid has the same gift. Jim Brown and O.J. Simpson didn't have it, but Gale Sayers did and Tim Brown does."

Years ago many Heisman voters were influenced by publicity campaigns. But now virtually every serious Heisman candidate can be seen on television. And after watching Brown in Notre Dame's 37–6 rout of Alabama last Saturday on television, he'll get my vote, with Lorenzo White second and Don McPherson third.

If the six-foot, 195-pound Notre Dame senior from Dallas wins the Heisman, he will be the first modern wide receiver to do so. Leon Hart, the 1949 winner, was what now is considered a tight end as well as a fullback and a

defensive end. Larry Kelley, the 1936 winner, was a Yale end in the single-wing formation who also played defense. Each of the other 50 Heisman winners has been either a running back, a quarterback or a single-wing tailback.

Although Notre Dame's national mystique will influence some voters, Brown is hardly a product of that appeal. Jack Butler and Harry Buffington, who supervise the two National Football League scouting combines, believe that Brown might be the very first choice in next year's NFL draft.

"If I had a vote for the Heisman," said Butler, "I would vote for Tim Brown. He does everything. He's a great wide receiver. He does the kick returns better than anybody. I think Don McPherson can be a pro quarterback, but he's not in Brown's class as a prospect. And it's not like Brown is just having a big year all of a sudden. He's been doing this ever since he's been at Notre Dame."

Buffington, if he had a vote, also acknowledged that he would choose Brown, with Lorenzo White second and Scott Davis, a 6'7", 270-pound defensive end at Illinois, third.

"Our scouts think Brown is terrific," Buffington said. "He's got good speed, he's strong and he's big. He could be the No. 1 choice, depending on which team has that choice and what it needs. Whatever happens, he'll be a very early pick in the first round, but I doubt that he'll return punts and kickoffs in the NFL. He's too valuable a wideout to risk on returns."

Once the Cotton Bowl is over, Tim Brown will be asked to return only his Heisman Trophy to Notre Dame's 100th anniversary exhibit.

downs. The Irish reached 8–1 before losing their last two regular-season games as well as the Cotton Bowl.

Brown won the Heisman by a comfortable margin over Syracuse quarterback Don McPherson. While at the D.A.C. on that first Saturday in December, Brown received a congratulatory phone call from President Ronald Reagan. "Yes, sir," Brown said when he picked up the phone. "How ya doin'?"

Brown's award made history. Woodrow Wilson High, the alma mater of 1938 Heisman winner Davey O'Brien, became the first high school to have two alumni win the award. [It did not become the first high school with two Heismans. That was Columbus (Ohio) Eastmore, the alma mater of Archie Griffin.]

The Los Angeles Raiders made Brown the sixth pick of the 1988 NFL draft. He quickly proved himself as a kick returner, winning a Pro Bowl berth in his rookie season. Brown also proved to be a durable star. In 1994 he led the AFC in receiving yardage (1,309) and caught nine scoring passes. In 1993 Brown signed a four-year, $11 million contract with the Raiders.

His Heisman legacy may be that he opened it up to players at his position. After Rodgers won in 1972, it took 15 years for the voters to recognize another receiver. Just four years after Brown's magical performance in 1987, Desmond Howard of Michigan won the Heisman.
—IVAN MAISEL

In many ways Barry Sanders struck a blow to America's free enterprise system. He won the 1988 Heisman Trophy on achievement alone. Neither publicity nor politics helped him. He wasn't from a school with a great Heisman tradition, and he didn't play near a major media center or on television. He hadn't been a starter heading into his junior season at Oklahoma State. All of the above have been considered prerequisites to winning the Heisman.

If a central planning office had been in charge of the Heisman, it couldn't have come up with a better formula to determine the winner than the setup at the start of the 1988 season. In a story line straight out of Hollywood, the top preseason Heisman candidates were from Los Angeles—UCLA's Troy Aikman and USC's Rodney Peete. Both were tall, handsome quarterbacks from high-profile programs. The plan called for them to meet in a late-season showdown to determine who would win the Heisman as the nation's best player.

Aikman and Peete had good seasons. Sanders had a remarkable one.

Central planning could not have forecast that Sanders would burst from obscurity and set more than two dozen NCAA records. No one could have predicted that this 5' 8", 197-pounder would create a new style for running backs, which former Oklahoma coach Barry Switzer would describe as "flying through a keyhole."

At Wichita North High School, Sanders played football with his older brother Byron, who would become a starting running back at Northwestern. Because Byron already played tailback, Barry switched to wingback. He didn't get a spot as running back until four games into his senior season at Wichita North. Sanders gained 1,417 yards, but a 5' 7", 175-pound high schooler was considered too small even for the local Wichita State Shockers, which would later drop its football program.

Sanders had been interested in Oklahoma, but Oklahoma, with a reputation for developing great running backs, wasn't interested in him. "We just blew it," Switzer said. "He was small and a wingback when we saw him."

Oklahoma State assistant coach George Walstad saw Sanders as a running back and hoped no one else found out about him. "I kept the tape [of Sanders] for two weeks to make sure no other coaches

Sanders' powerful but elusive style allowed him to top 300 yards four times and average 238.9 yards per game.

Darting through the Keyhole

would see it," Walstad said.

Sanders showed early signs of promise at Oklahoma State, proving his athleticism with a 4.5 time in the 40-yard dash and a 41-inch vertical leap, but nothing foreshadowed the record-breaking juggernaut of his junior year. His first two years Sanders played behind the All-America running back Thurman Thomas, who set a school record for a season's rushing, with 1,613 yards, in Sanders' sophomore season. Sanders primarily developed a reputation as a kickoff return specialist. He returned the first kickoff of his sophomore season for a touchdown. That year he led the nation in kickoff returns with a 31.6 yard average and had four touchdown returns—two on kickoffs and two on punts. He's the only NCAA player to ever return his team's season-opening kickoffs for touchdowns in consecutive seasons.

It has often been said that true superstars burst onto the scene, but that's not true for Sanders. He exploded.

Two months into his junior season Sanders had gone from being a no-name to being *the* name. He took over the starting spot in 1988 with little fanfare. But by the middle of the season, even former doubter Switzer was convinced of Sanders' ability. "Barry Sanders is the best college player in America and ought to be the favorite for the Heisman Trophy," Switzer said. "I admire talent, and Barry Sanders is a phenomenal talent." Sanders had 304 yards in his third game, against Tulsa. He had more than 1,000 yards in his first five games.

Not only was Sanders breaking records—he was also creating them. "We didn't list the number of 300-yard games, because no one had ever rushed for more than one," said Steve Boda, an NCAA statistician. When Sanders did it four times, it became an NCAA record.

Sanders had big days against mediocre competition, but the top teams couldn't stop him either. Against the Big Three (Colorado, Nebraska and Oklahoma) of the Big Eight Conference, Sanders had 578 yards rushing and 10 touchdowns. His most anticipated challenge came against Nebraska. In 1986 the Cornhuskers had ended the Heisman hopes of Thomas, holding him to seven yards rushing on nine carries and beating Oklahoma State 35–0. This year Nebraska would again win, but in a tougher battle. Sanders ended the game with 189 yards and four touchdowns in a 63–42 loss. "If there was ever any doubt—and I don't believe there was—this proves that Barry Sanders is the real thing," Oklahoma State coach Pat Jones said following the game.

Sanders' season became a statistician's delight. He even broke the oldest record in the books: The all-purpose yardage mark (246.3) set by Byron (Whizzer) White in 1937 was the only record remaining from the first year the NCAA started keeping records. Sanders shattered the record with 295.5 all-purpose yards per game. He had 2,628 yards rushing, 106 yards receiving, 95 yards in punt returns and 421 yards in kickoff returns. "He [Sanders] averaged almost as many yards rushing alone [238.9] as Whizzer had in the categories put together," said Jim Van Valkenburg of the NCAA.

The most recognizable NCAA records that Sanders broke were for single-season rushing and touchdowns. Marcus Allen of USC had set the rushing record with 2,342 yards, which Sanders beat by 286 yards. His 37 touchdowns shattered the record of 29 shared by both Lydell Mitchell of Penn State and Mike Rozier of Nebraska. Sanders' 7.6 yards per carry average was so far ahead of Allen's NCAA record (5.81 for more than 300 carries) that Sanders could have rushed 95 times for no gain in his season finale and still beaten the mark.

His size, which looked to be such a liability at first, proved to be an asset. Sanders combined his compact strength and quickness with an unusual ability to see and make quick cuts. He was a master at weaving, dodging and bursting upfield, and his 37-inch thighs made arm-tackling useless. The Sanders style of running with short, quick steps changed the way some coaches looked for running backs, away from big sprinters with long strides. "There's no real secret to running," Sanders said. "You just try to avoid people. It's no trick at all. But it's weird sometimes. You keep pounding and pounding away, and then you see a hole open up. And it's like a big boost of energy from inside you."

Sanders was not a one-season wonder. Picked by the Detroit Lions in the first round of the 1989 NFL draft, Sanders was the NFL Rookie of the Year in 1990 and the NFC's Most Valuable Player in 1991 and 1994.

The player who had started out on nobody's Heisman list ended up on top of nearly everybody's. Sanders won the Heisman with the 10th-largest margin and had 559 first-place votes. Peete finished second with 70 first-place votes and Aikman third with 31 first-place votes.

Sanders was only the eighth junior to win the Heisman. He decided not to try to become the second to win it back-to-back, opting for the NFL primarily because the only NCAA records left to break were his own. —*DAVID MCNABB*

Andre Ware

A Winner in the Womb

When Joyce Ware was carrying her firstborn, she detected some unusual movement. So did her mother, Marie Gentry, who placed her hand on her daughter's belly one day in 1968 and issued her verdict: "You've got a football player in there."

In the annals of prenatal prognostication, Granny Gentry's pronouncement ranks as understatement. She did not happen to mention that the baby would grow up to shatter collegiate passing records at the University of Houston, win the 1989 Heisman Memorial Trophy as a junior and then sign a multimillion-dollar contract as a first-round draft choice of the Detroit Lions.

His career as a football player may have been foreordained, but for Andre Ware, who was born in Dickinson, Texas, the road to stardom would not be easy. When Andre was three, his parents were divorced. Four years later his father, a teacher, died of viral pneumonia. His mother, who supported her son by working as a maid and busing tables until she became a clerk at the post office, did her best to make up for the loss. Joyce Ware, admittedly overprotective of her only child, also did her best to keep her mother's prediction from coming true. She encouraged her son to play baseball, but when it came to youth football she made it a point to miss the sign-up deadline two years in a row.

But for all her fear of football, Joyce Ware was Andre's fiercest supporter when he went out for the junior high team. When he came home in tears one day after his teammates had teased him about having a weak arm, she persuaded him to lift weights. "Never be a quitter, no matter how tough times get," she said.

Andre was the starting quarterback his last two years at Dickinson High School. The team used a winged-T formation with an emphasis on the run, and as an option quarterback, Ware threw just 71 passes as a senior in 1985, only one for a touchdown. But he was good enough to attract the interest, if not the enthu-

The first black quarterback to win the Heisman, Ware more than lived up to his grandmother's expectations.

siasm, of college recruiters, who tended to look at the 6'2", 205-pound quarterback and see a defensive back.

At the University of Houston, the story was different. Faced with an NCAA investigation into recruiting violations committed under coach Bill Yeoman, Houston was prepared to let Ware, or any other promising prospect, write his own ticket. Besides, Yeoman used a run-oriented veer offense, and with his high school experience, Ware would fit right in. But there was an obstacle. Ware learned that he had taken his SAT tests on a date not approved by the NCAA. Even though the Southwest Conference had listed the date, Ware and about 20 other conference recruits were out of luck. Only by taking the SATs again on the next approved date and enrolling in the spring could Ware preserve his eligibility.

After passing the SATs a second time, he arrived at the University of Houston in 1987 just in time for spring practice and another shock. Yeoman had been forced out as coach and his vaunted veer offense had gone with him.

The new coach, Jack Pardee, who had plans to install a run-and-shoot passing offense, hardly knew what to do with his hand-me-down option quarterback, but he gave him a chance. After a blowout loss the first game of the season, Ware was promoted to starter, but he broke an arm in the fifth game and was out for the season. As an alternate starter the following year, Ware played in all 11 games, completing 212 of 356 passes for 2,507 yards and a Southwest Conference-record 25 touchdowns.

Even before the 1989 season began, Ware was a hero on the Houston campus. After completing its investigation into past recruiting violations and imposing a three-year probation, including a ban on television and bowl games, the NCAA allowed Houston players a chance to transfer to other schools without the usual loss of a year's eligibility. Ware decided to stay, but then, he had always thrived on adversity.

His 1989 drive for the Heisman would have adversity aplenty, not to mention the undertones of a morality play. For one thing, he began the season as a distinct underdog, barely known outside the Southwest Conference. In a season in which Houston would not play a single game before a national television audience, it hardly seemed possible that Ware could overcome such a disadvantage, while rivals such as quarterbacks Major Harris of West Virginia and Tony Rice of Notre Dame dominated the highlight shows every week.

Houston played its first two games at night, too late for Ware's statistics to be included in the next day's East Coast reports. That meant few in the nation knew that Ware completed 30 of 48 passes for 390 yards and five touchdowns in a 69–0 drubbing of Nevada–Las Vegas or that he completed 41 of 69 passes for 503 yards and two touchdowns in a 36–7 victory over Arizona State.

When word of Ware's remarkable exploits did begin to get around, after he completed 30 of 45 passes for 413 yards and seven touchdowns in a 65–7 victory over Temple, the response tended to be, "So what?" Houston, it was claimed, was beating up on pushover opponents, and besides, Pardee's run-and-shoot offense practically guaranteed big passing numbers against weak opponents. Wait and see what happens when Houston faces a tough opponent, such as, say, Baylor, which was ranked first in the nation in pass defense.

The next week, when Houston beat Baylor 66–10, with Ware completing 33 of 53 passes for 514 yards and six touchdowns, Ware's Heisman bid had to be taken seriously. So seriously, in fact, that the long knives began to come out. Houston, it was repeatedly pointed out, was on probation for grave rules violations. Never mind that Ware was in junior high school when those violations were committed, no player from a probation team had ever won the Heisman.

It didn't help that Ware's chief rival, Anthony Thompson, a devout Indiana running back who dropped to his knees after every touchdown, spent a good part of the season praying in other team's end zones.

Amid the growing controversy, Ware's six-touchdown performance against the crack Baylor defense, which allowed only two other passing touchdowns all season, helped him weather a 17–13 loss to Texas A&M the next week. Then a 95–21 victory over Southern Methodist almost did him in. The outsized win over SMU, which was just returning to football after a two-year NCAA "death penalty," drew cries of outrage and accusations that Pardee was running up scores against hapless opponents simply to inflate Ware's statistics. Whatever Pardee may have been guilty of, including achieving the first 1,000-yard offensive performance in a college game, it hardly seemed fair to hold it against Ware, who played only 12 minutes, just long enough to complete 25 of 41 passes for 517 yards, six touchdowns and three NCAA records.

Besides, the complaint struck some as outlandish in the context of the Heisman Trophy, which is, after all, named for the man who coached Georgia Tech to its famous 222–0 victory over Cumberland in 1916.

Even so, it was becoming increasingly clear that Ware could win the Heisman only if his rivals lost it. As a result, a 352-yard, three-touchdown game in a 46–34 loss to Arkansas and a 477-yard, six-touchdown game in a 55–10 victory over Texas Christian seemed to matter little.

Neither, for that matter, did a routine 475-yard, four-touchdown outing in a 40–24 victory over Texas Tech on Thanksgiving weekend, the last game before the Heisman ballots were due.

What *did* make a difference, by most accounts, was that Thompson and Rice both faltered in their final games that weekend, leaving reasonable voters little choice. Even so, Ware barely squeaked to victory, edging Thompson by 70 points in the fourth-closest vote in Heisman history and becoming the first black quarterback to win the award.

Ware was not at the announcement ceremony at the Downtown Athletic Club. He was otherwise engaged, leading Houston to a 64–0 victory over Rice at Rice Stadium, the very campus where John W. Heisman himself had ended his 36-year coaching career in 1927. Playing less than three quarters, Ware completed 36 of 51 passes for 400 yards and two touchdowns, adding eight NCAA records to his total, including season marks for completions (365), passing offense (4,699 yards) and touchdowns per game (4.2).

His mother accepted the Heisman Trophy for him in New York, and in a television hookup from Houston, Ware gave a graceful speech, accepting the award, "for my teammates and the University of Houston." He did not mention his grandmother who many years earlier had predicted his football success.

Although he said at the time that he would return for his senior season, Ware decided he could not justify making his mother work another year. After the Detroit Lions chose him with the seventh pick in the first round of the NFL draft, he signed a four-year, $8 million contract.

But Ware's years in Detroit proved frustrating. After playing in only four games in 1990 and one in 1991, he started the last three games of the 1992 season, leading the Lions to two victories. However, 1993 again found him serving as a backup for most of the season. Having played out his contract, Ware moved to the Canadian Football League in 1994, but limited playing time still left the football world wondering whether he would ever live up to the promise he showed in college.

Not that he had to. Nobody who saw him play for Houston in 1989 could give his grandmother any argument. —ROBERT MCG. THOMAS JR.

Despite pressure from defenders and moralists alike, Ware set marks for yards and completions in a season.

The package came in the mail just before the start of the season. It was one of many that sportswriters find jammed into their mailboxes in August, the official start of the hype season. Hype for All-American, hype for the Outland Trophy, hype for all sorts of awards, including the ultimate one: the Heisman Trophy.

Heisman hype has come in many forms over the years. But it's safe to say it never came like this. Inside their mailboxes the sportswriters found a blue cardboard tie. The slogan said it all: "The official Heisman Ty."

The tie never went out of style that season. When it came to college football in 1990, Brigham Young's Ty Detmer was the sport's best-dressed man.

Detmer accomplished a feat that eluded all the great modern BYU quarterbacks, including Jim McMahon, Steve Young and Robbie Bosco. He won the school's first Heisman. In accepting the award Detmer said he won it for his predecessors who had eye-popping numbers yet were slighted because only a few eyes ever saw them. "They all had great seasons, and a couple of them could have won it," said Detmer, who was a junior at the time. "They set the tone here. It would have been a devastating blow to BYU if we hadn't won it this year. Now, we finally have it."

Detmer won it in grand fashion, easily outdistancing Notre Dame's Rocket Ismail. It's fitting that Detmer won the award over a player from football's most publicized school. Even though Detmer didn't get the same kind of exposure, there was no denying his numbers. He completed 361 passes for 5,188 yards and an amazing 41 touchdowns for the 10–3 Cougars. "After seeing those numbers, I would have voted for Detmer," Ismail said.

The Heisman winner-to-be launched his campaign with a bang. In the second game of the season, against defending national champion Miami, Detmer put on one of the greatest shows in Brigham Young history. He completed 38 of 54 passes for 406 yards in the Cougars' stunning 28–21 win. Detmer's frenetic runs left the Miami defenders grabbing for air all night. Their best hits came in pounding the ground in frustration. Detmer, off and running for the Heisman, modestly insisted that the Miami game was "just one game. If somebody makes their decision on the Heisman just based on one game, then it's not worth having."

Detmer, a San Antonio native, was relentlessly pursued in

Ty for the Win

high school, but he didn't even make a recruiting trip. He had been convinced by a family trip to Provo that it was the place for him. "My lifestyle fits the lifestyle at Brigham Young," said Detmer, who grew up as a Methodist. "I wanted a good, clean school with no distractions. I knew about BYU's passing game and their great quarterbacks, so my dad [a football coach] and I came on a trip to BYU the summer before my senior year of high school. We saw the facilities, and I was ready. We didn't visit any other school."

Detmer hardly fit the profile of a big-time quarterback when he arrived at BYU. The press guide listed him at 6' 1" and 175 pounds. Don't believe everything you read in press guides. "He was probably 5'11" and 155 pounds," recalled Brigham Young coach LaVell Edwards after his first meeting with Detmer. "I expected to see a John Elway and instead I saw a Pee Wee Herman. He looked like he was 15."

Edwards, though, soon found out that looks can be deceiving. Detmer had the scrambler's knack for making something out of nothing. Just when it appeared he would be sacked, he would turn a loss into a touchdown. He was also extremely competitive and unafraid of keeping other players in line. During one game Detmer noticed an offensive lineman's attention straying to a cheerleader. A whack in the head was his wake-up call.

"[McMahon and Detmer] are both excellent leaders," Edwards said. "Coming out of high school [they] were probably as advanced as any quarterbacks we've had. They each have the innate ability to make something out of nothing. Jim makes things happen. So does Ty. On that last drive you want them to be your quarterback."

Against Washington State, Detmer proved just how right Edwards was. BYU was hopelessly behind at halftime, but Detmer rallied his team for a 43-point second half to take a 50–36 victory. Then in the 1989 Holiday Bowl, Detmer riddled Penn State for 576 yards through the air, even though the Nittany Lions won 50–39. "Dan Marino never had that kind of night against us," Penn State coach Joe Paterno said. "Detmer is a great one. He smells of confidence. He has a great feel for the field and was not confused by anything we threw at him. We threw a lot of things at Detmer that a lot of good

Rather than let people down after winning the Heisman (in his junior year), Detmer decided to return to school for his senior year. He graduated owning virtually every NCAA passing record.

quarterbacks have not handled well over the years and were confused with. He wasn't."

Added Penn State linebacker Andre Collins: "He had me running around like a chicken with my head cut off. We didn't play that bad. Detmer is just that good."

Detmer typically reacted to praise as if he were going for the Heisman Trophy for modesty. "I get too much credit," he said. "The credit should go to the team." A good time for the polite Detmer is a hunting or fishing trip, although he does like a practical joke. Once after a barbecue he took a hog's head and left it on a teammate's pillow, a move that would have made Marlon (the "Godfather") Brando proud. Another time he invited teammate David Henderson to an ESPN taping. When Henderson got there, Detmer stuck a pie in his face.

"I like to loosen things up sometimes," Detmer said. Detmer also enjoyed mixing it up on the field but in a different way. "Whenever there's a brawl on the field, he's always in there," said Detmer's tight end Chris Smith. "He goes after tackles and linebackers, always someone big. It seems like he's a magnet to the largest guy out there. The coaches get mad at him, of course. We tell him if he's going to swing, do it with his left hand."

"Off the field I never get upset at anything," Detmer said. "But on the field, I've never been one to back down. I'm a competitive person." Little wonder that one writer said Detmer was a cross between Richie Cunningham and Bart Simpson. The combination, though, couldn't have been better. "If there's such a thing as a coach's dream," Edwards said, "Ty's it."

After winning the Heisman, Detmer didn't think twice about staying in school for his senior year. He said, "I'd be letting people down if I didn't stay." With just 12 interceptions compared to 28 during his Heisman year, his game was cleaner, and he threw for 4,031 yards and 35 touchdowns. Those would be Heisman numbers in most years, but when the Cougars got off to a slow start, Detmer lost pace with the eventual winner, Desmond Howard, and finished third in the voting. It didn't matter to the folks at Brigham Young. His status as an icon was already secure. He left the school owning virtually every NCAA passing record. Detmer was the career leader in, among other categories, passing efficiency (162.7), passing yards (15,031) and touchdowns (121).

Then, of course, there's the Heisman. For one year Detmer had Brigham Young at the center of the college football universe. He made sure he lived up to his slogan. The Heisman did indeed finish in a Ty.

—ED SHERMAN

Desmond Howard

Magic Fingers

The spectacular feat performed by Desmond Howard against Notre Dame doesn't have a fancy label such as the Immaculate Reception or even the Catch.

Perhaps it's just as well. History now should call it the Heisman, because it was this game-clinching, diving reception that propelled Howard to college football's highest honor in 1991. Before the Notre Dame game, the Wolverines' second of the season, Howard, a wide receiver, wasn't even a serious candidate for the Heisman. After that game he was the front-runner.

In a landslide victory Howard received 640 out of 753 first-place votes for the 57th Heisman Memorial Trophy, an 85% ratio, and followed Tom Harmon (1940) as Michigan's second Heisman winner.

Howard's hands, along with his fleet legs and uncanny concentration, brought him to this pinnacle. Never did the combination work better than against Notre Dame. Sitting on a narrow 17–14 lead in the fourth quarter, Michigan faced a fourth down and one from the Irish 25. In a shocking decision quarterback Elvis Grbac went back to pass. It was the kind of call that could ruin a coach's career. But Gary Moeller was confident, for he had Howard. As the ball went up in the air, the 106,000 fans in Michigan Stadium let out a huge gasp. The ball seemed destined for the stands, and Notre Dame seemed on the verge of making a huge stop.

Howard, though, wouldn't allow it. He stretched and stretched his body until he hung parallel to the ground, as if in suspended animation. Somehow, with not even an inch to spare, Howard pulled the ball in for a touchdown.

Michigan Stadium exploded. Notre Dame coach Lou Holtz couldn't believe what he saw. Only the Irish are supposed to produce such miracles.

The player nicknamed Magic tried to explain his illusion against Notre Dame. "I remember it got silent. Everybody was looking for the ball. I hit this fifth gear and kept my eye on the ball, and I dove for it. I wanted that

Howard scored 23 touchdowns in 1991, one on a 93-yard kickoff return against Ohio State.

1991 Desmond Howard

ball. Nobody else was going to get to it."

It was the play of the season, of any season. The catch went beyond numbers, although Howard had those, too. In 1991 he scored 23 touchdowns, at least one in every game; in all but two games he reached the end zone at least twice. He had 61 receptions for 950 yards and averaged 17.4 yards per punt return. And he did it all with a flair befitting his nickname. The Notre Dame miracle wasn't a one-time event. Howard never seemed to catch a touchdown when he wasn't flinging his body parallel to the ground.

Howard was hardly the Heisman front-runner entering his junior season. While he had come off a good sophomore year, the 1990 winner, Ty Detmer, was the favorite to repeat. But Howard burst onto the scene in the season opener, against Boston College, scoring four touchdowns. Then the Notre Dame touchdown propelled him into the national spotlight. Howard never let up. He punctuated his season with a 93-yard punt return for a touchdown against Ohio State. After he ran into the end zone, he cast himself into the classic Heisman pose. He was merely rehearsing for receiving the real thing. "All I wanted to do was be consistent," Howard said. "I tried not to think about the Heisman, but it was very difficult. You guys [the reporters] reminded me of it every day. I just wanted to keep my focus."

Howard said his mother's reaction to the award summed up his feelings. Watching from her Cleveland home, she broke into tears at the announcement. "Besides having me in 1970, this is the most emotional day of her life," Howard cracked, then flashed a bright smile, a grin comparable to that of the original Magic. Howard also has an engaging, unusual laugh, a staccato, "Hehehehhehheh."

> As the Irish discovered, levitation was one of the countless tricks "Magic" had up his sleeve.

That's the public side of Howard. In 1991 he not only was the nation's best player, he also was the most charismatic. But there was another side to Howard, one completely different from the showman on the football field. "Being a football player is a part of me," Howard said. "But it's not the biggest part of me. There's a lot to me people don't know about." During a 90-minute lunch interview the conversation never focused on football. Instead, the serious and thoughtful Howard preferred to talk about such topics as his desire to become a Ph.D.

Michigan wasn't a pit stop for Howard on his way to the pros. He earned a degree in communications, which meant as much to him as winning the Heisman. "Nobody else in my family has their degree," Howard said at the

time. He would go to classes in a dress shirt and tie, carrying a briefcase. "You should look like you aspire to be," he said. Despite his coaches' wishes, he lived off-campus in nearby Ypsilanti, away from distractions that could keep him from concentrating on school.

While at Michigan, Howard became interested in his black heritage. "You don't learn about history by just reading books," Howard said. "I like to seek out knowledge. Being a scholar has been very rewarding. I want to investigate things for myself." A visit with noted sociologist and black leader Harry Edwards prompted Howard to work on his public speaking. He knew his status as an athlete opened up doors with young people, and he wanted the chance to influence them.

"I didn't grow up in a ghetto, but drugs were pervasive in my neighborhood," Howard said. "I was chased by gangs. Some of the people I knew are now in juvenile homes, or even were killed. I know it's not easy, but I came from that environment, and I did something with myself. I try to leave them with something positive. I don't think you reach everyone in a crowd. That's virtually impossible. But if each one teaches one, then you're doing your job."

After he won the Heisman, Howard spoke of coming back for his senior year. But the following Rose Bowl, a crushing loss to Washington, was a major disappointment. Howard reconsidered his options and came to the conclusion that he had accomplished all his goals at Michigan. He bypassed his senior year and was chosen in the first round by the Washington Redskins.

No matter what he does in the pros, they will always talk about Howard at Michigan. He was a fine ambassador for the school and, along with Harmon, holds a special place there. The fans will remember him as a thrilling and game-breaking player. Yet, at the end of an interview, Howard was asked how he would like to be recalled—as Dr. Howard or as a football player. Howard flashed his grin and let out a short "Hehhehheh."

"I'd rather be remembered as Dr. Howard who broke all the records at Michigan."   —*ED SHERMAN*

On the day that Miami quarterback Gino Torretta won the Heisman Memorial Trophy, more than 125 people squeezed their way into Antler's Tavern in tiny Pinole, California.

Had the town's fire marshal seen the crowd on that December 12, 1992, there would have been citations galore for the Torrettas, who own the bar and the two-story building that houses it at town's center. Friends and neighbors were happily pinned shoulder to shoulder in the cozy confines. They were there to honor one of their own, the local boy made good. As the minutes ticked down before the announcement, someone in the bar began chanting, "Gi-no, Gi-no, Gi-no!" Soon the entire tavern was alive with the chant.

At last it was time. A name was read—Torretta's name. Smiles in Manhattan. Bedlam in Pinole.

Torretta, who wore his lucky white socks with his newly purchased double-breasted suit, walked quickly to the podium where he was presented with the 25-pound stiff-arming statuette. His mother, Connie, and his three brothers sat nearby. Look hard and you could see the pride. Tears weren't so difficult to detect, either.

Torretta had received 1,400 points, a 320-point margin over second-place finisher Marshall Faulk, the sophomore running back from San Diego State. Out of the 779 ballots, Torretta earned 310 first-place votes, which was more than the combined total of Faulk and third-place finisher Garrison Hearst of Georgia.

At the microphone Torretta thanked the members of the Downtown Athletic Club, his coaches and teammates at Miami, his athletic director, his university president, his mother and brothers. Then Torretta took a deep breath and, as his lower lip quivered with emotion, said, "To my dad: without whom I would not be here today."

Al Torretta died of a stroke-induced brain hemorrhage on September 4, 1988, and never saw his youngest son play a single down of football for the Miami Hurricanes. He didn't see Gino work his way from depth-chart oblivion to an unexpected debut as a redshirt freshman in 1989. Nor did he see Gino enter the starting lineup when Craig Erickson broke a finger during the Michigan State game that same season. Most important, he couldn't comfort his son when Gino threw four interceptions against archrival Florida State, which marked his one and only regular-season loss as a Hurricane starter.

With Torretta as its quarterback, Miami won one

Gino Torretta

Doing it for Dad

national championship and almost a second. It lost only two games during his entire tenure, one against the Seminoles, one against Alabama in the 1993 Sugar Bowl. Along the way the 6' 3", 205-pound Torretta won more games (26) than any quarterback in the Hurricanes' distinguished football history, including such stars as Heisman winner Vinny Testaverde, Bernie Kosar, Jim Kelly, Steve Walsh and Craig Erickson. Torretta also finished his Miami career as the school's alltime leader in passing yards, completions, attempts and total offense.

"Gino is smart, he makes few mistakes and he probably operates the offense better than anyone I've ever had," Miami coach Dennis Erickson once said.

As early as his junior year in high school Torretta promised his mother that he would win the Heisman for her. It was a nice thought, but no one truly believed he would make good on his pledge. Or did they? Torretta's name was nowhere to be found among the top 100 high school recruits. His arm strength was suspect and his foot speed not overly impressive. Still, his brother Geoff, who served as backup quarterback to Testaverde at Miami, detected something that others missed. "After his freshman camp he looked impressive," Geoff said. "I remember thinking, He's gonna play here."

Gino did, but on the day after the start of the Hurricanes' 1988 season, his father had a stroke. "I always felt bad for Gino," said Connie Torretta, whose nickname for her youngest son is Precious. "In [Gino's] accomplishments, Al wasn't there to say, 'Good boy.' We raised our kids with the thought that you can do anything you set your mind to. With Gino, he's received the best, achieved the best and made it all come true. But Al's not here to say, 'See, I knew you could do it.'"

When the town of Pinole needed a new scoreboard for the baseball field, Al bought it. If a team needed a sponsor, Al would foot the bill. When workers from the local sugar factory went on strike, Al took several of them aside and sent them each off with $50 worth of groceries from his store. "Al, I can't pay for any of this," one worker said. "Don't worry about it," Al replied.

When Al died there wasn't an empty seat to be found at the funeral Mass at St. Joseph's Church. "You would have thought the Pope passed away," said family friend Bill

Torretta's leadership was just as critical to his Heisman success as his statistics.

218

McCombe.

Maybe it was just coincidence, but after every touch-down pass Gino threw for the Hurricanes he seemed to glance upward, as if making sure Al had noticed. And in his final home game at Miami, Torretta paid another private tribute to his father. On the sidelines that day was his brother Gary, who approached Gino after the game. "You know, it's Dad's birthday today," Gary said.

"I know," said Gino, flashing his wristbands with the word *Dad* on them.

Torretta's game-by-game statistics in 1992 were impressive but not always overpowering. He threw for 433 yards and two touchdowns against Iowa, 350 yards and three touchdowns against Texas Christian, 363 yards and three touchdowns against West Virginia, 343 yards against Syracuse and 310 yards and one touchdown against San Diego State. Better yet, he threw just seven interceptions during the regular season. And he won. Eleven regular-season games, 11 victories.

In a 19–16 win against Florida State, Torretta completed just 20 of 48 passes for 252 yards. But when asked afterward who was the difference in the game, glum Seminole coach Bobby Bowden issued a one-word answer. "Torretta," he said. Against Penn State, Torretta had only 11 completions in 31 attempts for 80 yards and no touchdowns. Still, he somehow helped the Hurricanes squeak past the Nittany Lions 17–14. "I feel I did a lot more things as an individual," said Faulk later, who rushed for 1,630 yards that year. "But Gino was a great team leader. He's helped his team to two successful seasons."

For Torretta those were words to live by. Taught to him, of course, by his father. "He'd be happy, and he'd be proud, but he wouldn't say much," said Gino of his father. "He'd probably still treat me like I was his youngest kid. He wasn't really one to talk much."

Upon arriving home to Pinole after the Heisman ceremony, Torretta was honored with a parade and a standing-room only banquet. Torretta had only one favor to ask of the organizers: Could the autographed pictures he planned to sign please be sold to benefit some of the local youth basketball and football leagues?

The organizers of Gino Torretta Day couldn't say yes fast enough. Of course, Torretta's request shouldn't have surprised anyone. After all, like father, like son.

—*Gene Wojciechowski*

Charlie Ward

The Renaissance Man

No one quite remembers the year, but Charlie Ward Sr. remembers the day a friend came to him and boldly predicted that Charlie Ward Jr., still in grade school at the time, would someday win the Heisman Trophy. The thought made Junior, as he is still called in his hometown of Thomasville, Georgia, uncomfortable. The idea of personal honors was not part of his makeup. Do everything you can to make your team successful, said his father, and the individual glory will take care of itself.

Charlie Ward was to find glory for himself and his team in a brilliant career that saw him play two sports, football and basketball, at the very highest level of college competition. On December 11, 1993, the Florida State quarterback became the 59th recipient of the Heisman Memorial Trophy after a season in which he set 19 school records, including a total offense mark of 3,371 yards.

Two weeks after receiving the Heisman, Ward helped his team enjoy the ultimate accomplishment. Trailing 16–15 with less than two minutes to go in the Orange Bowl, Ward led his team down the field and put the Seminoles into position to kick a game-winning field goal. The next morning Florida State was declared college football's national champion, making Ward the first Heisman Trophy winner since Pittsburgh's Tony Dorsett in 1976 to play for a national champion.

And Ward's collegiate athletic career was far from over. He reported for basketball practice the next day and went on to lead the Seminoles to a 25–10 record and the final eight in the NCAA tournament. "Charlie is the best point guard in the nation," said veteran NBA scout Marty Blake. The New York Knicks must have agreed, making him a first-round selection in the NBA draft.

Unlike that of many great players, Ward's star did not suddenly burst onto the horizon with his arrival on the Florida State campus. After signing with the Seminoles in February 1988, he sat out a year for academic reasons and attended community college. In 1989

Ward had to wait several years before Bowden gave him the ball and the Seminole offense.

he was Florida State's punter, and in 1990 there were so many good quarterbacks in the program he took a red-shirt year. He was a little-used backup in 1991.

Doesn't sound like a Heisman story so far, does it?

Even after Ward finally became the starter, in 1992, there were lingering doubts about his ability to play quarterback at such a high level. He threw eight interceptions in his first two games as starting quarterback. In a nationally televised game against Clemson, he had four interceptions, and as a result Clemson led 20–17 with time running out. But in the final minutes Ward directed a 77-yard drive that ended with his throwing a nine-yard touchdown pass. Florida State won the game 24–20, and no one ever doubted Charlie Ward again.

"That's when I knew that nothing would ever bother him," said Bowden. "Another kid would have folded up his tent after four interceptions. Not Charlie. He wanted to win."

While the Clemson comeback solidified Ward's place in the minds of the Florida State coaches, the final turning point did not come until a month later, on October 17, when the Seminoles faced Georgia Tech in Atlanta. Ward was still making mistakes, and Georgia Tech took a 21–7 lead in the second half. At the insistence of FSU assistant Brad Scott, Bowden switched to a no-huddle, shotgun offense. The rest is football history: Ward rallied Florida State for three touchdowns in the fourth quarter and a 29–24 victory.

After the Georgia Tech game Bowden & Co. went exclusively with the fast-break offense, which proved to be just the right vehicle to maximize Ward's special talents. Florida State finished 11–1 after beating Nebraska in the Orange Bowl, and Ward garnered a season-total 2,647 yards passing and 22 touchdowns.

While his numbers were impressive in 1992, in 1993 they were staggering. The year before, while still learning the position, Ward threw 17 interceptions. In 1993 he attempted 15 more passes but threw only four interceptions while completing almost 70%.

But Ward transcended mere statistics. He brought magic to the team in addition to communicating the sense that he was in total control. At no time was this trait more evident than in the regular-season finale at archrival Florida. In four years under coach Steve Spurrier the Gators had won 23 straight games at home. Florida State already had one loss, and another would knock them out of the national championship picture. To that end the Gators and the

Ward was not a classic passer but he got the job done, throwing for 49 TDs in his two years as a starter.

boisterous crowd at Florida Field were primed.

In the fourth quarter Florida had rallied from a 27–7 deficit and scored to come within six points with 5:58 remaining in the game. A penalty on the ensuing kickoff forced FSU to start its next drive from its own 21-yard line. The noise at Florida Field was deafening.

After Ward's first two passes were batted down, the crowd grew louder still. Inside the nervous Florida State huddle Ward was an island of calm. He called the season's crucial third-down play and sent his team to the line of scrimmage.

Ward's primary receiver was covered down the middle. Ward slipped away from pressure and found his roommate, freshman running back Warrick Dunn, just one step behind a linebacker out in the flat. It was a perfect touch pass that Dunn caught without ever breaking stride. He raced 79 yards for a touchdown. Florida State won 33–21 and kept its national championship hopes alive.

Ward ended that game completing 38 of 53 passes for 446 yards, the best day ever for an opposing quarterback against Florida. It also ended all speculation about who would be receiving the Heisman two weeks later. Ward won the Heisman by 1,622 points, the second-largest margin of victory ever next to O.J. Simpson's in 1968.

Ward accepted the trophy with all the calm and gratitude that had marked his tenure at FSU. "It says my name on the trophy, but behind my name are the names of all the coaches and players and family who put me here," said Ward.

Bowden, for one, thought Ward was being too modest. And no wonder: When Charlie Ward left Florida State he had a 23–2 record as the Seminoles' starting quarterback. In just two seasons he had thrown 49 touchdown passes. He also had two bowl victories and a national championship to his credit. Forget the fact that Ward wasn't drafted by an NFL team, an oddity easily explained by the fears—well founded as it turned out—that Ward would pick the NBA as his next destination. In the end, no one doubted his talent or his character. "Hey, it was a great ride for all of us," said Bowden. "We just appreciated the fact that Charlie let us go along." —*Tony Barnhart*

1994
Rashaan Salaam

Like A Political Campaign

Football is more of a team game than ever before. As many as 50 sound players are now deemed necessary every Saturday by those aspiring to a conference title, a major bowl bid, or the so-called national championship.

Nevertheless the spotlight on a single player—the Heisman Trophy winner—has intensified so much, that the candidates are examined, shuffled and re-examined from September to December.

The process, very much like a national political campaign. begins with the media's preseason previews of the most likely candidates and continues each week driven by the numbers—yards gained by run, by pass or catch. The Heisman victor is determined by these statistics,as there is no other way for a consensus to emerge from the 800 electors. Players who either run with the ball, throw it or catch it, can forget the Heisman.

It helps if a candidate's team is a winning one, near the top in the weekly polls. The other vital elements are the fates—what happens to the other guys.

Rashaan Salaam's Heisman season of 1994 was so perfect, it could have been scripted by a political scientist teaching a seminar on how to become President.

The Colorado tailback had been a secondary candidate in the previews found in the college football annuals, the daily sports pages. the television studio discussions and the radio talk shows. He was just another running back, without the renown of one like Washington's flashy Napoleon Kaufman.

The Salaam campaign began quietly. Like the New Hampshire primary, it was not to be taken too seriously. Colorado routed Northeast Louisiana, 48 - 13, as Salaam rushed for 184 yards and scored three touchdowns. So what.

Against an unformidable opponent, one playing a Division I-A foe for the first time in over a decade, such a performance was an expectation rather than a surprise. Salaam, a 21-year-old junior from San Diego, Calif., 6'1", 215 pounds, had been programmed since spring practice to be the No. 1 tailback in Colorado's powerful single-back option offense, after sharing the position with Lamont Warren the season before. Warren, then a junior, had left school early to turn pro, the first of many fates to turn Salaam's way.

Rashaan needed national exposure to become a household name. Deion Sanders put it best, "I'm household."

He got it the next two Saturdays. Colorado hosted Wisconsin, the defending Rose Bowl team ranked No. 10 in the polls, in an ESPN nationally televised event and it won, 55 -17. The size of the score, was noteworthy as were Salaam's four touchdowns.

The Buffaloes caught everyone's attention at Ann Arbor the following Saturday. The game's last play, a 64 - yard touchdown pass and ricochet catch from Kordell Stewart to Michael Westbrook with 00:00 showing on the clock, was called "The Miracle in Michigan," or "The Throw." Colorado had won, 27-26.

The play put Salaam's 141 rushing yards and two touchdowns in the shade but significantly he had outgained the Wolverines' Tyrone Wheatley by 91 yards.

Wheatley, a somewhat bigger running back and the foremost Heisman candidate, would soon be injured and miss the bulk of the season. A similar fate had befallen the other prime candidate before the season began, J.J. Stokes, the U.C.L.A. wide receiver.

Colorado's fourth game, on October 1, was like the California primary for Salaam. The Buffaloes, now ranked No. 5, beat No. 16 Texas, 34-31, thanks to a 24-yard field goal by Neil Voskeritchian with one second remaining. More important to the Heisman candidacy,were Salaam's 35 carries for 317 yards and his 362 all-purpose yards, the latter a C.U. record.

A 300-yard game like that one serves as a cattle prod on the Heisman electors.

Salaam had become the front runner in what the media hyperbolically described as the Heisman "race," and matters moved smoothly from then on. Colorado won the rest of its games, save the one to national champion Nebraska. The 24 - 7 defeat made no difference to the Heisman chronology as Salaam distinguished himself with 134 rushing yards.

To become only the fourth Division I-A player in the annals of the National Collegiate Athletic Association to gain more than 2,000 yards in a single season, Salaam needed 205 in the final regular-season contest. He got 259 in a 41-20 win over Iowa State and concluded as the nation's rushing leader for Division I with a 186.8 yards-per-game average.

Marcus Allen of Southern California in 1981; Nebraska's Mike Rozier in

Salaam, became only the fourth Division IA player in NCAA history to gain more than 2,000 yards in a single season.

224

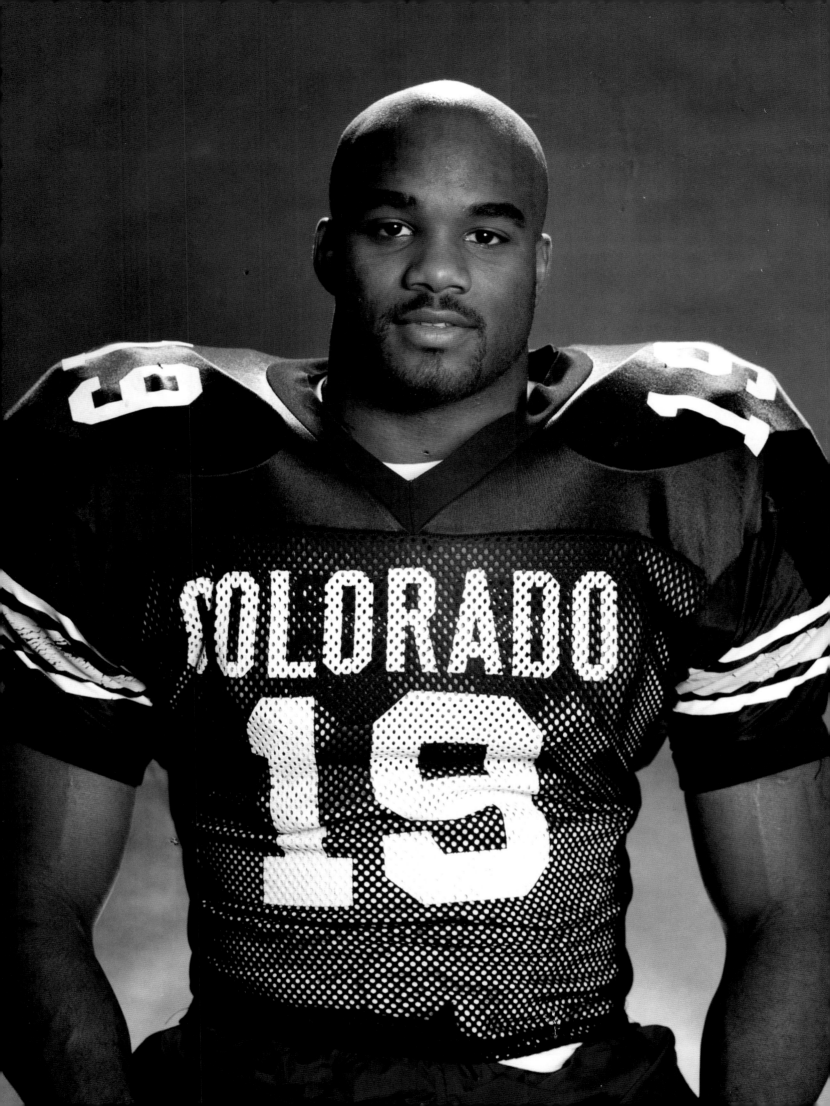

1983, and Barry Sanders of Oklahoma State in 1988 were the 2,000 - yard predecessors and each had been voted the Heisman Trophy.

There was no denying Salaam. The electors gave him 1,743 points, 842 more than second-place Ki-Jana Carter of undefeated Penn State.

The Nittany Lions had won many of their games so easily that Carter was withdrawn early. He played into the fourth quarter only four times, curbing his rushing numbers somewhat. Fateful? Of course. Carter had 100 fewer carries than Salaam and his average per rush was higher, 7.8 yards to 6.9. No matter.

In the Fiesta Bowl game, January 2, 1995, Colorado defeated Notre Dame easily, 41 - 24. Salaam had his least productive game of the jubilant campaign, 83 yards on 23 carries, and immediately announced he would forego his senior season in favor of the National Football League draft. In April he was the first round choice of the Chicago Bears, the 21st player selected. Carter, also a junior, was the first one.

Only 30 months before, it was hard to believe any of these events would come to pass for Rashaan Salaam, a gifted but raw athlete, who came to the campus at Boulder, from a small private school, La Jolla Country Day.

His mother, Khalada Salaam - Alaji, was a formidable woman educator who had established and ran a private elementary school in San Diego. She sent her son, age 13, to another private school with a $7,700 tuition fee in upperclass La Jolla, a 45-minute bus trip each way, after his ninth grade in an inner-city public school. His grades had dipped and he had begun to hang out with lads who leaned to gangs.

Salaam at first hated the new environment, but he stuck with the program because of his mother's persistence. They had a football team, of the eight-man kind. Despite the stigma of eight rather than 11 on a side, this was not kindergarten football because the coaching was good and there was a schedule.

Salaam's talents exceeded that of his peers. By the time he was done, he had rushed for 4,965 yards and scored 112 touchdowns. There were 1,600 yards and 31 touchdowns in his final season even though six of the eight games were cut short because his team was ahead by 45 points or more. That is a rule in California eight-man prep football. "It was too easy," Salaam later said. The recruiters had found him and offers came. He chose Colorado. although his mother would have preferred Stanford or California-Berkeley.

Ben Gregory, Colorado's running backs coach, said, "Rashaan came to Division I with very little football experience. After our second meeting his freshman year, I realized Rashaan didn't even know what I was talking about."

He watched more than he played that freshman season. In the spring he was arrested for giving the police a wrong name, after being a bystander in a liquor store robbery. He was ready to quit but once again his strong mother prevailed.

He had come from football stock. His father, Harold (Teddy) Washington, had played freshman football at Colorado in 1963; transferred to San Diego State and had a fling in pro ball with the Cincinnati Bengals and in the Canadian League.

The family became Muslim converts when the son was a year old and his name, Rashaan Iman Salaam, translates to Righteous, Faith, Peace. The parents soon divorced and his mother then remarried. His father, a Las Vegas fireman, Sultan Abdus-Salaam, twice went through substance rehabilitation programs and became a dedicated Muslim.

The mother, father and step-father were all present for the Heisman ceremonies at the Downtown Athletic Club in New York. Rashaan said, "This trophy is for my mom. I played for her, and I was really glad I could win it for her."

His mother had a different perspective. She said, "Not in my wildest dreams did I expect any of this. I never planned for this. You make plans. But God makes plans and God is the best of planners."

"I still feel Rashaan will have a bigger impact off the field in the scheme of things. He is more special than this. He has his own mind, and his thinking is rational. He is not swept up by the moment."

What about the team concept? At Colorado it was still in place. Derek West, the senior offensive tackle.so helpful in making the award come about, said it best.

"His Heisman is my Heisman. That's how we view it."

A combination of fate, exceptional talent and a loving mother's persistence helped Rashaan Salaam prevail.

HONORING THE WINNERS

Downtown Athletic Club was honored to have John Wayne as featured speaker at the 1971 awards ceremony.

It is late afternoon on a Saturday early in December. In the Heisman Room on the 13th floor of The Downtown Athletic Club overlooking the Hudson River in lower Manhattan you can almost feel the suspense. As the television lights go up and the president of the club steps to the lectern, the hubbub dies and there is a hush in the room.

The five leading candidates for The Heisman Memorial Trophy sit nervously in the front row. Behind them are scores of club officials and invited guests, some standing at the back, blocking the door and spilling out into the elevator lobby.

Four floors above, a horde of reporters keep their eyes on the television monitor as they await the announcement now moments away. If the excitement seems palpable, there is a reason. It has been building for 60 years. Bill Prince, what have thou wrought!

It was not John W. Heisman, the club's athletic director, but Willard B. Prince, the editor of *The D.A.C. Journal,* who dreamed up the idea of an annual award honoring the year's outstanding college football player. Indeed, Heisman was actually cool to the idea, believing that it would be inappropriate to honor individual achievement in a team sport. But when Heisman mentioned Prince's idea at a lunch with a group of sportswriters, their response was so enthusiastic he changed his mind.

Still, Heisman rejected Prince's idea that the award be named for him, so the first award,

President Richard Nixon swaps Presidential cufflinks for Heisman cufflinks with Steve and Barbara Owens aboard Air Force One.

given in 1935 and limited to players east of the Mississippi, was known as The Downtown Athletic Club Trophy.

The next year, after Heisman's death, it became The Heisman Memorial Trophy and was broadened to include the entire country.

From the beginning, sportswriters and broadcasters have determined the winner, and to balance sectional favoritism they have been divided evenly among geographic regions. The number of regions and selectors have varied, but since 1988 there have been a total of 870 media voters, 145 from each of six regions. Since 1988 former Heisman winners have also voted.

Prince died in 1949, but many of the principles he laid down have not varied. Each elector is still required to vote for three players, with points awarded on a 3-2-1 basis and the winner being the player who receives the most points, whether or not he has received the most first-place votes.

Part of Prince's methodology though~has changed a lot. For the first award his son John helped him address hundreds of envelopes mailed to the initial electors, and when the ballots came back, Prince's daughter helped him count them at the dining room table.

Now the ballots are received and tallied by auditors at the accounting firm of Deloitte &Touche, who are sworn to secrecy. Although they give the club a list of top vote getters so the leading candidates may be invited to the announcement ceremony, only the auditors know the winner until an afternoon in December when the club president steps to the lectern, opens a sealed envelope and reads the name to an expectant nation.

Like each award for 60 years, Bill Prince, this one's for you. The envelope, please.

Vice-President George Bush addresses the audience during the 1983 Heisman presentation ceremony.

Selecting a winner based on size is not a prerequisite of the Heisman selection process. Nile Kinnick was only five feet eight inches and 170 pounds. He passed, he punted, he carried the ball, he kicked extra points, he played tenacious defense. Small in size but large in stature in the game of football and the game of life, which was cut short at age 24. Kinnick's greatness was legendary as he died defending his country.

As part of its 100th anniversary celebration early next year, Notre Dame intends to display each of the Heisman trophies that its football players have won. Asked to return his trophy for the exhibit, Paul Hornung preferred to bring it to the campus himself rather than risk shipping it. So not long ago the 1956 winner was walking through the South Bend, Ind., airport, carrying the bronzed statue of a running back as if it were a football.

Suddenly a stranger stared "Showoff," the man said. Must've been a South Bend old-timer who remembers when the Heisman Trophy was considered a campus fixture. Angelo Bertelli, John Lujack and Leon Hart have also returned their trophies. Johnny Lattner and John Huarte have yet to comply. But before the exhibit opens, Notre Dame is expected to be applauding its seventh Heisman winner, its first in 23 years: Tim Brown, the wide receiver and kick-returner on the 8-1 team apparently on its way to the Cotton Bowl in only Lou Holtz's second season as coach.

Over the years, The Heisman Memorial Trophy, awarded annually to the nation's "most outstanding college football player," has created one of America's most controversial elections. For many of the more than 1,000 sportswriters and sports broadcasters who vote, publicity is often more important than performance, psychology often more important than skill.

Of this year's other candidates, a strong case can be argued for Don McPherson, the Syracuse quarterback, and Lorenzo White, the Michigan State running back. Gordon Lockbaum, the Holy Cross two-way throwback, had 32 first-place votes last year, more than anybody except the winner, Vinny Testaverde, now the Tampa Bay Buccaneers' rookie quarterback. And if Gaston Green, the U.C.L.A. tailback, had not missed almost all of three games because of a pinched nerve in his neck, his yardage would be even more impressive.

The Favorite to Win

Most candidates shrug modestly that their team's record is more important than the Heisman Trophy, but Don McPherson says quietly and refreshingly, "I think I've done the type of job that's worthy of the Heisman Trophy." And he has. But even the campus campaign managers for the Syracuse quarterback, and this year's other leading candidates sound willing to concede that Tim Brown will be the winner when the announcement is made Dec. 5 at The Downtown Athletic Club.

With two more nationally-televised games remaining, against Penn State and Miami (Fla.), the Notre Dame all-American appears to have everything going for him: the publicity, the performance, the psychology and the skill.

"I think Tim came into the season as the favorite to win the Heisman," said Roger Valdiserri, his campaign manager as Notre Dame's associate athletic director. "And I can't think of a week when he's lost it." Brown has caught 32 passes for 729 yards, averaged 21 yards on kickoff returns and 12.3 yards on punt returns. As an occasional

ANOTHER HEISMAN IS NOTRE DAME BOUND

By Dave Anderson

running back, he has rushed for 133 yards in 29 carries. He has scored seven touchdowns. I've never seen a flanker put so much pressure on the defense as this kid does, and he's the best kick-returner since Johnny Rodgers won the Heisman at Nebraska," said Hornung, hardly an unbiased observer but certainly a respected one. "I've only known one other football player who brings the crowd to its feet every time he touches the ball, Gale Sayers when he was with the Bears. This kid has the same gift. Jim Brown and O.J. Simpson didn't have it, but Gale Sayers did and Tim Brown does."

Years ago many Heisman voters were influenced by publicity carnpaigns. But now virtually every serious Heisman candidate can be seen on television. And after watching Brown in Notre Dame's 37-6 rout of Alabarna last Saturday on television, he'll get my vote, with Lorenzo White second and Don McPherson third.

The First Receiver Since Rodgers

If the 6-foot, 195-pound Notre Dame senior from Dallas wins the Heisman, he will be the first modern wide receiver to do so. Leon Hart, the 1949 winner, was what now is considered a tight end as well as a fullback and a defensive end. Larry Kelley, the 1936 winner, was a Yale end in the single-wing formation, who also played defense. Rodgers, the Nebraska flanker, kick returner and occasional tailback, won the award in 1972.

Each of the other 49 Heisman winners has been either a running back, a quarterback or a single-wing tailback.

Although Notre Dame's national mystique will influence some voters, Brown is hardly a product of that appeal. Jack Butler and Harry Buffington, who supervise the two National Football League scouting combines, each believes that Brown might be the very first choice in next year's N.F.L. draft. "If I had a vote for the Heisman," said Butler, "I would vote for Tim Brown. He does everything. He's a great wide receiver. He does the kick returns better than anybody. I think Don McPherson can be a pro quarterback, but he's not in Brown's class as a prospect. And it's not like Brown is just having a big year all of a sudden. He's been doing this ever since he's been at Notre Dame."

Buffington, if he had a vote, also acknowledged that he would choose Brown, with Lorenzo White second and Scott Davis, a 6-foot-7, 270-pound defensive end at Illinois, third.

"Our scouts think Brown is terrific," Buffington said. "He's got good speed, he's strong and he's big. He could be the No. 1 choice, depending on which team has that choice and what it needs. Whatever happens, he'll be a very early pick in the first round, but I doubt that he'll return punts and kickoffs in the N.F.L. He's too valuable a wide-out to risk on returns."

Once the Cotton Bowl is over, Tim Brown will be asked to return his Heisman Trophy to Notre Dame's 100th anniversary exhibit.

NOTRE DAME HEISMAN TROPHY WINNERS

1943 QB ANGELO BERTELLI

1947 QB JOHN LUJACK

1949 E LEON HART

1953 HB JOHN LATTNER

1956 QB PAUL HORNUNG

1964 QB JOHN HUARTE

1987 FL TIM BROWN

Notre Dame's seven Heisman Trophy winners (from left to right): John Lujack, 1947; Angelo Bertelli, 1943; Leon Hart, 1949; Tim Brown, 1987; Paul Hornung, 1956; John Huarte, 1964; and John Lattner, 1953.

BUCKEYE HEISMAN TROPHY WINNERS

1955 HB HOWARD "HOPALONG" CASSIDY   1944 QB LES HORVATH   1974-1975 RB ARCHIE GRIFFIN   1953 RB VIC JANOWICZ

TROJANS HEISMAN TROPHY WINNERS

1965 RB MIKE GARRETT   1968 RB O. J. SIMPSON   1979 RB CHARLES WHITE   1981 RB MARCUS ALLEN

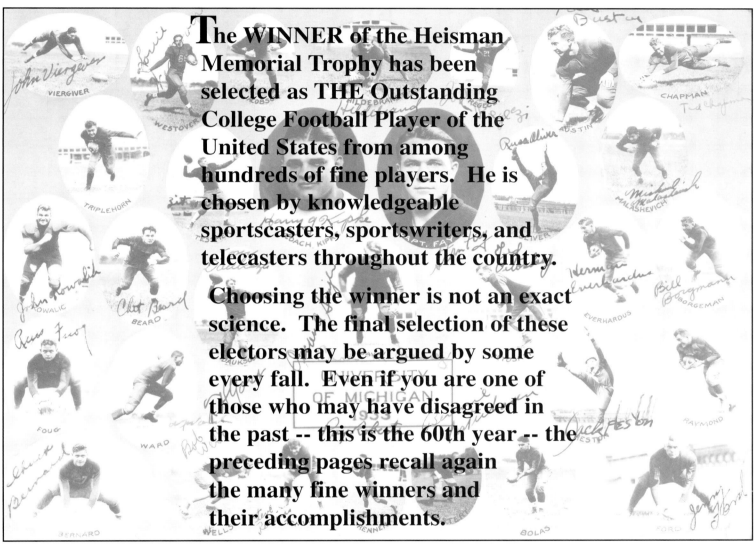

The WINNER of the Heisman Memorial Trophy has been selected as THE Outstanding College Football Player of the United States from among hundreds of fine players. He is chosen by knowledgeable sportscasters, sportswriters, and telecasters throughout the country.

Choosing the winner is not an exact science. The final selection of these electors may be argued by some every fall. Even if you are one of those who may have disagreed in the past -- this is the 60th year -- the preceding pages recall again the many fine winners and their accomplishments.

Balloting Over the Years and How They Finished 1935 to 1994

1935
1. JAY BERWANGER, *Chicago*
2. MONK MEYER, *Army*
3. WILLIAM SHAKESPEARE, *Notre Dame*
4. PEPPER CONSTABLE, *Princeton*
    No player west of the Mississippi was eligible
    for the trophy this year.

1936
1. LARRY KELLEY, *Yale*
2. SAM FRANCIS, *Nebraska*
3. RAY BUIVID, *Marquette*
4. SAMMY BAUGH, *TCU*
5. CLINT FRANK, *Yale*

1937
1. CLINT FRANK, *Yale*
2. BYRON WHITE, *Chicago*
3. MARSHALL GOLDBERG, *Pitt*
4. ALEX WOJCIECHOWICZ, *Fordham*
5. JOE KILGROW, *Alabama*

1938
1. DAVEY O'BRIEN, *TCU*
2. MARSHALL GOLDBERG, *Pitt*
3. SID LUCKMAN, *Columbia*
4. BOB MacLEOD, *Dartmouth*
5. VIC BOTTARI, *California*

1939
1. NILE KINNICK, *Iowa*
2. TOM HARMON, *Michigan*
3. PAUL CHRISTMAN, *Missouri*
4. GEORGE CAFEGO, *Tennessee*
5. JOHN KIMBROUGH, *Texas A & M*

1940
1. TOM HARMON, *Michigan*
2. JOHN KIMBROUGH, *Texas A & M*
3. GEORGE FRANCK, *Minnesota*
4. FRANKIE ALBERT, *Stanford*
5. PAUL CHRISTMAN, *Missouri*

1941
1. BRUCE SMITH, *Minnesota*
2. ANGELO BERTELLI, *Notre Dame*
3. FRANKIE ALBERT, *Stanford*
4. FRANK SINKWICH, *Georgia*
5. BILL DUDLEY, *Virginia*

1942
1. FRANK SINKWICH, *Georgia*
2. PAUL GOVERNALL, *Columbia*
3. CLINT CASTLEBERRY, *Georgia Tech*
4. MIKE HOLOVAK, *Boston College*
5. BILL HILLENBRAND, *Indiana*

1943
1. ANGELO BERTELLI, *Notre Dame*
2. BOB ODELL, *Pennsylvania*
3. OTTO GRAHAM, *Northwestern*
4. CREIGHTON MILLER, *Notre Dame*
5. EDDIE PROKOP, *Georgia Tech*

1944
1. LES HORVATH, *Ohio State*
2. GLENN DAVIS, *Army*
3. FELIX BLANCHARD, *Army*
4. DON WHITMIRE, *Navy*
5. BUDDY YOUNG, *Illinois*

1945
1. FELIX BLANCHARD, *Army*
2. GLENN DAVIS, *Army*
3. BOB FENIMORE, *Okla. A & M*
4. HERMAN WEDEMEYER, *St. Mary's*
5. HARRY GILMER, *Alabama*

1946
1. GLENN DAVIS, *Army*
2. CHARLES TRIPPI, *Georgia*
3. JOHN LUJACK, *Notre Dame*
4. FELIX BLANCHARD, *Army*
5. HERMAN WEDEMEYER, *St. Mary's*

1947
1. JOHN LUJACK, *Notre Dame*
2. BOB CHAPPUIS, *Michigan*
3. DOAK WALKER, *Southern Methodist*
4. CHARLEY CONERLY, *Mississippi*
5. HARRY GILMER, *Alabama*

1948
1. DOAK WALKER, *Southern Methodist*
2. CHARLIE JUSTICE, *North Carolina*
3. CHUCK BEDNARIK, *Pennsylvania*
4. JACKIE JENSEN, *California*
5. STANLEY HEATH, *Nevada*

1949
1. LEON HART, *Notre Dame*
2. CHARLIE JUSTICE, *North Carolina*
3. DOAK WALKER, *Southern Methodist*
4. ARNOLD GALIFFA, *Army*
5. BOB WILLIAMS, *Notre Dame*

1950
1. VIC JANOWICZ, *Ohio State*
2. KYLE ROTE, *Southern Methodist*
3. RED BAGNELL, *Pennsylvania*
4. BABE PARILLI, *Kentucky*
5. BOBBY REYNOLDS, *Nebraska*

1951
1. DICK KAZMAIER, *Princeton*
2. HANK LAURICELLA, *Tennessee*
3. BABE PARILLI, *Kentucky*
4. BILL McCOLL, *Stanford*
5. JOHN BRIGHT, *Drake*

1952
1. BILLY VESSELS, *Oklahoma*
2. JACK SCARBATH, *Maryland*
3. PAUL GIEL, *Minnesota*
4. DON MOOMAW, *UCLA*
5. JOHN LATTNER, *Notre Dame*

1953
1. JOHN LATTNER, *Notre Dame*
2. PAUL GIEL, *Minnesota*
3. PAUL CAMERON, *UCLA*
4. BERNIE FALONEY, *Maryland*
5. BOB GARRETT, *Stanford*

1954
1. ALAN AMECHE, *Wisconsin*
2. KURT BURRIS, *Oklahoma*
3. HOWARD CASSADY, *Ohio State*
4. RALPH GUGLIELMI, *Notre Dame*
5. PAUL LARSON, *California*

1955
1. HOWARD CASSADY, *Ohio State*
2. JIM SWINK, *Texas Christian*
3. GEORGE WELSH, *Navy*
4. EARL MORRALL, *Michigan State*
5. PAUL HORNUNG, *Notre Dame*

1956
1. PAUL HORNUNG, *Notre Dame*
2. JOHN MAJORS, *Tennessee*
3. TOM McDONALD, *Oklahoma*
4. GERRY TUBBS, *Oklahoma*
5. JIMMY BROWN, *Syracuse*

1957
1. JOHN CROW, *Texas A & M*
2. ALEX KARRAS, *Iowa*
3. WALT KOWALCZYK, *Michigan State*
4. LOU MICHAELS, *Kentucky*
5. TOM FORRESTAL, *Navy*

1958
1. PETER DAWKINS, *Army*
2. RANDY DUNCAN, *Iowa*
3. BILLY CANNON, *LSU*
4. BOB WHITE, *Ohio State*
5. JOE KAPP, *California*

1959
1. BILLY CANNON, *LSU*
2. RICHIE LUCAS, *Penn State*
3. DON MEREDITH, *Southern Methodist*
4. BILL BURRELL, *Illinois*
5. CHARLES FLOWERS, *Mississippi*

1960
1. JOE BELLINO, *Navy*
2. TOM BROWN, *Minnesota*
3. JAKE GIBBS, *Mississippi*
4. ED DYAS, *Auburn*
5. BILL KILMER, *UCLA*

1961
1. ERNIE DAVIS, *Syracuse*
2. BOB FERGUSON, *Ohio State*
3. JIMMY SAXTON, *Texas*
4. SANDY STEPHENS, *Minnesota*
5. PAT TRAMMEL, *Alabama*

1962
1. TERRY BAKER, *Oregon State*
2. JERRY STOVALL, *Louisiana State*
3. BOB BELL, *Minnesota*
4. LEE ROY JORDAN, *Alabama*
5. GEORGE MIRA, *Miami*

1963
1. ROGER STAUBACH, *Navy*
2. BILLY LOTHRIDGE, *Georgia Tech*
3. SHERMAN LEWIS, *Michigan State*
4. DON TRULL, *Baylor*
5. SCOTT APPLETON, *Texas*

1964
1. JOHN HUARTE, *Notre Dame*
2. JERRY RHOME, *Tulsa*
3. DICK BUTKUS, *Illinois*
4. BOB TIMBERLAKE, *Michigan*
5. JACK SNOW, *Notre Dame*

1965
1. MIKE GARRETT, *Southern California*
2. HOWARD TWILLEY, *Tulsa*
3. JIM GRABOWSKI, *Illinois*
4. DON ANDERSON, *Texas Tech*
5. FLOYD LITTLE, *Syracuse*

1966
1. STEVE SPURRIER, *Florida*
2. BOB GRIESE, *Purdue*
3. NICK EDDY, *Notre Dame*
4. GARY BEBAN, *UCLA*
5. FLOYD LITTLE, *Syracuse*

1967
1. GARY BEBAN, *UCLA*
2. O. J. SIMPSON, *Southern California*
3. LEROY KEYES, *Purdue*
4. LARRY CSONKA, *Syracuse*
5. KIM HAMMOND, *Florida State*

1968
1. O. J. SIMPSON, *Southern California*
2. LEROY KEYES, *Purdue*
3. TERRY HANRATTY, *Notre Dame*
4. TED KWALICK, *Penn State*
5. TED HENDRICKS, *Miami*

1969
1. STEVE OWNES, *Oklahoma*
2. MIKE PHIPPS, *Purdue*
3. REX KERN, *Ohio State*
4. ARCHIE MANNING, *Mississippi*
5. MIKE REID, *Penn State*

1970
1. JIM PLUNKETT, *Stanford*
2. JOE THEISMANN, *Notre Dame*
3. ARCHIE MANNING, *Mississippi*
4. STEVE WORSTER, *Texas*
5. REX KERN, *Ohio State*

1971
1. PAT SULLIVAN, *Auburn*
2. ED MARINARO, *Cornell*
3. GREGG PRUITT, *Oklahoma*
4. JOHN MUSSO, *Alabama*
5. LYDELL MITCHELL, *Penn State*

1972
1. JOHNNY RODGERS, *Nebraska*
2. GREGG PRUITT, *Oklahoma*
3. RICH GLOVER, *Nebraska*
4. BERT JONES, *LSU*
5. TERRY DAVIS, *Alabama*

1973
1. JOHN CAPELLETTI, *Penn State*
2. JOHN HICKS, *Ohio State*
3. ROOSEVELT LEAKS, *Texas*
4. DAVID JAYNES, *Kansas*
5. ARCHIE GRIFFIN, *Ohio State*

1974
1. ARCHIE GRIFFIN, *Ohio State*
2. ANTHONY DAVIS, *Southern California*
3. JOE WASHINGTON, *Oklahoma*
4. TOM CLEMENTS, *Notre Dame*
5. DAVE HUMM, *Nebraska*

1975
1. ARCHIE GRIFFIN, *Ohio State*
2. CHUCK MUNCIE, *California*
3. RICKY BELL, *Southern California*
4. TONY DORSETT, *Pittsburgh*
5. JOE WASHINGTON, *Oklahoma*

1976
1. TONY DORSETT, *Pittsburgh*
2. RICKY BELL, *Southern California*
3. ROB LYTLE, *Michigan*
4. TERRY MILLER, *Oklahoma State*
5. TOM KRAMER, *Rice*

1977
1. EARL CAMPBELL, *Texas*
2. TERRY MILLER, *Oklahoma*
3. KEN MacAFEE, *Notre Dame*
4. DOUG WILLIAMS, *Grambling College*
5. ROSS BROWNER, *Notre Dame*

1978
1. BILLY SIMS, *Oklahoma*
2. CHUCK FUSINA, *Penn State*
3. RICH LEACH, *Michigan*
4. CHARLES WHITE, *Southern California*
5. CHARLES ALEXANDER, *Louisiana State*

1979
1. CHARLES WHITE, *Southern California*
2. BILLY SIMS, *Oklahoma*
3. MARC WILSON, *Brigham Young*
4. ART SCHLICHTER, *Ohio State*
5. VAGAS FERGUSON, *Notre Dame*

1980
1. GEORGE ROGERS, *South Carolina*
2. HIGH GREEN, *Pittsburgh*
3. HERSCHEL WALKER, *Georgia*
4. MARK HERRMANN, *Purdue*
5. JIM McMAHON, *Brigham Young*

1981
1. MARCUS ALLEN, *Southern California*
2. HERSCHEL WALKER, *Georgia*
3. JIM McMAHON, *Pittsburgh*
4. DAN MARINO, *Pittsburgh*
5. ART SCHLICHTER, *Ohio State*

1982
1. HERSCHEL WALKER, *Georgia*
2. JOHN ELWAY, *Stanford*
3. ERIC DICKERSON, *Southern Methodist*
4. ANTHONY CARTER, *Michigan*
5. DAVE RIMINGTON, *Nebraska*

1983
1. MIKE ROZIER, *Nebraska*
2. STEVE YOUNG, *Brigham Young*
3. DOUGH FLUTIE, *Boston College*
4. TURNER GILL, *Nebraska*
5. TERRY HOAGE, *Georgia*

1984
1. DOUG FLUTIE, *Boston College*
2. KEITH BYARS, *Ohio State*
3. ROBBIE BOSCO, *Brigham Young*
4. BERNIE KOSAR, *Miami*
5. KEN DAVIS, *Texas Christian*

1985
1. BO JACKSON, *Auburn*
2. CHUCK LONG, *Iowa*
3. ROBBIE BOSCO, *Brigham Young*
4. LORENZO WHITE, *Michigan State*
5. VINNY TESTAVERDE, *Miami*

1986
1. VINNY TESTAVERDE, *Miami*
2. PAUL PALMER, *Temple*
3. JIM HARBAUGH, *Michigan*
4. BRIAN BOSWORTH, *Oklahoma*
5. GORDON LOCKBAUM, *Holy Cross*

1987
1. TIM BROWN, *Notre Dame*
2. DON McPHERSON, *Syracuse*
3. GORDON LOCKBAUM, *Holy Cross*
4. LORENZO WHITE, *Michigan State*
5. GRAIG HEYWARD, *Pittsburgh*

1988
1. BARRY SANDERS, *Oklahoma State*
2. RODNEY PEETE, *Southern California*
3. TROY AIKMAN, *UCLA*
4. STEVE WALSH, *Miami*
5. MAJOR HARRIS, *West Virginia*

1989
1. ANDRE WARE, *Houston*
2. ANTHONY THOMPSON, *Indiana*
3. MAJOR HARRIS, *West Virginia*
4. TONY RICE, *Notre Dame*
5. DARIAN HAGAN, *Colorado*

1990
1. TY DETMER, *Brigham Young*
2. RAGHIB ISMAIL, *Notre Dame*
3. ERIC BIENIEMY, *Colorado*
4. SHAWN MOORE, *Virginia*
5. DAVID KLINGLER, *Houston*

1991
1. DESMOND HOWARD, *Michigan*
2. CASEY WELDON, *Florida State*
3. TY DETMER, *Brigham Young*
4. STEVE EMTMAN, *Washington*
5. SHANE MATTHEWS, *Florida*

1992
1. GINO TORRETTA, *Miami*
2. MARSHALL FAULK, *San Diego State*
3. GARRISON HEARST, *Georgia*
4. MARVIN JONES, *Florida State*
5. REGGIE BROOKS, *Notre Dame*

1993
1. CHARLIE WARD, *Florida State*
2. HEATH SHULER, *Tennessee*
3. DAVID PALMER, *Alabama*
4. MARSHALL FAULK, *San Diego State*
5. GLENN FOLEY, *Boston College*

1994
1. RASHAAN SALAAM, *University of Colorado*
2. KI-JANA CARTER, *Penn State University*
3. STEVE MC NAIR, *Alcorn State University*
4. KERRY COLLINS, *Penn State University*
5. JAY BARKER, *University of Alabama*

THE GAME

Yale Game 1935

HAS CHANGED...

Georgia Game 1981

...BUT THE ESSENCE OF THE

Charles White turns the corner in his glorious 1979 season

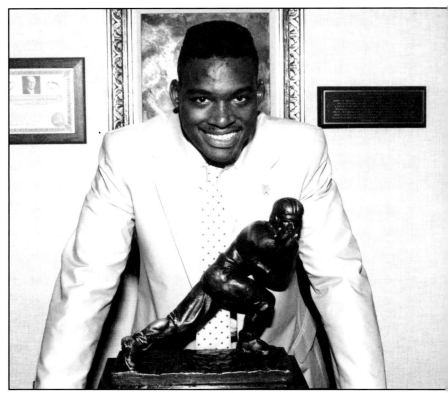

Andre Ware, 1989

Trophy presentation to Yale's Larry Kelley in 1937

238

WINNERS REMAINS THE SAME

Doug Flutie, the Miracle Man, hold his prize in 1984

Tommy Harmon, who made #98 famous, used the number as part of his Army bomber.

Jim Plunkett celebrates with Al Guage and Rudy Riska

EPILOGUE

Regardless of era, heritage or futures, what all Heisman Trophy winners share in common is one glorious football season forever theirs. To be acknowledged as the best, by a panel of authorities, is a memory and a reality that will be cherished forever. That season can never be diminished or distorted.

For a few early victors, like Clint Frank, the finale of that glorious season was the last game of football they were ever to play. For others it was a stepping stone to greater football fame and some riches. Six of the more famous come to mind: Doak Walker, Southern Methodist, 1948; Paul Hornung, Notre Dame, 1956; Roger Staubach, Navy 1963; O.J. Simpson, Southern California, 1968; Tony Dorsett, Pittsburgh, 1976; and Earl Campbell, Texas, 1977. They are the only Heisman winners, thus far, elected to the Pro-Football Hall of Fame.

The trophy itself has had different meaning to all the winners. Larry Kelly stored it in a closet. Roger Staubach allowed his children to play with it. Others have given it a place of prominence in their homes and professional lives.

When the award is made each December, at the Downtown Athletic Club in New York City, the acceptance speeches are often predictable. The honored athlete is disposed to thank his coaches, his parents and rightfully his teammates for making all this possible. After all, football is the ultimate team game.

Occasionally the Heisman victor will salute the game of football, which also made his celebrity possible. That is appropriate.

Colonel Earl (Red) Blaik, the late, great Army coach, described football as, "This fascinating game which has challenged the minds of men of culture and action."

In his foreword for Allison Danzig's "The History of American Football," written 40 year ago, Colonel Blaik continued, "That the game survived its primitive infancy attests to the fact that it appeals not only to our basic qualities of combat, but also to those of intellect, from which logical rules, strategy and techniques have evolved. The foundation of American football was laid by great men of character, imagination and ingenuity."

The Heisman Trophy is college football's greatest prize, it also reflects our founding fathers' qualities as well as a strive for perfection. It rewards the winners for their outstanding efforts and the Heisman heritage would have it no other way.

William N. Wallace

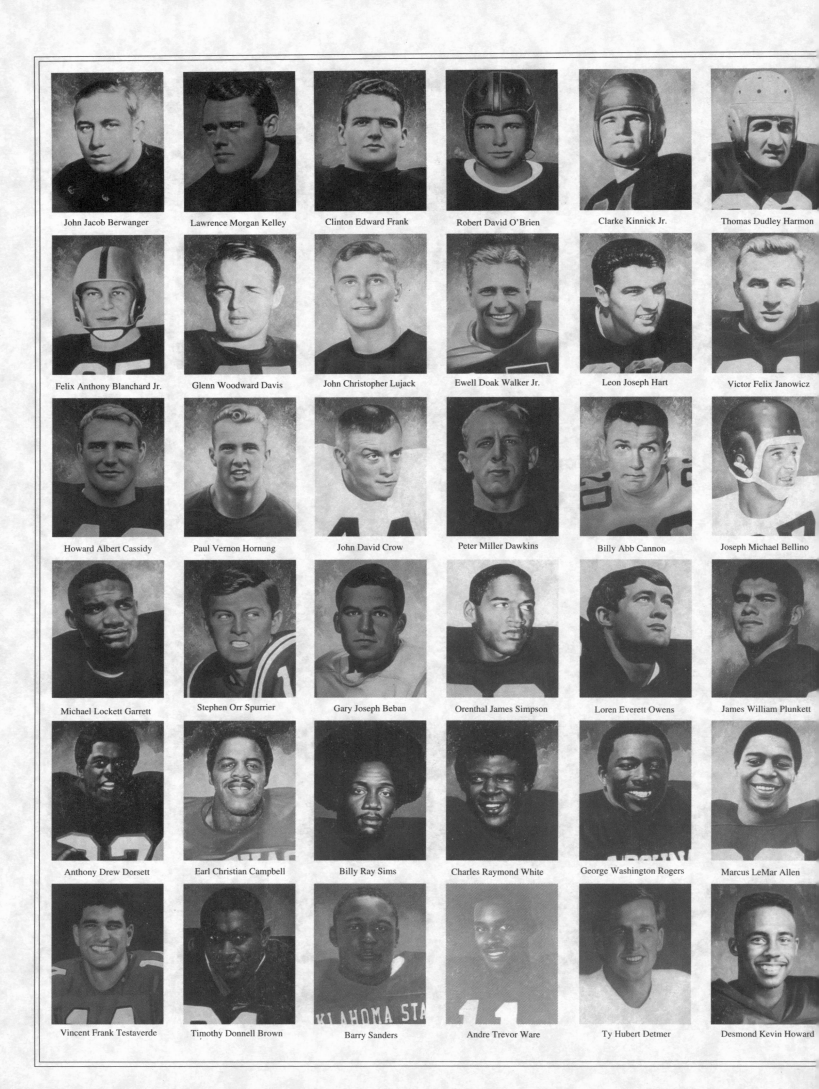

John Jacob Berwanger

Lawrence Morgan Kelley

Clinton Edward Frank

Robert David O'Brien

Clarke Kinnick Jr.

Thomas Dudley Harmon

Felix Anthony Blanchard Jr.

Glenn Woodward Davis

John Christopher Lujack

Ewell Doak Walker Jr.

Leon Joseph Hart

Victor Felix Janowicz

Howard Albert Cassidy

Paul Vernon Hornung

John David Crow

Peter Miller Dawkins

Billy Abb Cannon

Joseph Michael Bellino

Michael Lockett Garrett

Stephen Orr Spurrier

Gary Joseph Beban

Orenthal James Simpson

Loren Everett Owens

James William Plunkett

Anthony Drew Dorsett

Earl Christian Campbell

Billy Ray Sims

Charles Raymond White

George Washington Rogers

Marcus LeMar Allen

Vincent Frank Testaverde

Timothy Donnell Brown

Barry Sanders

Andre Trevor Ware

Ty Hubert Detmer

Desmond Kevin Howard